Library of
Davidson College

A HISTORY OF TORYISM.

A HISTORY OF TORYISM

by

T.E. Kebbel

New Introduction

by

E.J. Feuchtwanger

Rp

The Richmond Publishing Co. Ltd. 1972

329.942

K25-R

SBN 85546 168 3

73-8377

Republished in 1972 by The Richmond Publishing Co. Ltd.
Orchard Road, Richmond, Surrey, England.

Reprinted in Great Britain by Kingprint Limited
Richmond, Surrey.

INTRODUCTION

This book traces the history of the Tory party from the accession to power of the Younger Pitt in 1783 to the death of Beaconsfield in 1881. It also offers a Tory interpretation of the same century of English history, a counter to the Whig interpretation which was dominant at the time of its publication in 1886 and which, inspite of all modern corrections and historiographical refinements, still colours much of our thinking about the 19th century. The book is a reflection upon a period of history written at a time when much of it was still very recent and when the writer, at sixty years of age, could regard himself as a contemporary of many of the men and works he was discussing.

The History of Toryism raises many of the fundamental issues of 18th and 19th century history. What is party? What is a Tory and what a Whig? The modern notion of party grew up in the later 19th century and was customarily projected backwards as if it had equal validity in an earlier period. Whigs and Tories were seen as precursors of the "little Liberals and Conservatives" who were born into this world alive in the later Victorian age. Then came the Namier revolution which virtually blotted out the concept of party from 18th and much of 19th century English history. Our author, who had himself lived through the politics of the mid-19th century and had contact with men who operated in the unreformed political system before 1832, avoids either extreme. By adopting the term Toryism and not Tory party in his title, he shows from the outset that one cannot speak of a party continuous in organisation throughout the hundred years covered in his book. On the other hand he emphasizes the continuity of certain principles. At the beginning of his book he describes Tory principles as the combination of "the territorial and commercial interests in support of the Constitution and the Empire, the promotion of truly popular reforms and the jealous conservation of our naval and maritime preeminence." At the end of his journey through the century he declares that the Tories were always opposed to the three principles of compulsion, centralization and confiscation.

Paradoxically, if this is the Tory tradition, it is not too far removed from the Whig tradition. Perhaps the Whigs were more eager for reform than the Tories, but Kebbel rightly makes much of the fact that Tories were always prepared to contemplate timely and moderate reform. They experienced their real failures when they refused to carry moderate reforms in good time and within the widest possible consensus. Kebbel sees such a failure of Toryism over Catholic Emancipation and the first Reform Bill.

The Whigs were perhaps prepared to be more positively identified with reform but they too wanted reform primarily to avoid violent upheavals - a stitch in time, not change for change's sake. In foreign policy the Whigs were more enthusiastic in espousing liberal causes abroad than the Tories, from the French Revolution to Mazzini. However, in the 19th century support for liberal causes was usually in the best interests of Britain and the Tory Canning and the ex-Tory Palmerston found a moderately liberal foreign policy entirely compatible with a robust assertion of British advantage.

On many details Kebbel's interpretations are interesting and original. He defends the repressive domestic policies of the Liverpool Ministry after 1815 on grounds which are familiar to modern historians. The departures of Liverpool and his colleagues from liberal practice were, in Kebbel's view, slight and amply justified by the slender means available to the Government for the maintenance of public order. Kebbel rejects Spencer Walpole's "regulation Liberalism" on this issue (p 125) and even disagrees with Disraeli's unfavourable view of the whole post-war phase in the history of the Tory party (p 176).

Kebbel is critical of Peel and Wellington's conduct in the years between 1827 and 1832. He feels that his hero Canning, had he lived, would have carried out a moderate reform of the old electoral system and would have avoided the profound break in constitutional continuity which, in Kebbel's judgement, occurred in 1832. Peel and Wellington should have supported Canning in 1827 (p 184); instead, they initiated the process of Tory decay which brought about the return of the Whigs. In 1828 the Tories could have begun the process of modest electoral reform, they could have tackled Catholic Emancipation safely, need never have been committed to protection and could have ruled for most the 19th century. Kebbel is never afraid of such bold hypothetical speculations. Nevertheless, his account is firmly based on the sources available in his day, such as the Croker Papers, the Greville Memoirs and the standard political biographies.

Thomas Edward Kebbel was born in 1828, the son of a Leicestershire parson. He was educated at Merchant Taylor's and then went to Oxford where Mark Pattison was his tutor at Lincoln. He decided to enter the legal profession but his studies were interrupted by financial difficulties and he was not called to the bar until 1862. To maintain himself, he took to journalism and wrote for an ever-increasing number of papers and periodicals including the *Saturday, Quarterly* and *Fortnightly* Reviews and *The Times*. In 1867 he was active as a writer in defence of Disraeli's Reform Bill and from 1873 he was a regular contributor to the *Standard*, the leading Conservative daily in London. He published numerous books including short lives of Beaconsfield and the 14th Earl of Derby, an edition of Beaconsfield's speeches and a history of the agricultural labourer. From the 1860's onwards he was, therefore, deeply involved in Tory politics and journalism. Kebbel is not a major political writer in the class of Bagehot or even Goldwin Smith, but in this *History of Toryism* he offers a useful and refreshing challenge to the accepted orthodoxies of his day. For the modern student the book presents a contemporary document helpful in clarifying Victorian perceptions of political parties and principles.

E.J.Feuchtwanger
1972

A

HISTORY OF TORYISM:

FROM

THE ACCESSION OF MR. PITT TO POWER IN 1783

TO

THE DEATH OF LORD BEACONSFIELD IN 1881

BY

T. E. KEBBEL, M.A.

BARRISTER-AT-LAW, EDITOR OF "LORD BEACONSFIELD'S SPEECHES"

LONDON:

W. H. ALLEN & CO., 13 WATERLOO PLACE,
PALL MALL, S.W.
PUBLISHERS TO THE INDIA OFFICE.

1886.

A

HISTORY OF TORYISM:

FROM

THE ACCESSION OF MR. PITT TO POWER IN 1783

TO

THE DEATH OF LORD BEACONSFIELD IN 1881.

BY

T. E. KEBBEL, M.A.,

BARRISTER-AT-LAW, EDITOR OF "LORD BEACONSFIELD'S SPEECHES."

LONDON:

W. H. ALLEN & CO., 13 WATERLOO PLACE,
PALL MALL, S.W.

PUBLISHERS TO THE INDIA OFFICE.

1886.

PREFACE

I am been contemplating for some years presently well
as is here presented in the parties, these prepared to
me by the Editors of the Vansard Chronicle, with a
series of short studies of Tory Prime Ministers and afterwards for publication by the Nation Society, it struck me
that this might itself an opportunity of carrying out my
original design in connexion with the aid of these notes and
the materials I had and already collected, I might easily
expand these sketches into a connected history of
Toryism during the period in which I had occupied myself.
As I had previously contributed largely to selling over
some portions of the whole though by other periodicals
I have here and there interwoven with the present work
some matter which has already been printed. But such

PREFACE.

I HAD been contemplating for some years some such work as is here presented to the public, when it was proposed to me by the Editors of the *National Review* to write a series of short studies of Tory Prime Ministers, and afterwards to republish them by themselves. It struck me that this was an excellent opportunity of carrying out my original design, and that with the aid of the notes and the materials which I had already collected, I might easily expand these biographies into a connected history of Toryism during the period to which I had confined myself. As I had previously contributed Essays travelling over some portion of the same ground to other Periodicals, I have here and there interwoven with the present work some matter which has previously been printed. But such passages are few and brief. A great part of the work is entirely new; the rest has been completely recast; and I now offer it to the world in hopes that it may be accepted as an honest attempt to do justice to a great Party, whose actions have hitherto been recorded either by its avowed enemies, or by friends who were too much devoted to one aspect of Toryism to be able to appreciate the other.

T. E. K.

CONTENTS.

A HISTORY OF TORYISM.

CHAPTER I.

NORTH, SHELBURNE, AND PITT.

In writing a history of Toryism from the year 1783, it will be necessary to commence our enquiry from a point rather higher up the stream. To understand the new political departure which began with Mr. Pitt, whose traditions and principles the great Tory statesman of these latter days was so fond of recalling to us, we must first gain a clear idea of the long party struggle which preceded it. But before we embark on this enquiry, I may refer very briefly to what I hope hereafter to discuss more fully, the continuity, namely, of the political party whose fortunes I have undertaken to recount. When, in 1830, the Whigs returned to power after fifty years of Opposition, it was only to find the old *régime* moribund, and all the old conditions on which the maintenance of their supremacy had formerly depended on the brink of dissolution. The Whigs themselves finally put an end to them, and fancied they had won a great victory. In reality they only sealed their own doom. To the old Whig party, the party of

1

Newcastle and Rockingham, of Burke and Fox, of Lord
Grey and Lord Althorpe, the party which had beaten Lord
North and had been beaten by Mr. Pitt, the old borough
system was more necessary than it had been to the Tories,
and they perished with it. They left their sting in the Constitution and expired. Henceforth both Whigs and Tories
assumed other names, and became known as Liberals and
Conservatives. Yet there has been a continuity in the
one party which has not existed in the other. The terms
Tory and Conservative are still practically co-extensive,
and used indiscriminately by the public. Whig and Liberal
are not. The Whigs have now become part of another
party, in which their own idiosyncrasy is merged. Their
rivals have preserved their homogeneity, and, if I may
say so, their personal identity. By the Reform Bill of
1832 the balance of power established in 1784 was destroyed : while the growth of a revolutionary party has
caused the defensive or Conservative function of Toryism
to stand out with more exclusive prominence than it had
done in the previous century. But the Conservative
policy of the present day still runs upon the old lines
which were traced out by the younger Pitt—the combination of the territorial and commercial interests in support
of the Constitution and the Empire, the promotion of
truly popular reforms, and the jealous conservation of our
naval and maritime pre-eminence.

It is unnecessary to pursue the parallel into detail.
Nobody will contend that the metamorphosis of Tories into
Conservatives is not widely different, both in kind and
in degree, from the metamorphosis of Whigs into Liberals.
More than this, let us remember that the last Tory Prime
Minister who swayed the destinies of the country did
always contemplate the Toryism of the eighteenth century

as a model for ourselves, and seems to have believed at
one time that it was capable of revival, not merely in the
spirit but in the letter, and on a large scale. No one
has ever suggested that the Whiggism of the eighteenth
century could be revived by the Cavendishes or Fitz-
Williams. The proper place for the discussion of these
views will be found in the last of these biographies; but
I have said enough, I think, to show that the Toryism of
the last hundred years is capable, in a way in which the
Whiggism of the last hundred years is not, of being
discussed as a whole : and I will venture to add that,
while divisible into two very distinct halves, it will be
found that a period whole and complete within itself lies
between the accession to office of Mr. Pitt and the resignation of office by Lord Beaconsfield.

With the coronation of George the Third, we see two
rival principles of foreign policy contending for the mastery
in the counsels of the English Government. The House
of Hanover was now firmly established on the throne.
Disaffection was extinct in England and impotent in
Scotland; and though the French had not abandoned
all idea of using the Stuart family as a weapon against
Great Britain, nobody on this side of the Channel gave
himself a moment's uneasiness on the subject. Now,
therefore, as it seemed to one party in the State, was the
time for putting an end to the system which had brought
so much odium on George the First and George the
Second, and for once more making the King of England
"the most popular man in his dominions." We could
now at last afford to cut ourselves adrift from that net-
work of German alliances and German subsidies by which
the English people had been grieved for more than forty
years, and from which it had always been the object of

1 *

the Tory Party to extricate them. Granting, for the sake
of argument, that they had been necessary at one time,
that time had happily gone by. Nothing would cement
the young King's popularity so strongly as his willingness to enter into these views; and it might have
been said, perhaps, to be the only thing wanting to con-
solidate the power of his dynasty. This was the Tory
policy. It cannot be denied that it was a national policy,
and no one had been a more passionate adherent of it
at an earlier period than Pitt himself, who was now
Secretary of State.

On the other hand lay the alleged expediency of a
vigorous prosecution of the war, conducted chiefly by sea,
and leaving the safety of our Hanoverian dominions
dependent on our German allies. It might not have been
impossible, perhaps, after the Peace of Aix la Chapelle in
1748, to have reverted to the French alliance which had
been the policy of Bolingbroke, and which necessity and
his own sagacity had made the policy of Walpole. But
after the blows which we had inflicted on France both in
India and America during the Seven Years' War, it had
become useless to think of anything of the kind, and we
had only to consider how best we could disable her
hostility. The Family Compact concluded between France
and Spain in August 1761, came in to exasperate the
situation still further; and though the English Cabinet
refused to make the compact by itself a *casus belli* against
Spain, thereby causing the immediate resignation of Mr.
Pitt, they were obliged to do six months afterwards what
he would have done at once, and by the conquest of
Havannah and the Philippine Islands speedily brought
Spain upon her knees. The two Courts now recognized
the necessity for peace, and the only question with Eng-

land was whether it should be granted or not—whether she had yet done enough to secure herself from the future vengeance of the humiliated Powers. Pitt, who had now been joined in Opposition by the Duke of New-castle and Lord Temple, said, No; we must yet further humiliate the House of Bourbon. For this object he threw himself zealously into the German system, which he had once as strenuously condemned, and would have continued the war until the navies of France and Spain had been swept from the seas, and their colonies and commerce annihilated. This was the Whig policy. The Tories, whose object, as we have seen, was to disentangle England from Germany, thought enough had been done when the original object of the Seven Years' War had been attained, Great Britain at the same time receiving ample accessories of territory in compensation for her exertions and expenditure.

It is easy to see that there is a good deal to be said for each of these views, that both might well be inspired by wise and patriotic motives, and that both were pro-bably intermingled with elements of a less exalted cha-racter. There can be no question at all that the eman-cipation of England from the German system was a salutary and statesman-like policy; but there is reason to believe that Bute's anxiety for peace was quite as much dictated by his jealousy of Mr. Pitt as by his zeal for the interests of England. It is equally indisputable that it would have been much to the advantage of this country could she have reduced France and Spain to such utter prostration as to have disabled them from renewing the contest fifteen years afterwards. But it likewise remains to be considered, as Lord Macaulay very candidly admits, that Mr. Pitt had won his fame

and popularity in the prosecution of the war ; that this
was the sphere in which he felt himself best qualified to
shine ; and that if the war were continued he was pretty
sure to be recalled to power. He occupied, in fact, at the
end of the Seven Years' War much the same position
as was occupied by Marlborough at the end of the Spanish
Succession War. A man easily persuades himself that
what is for his own interest is for the interest of the
public as well, and there is no reason to suppose that
Pitt was an exception to the rule. It has been said
that the Peace of Paris, like the Peace of Utrecht, was
prompted by the wish to exclude a great man from
power who was pre-eminently fitted to carry on the
war. But if the great man's pre-eminent fitness for war
makes him indifferent to peace, and desirous of a perpetual theatre on which to exhibit his pre-eminence, there
is no alternative but to exclude him.

The further question remains whether it would have
been possible to reduce France and Spain to such a
condition of impotence as would alone have justified the
adoption of Mr. Pitt's policy ? I believe it would have
been totally impossible, and that it was idle, therefore,
to prolong hostilities which had no other object in view.
We had got all we wanted for ourselves, and by continuing
the war should only have added fuel to the French
desire for revenge, without succeeding, after all, in placing
it beyond their reach. The Tory peace of 1763 was described by Lord Granville, the greatest authority on foreign
politics in England, as " the most glorious and honourable
which this country had ever made." The modern Whig,
Mr. Massey, takes the same view. It secured for this
country, he says, everything that was worth having, or
that she was likely to be able to maintain. Lord

Edmond Fitzmaurice* is wholly in favour of it; and it
had, we know, the full approval and support of his celebrated ancestor, Lord Shelburne, who, whatever his fail-
ings, was a statesman of the first class, and honest even
to perversity.

We have dwelt with the more emphasis on the merits
of the Peace of Paris because it can hardly be doubted
that the circumstances by which it was accompanied
confirmed those impressions which the King had received
from his education, and determined the bias of his mind
in relation to political parties for the remainder of his
reign. With all these arguments in favour of concluding
peace, George the Third, on his accession to the throne,
found the Whig Party obstinately bent on war, solely, as
it would seem to him, because their own interests required
it. For a similar reason, as it appeared, Pitt, who had
formerly thundered against German engagements, was
now thundering against the abandonment of them. This
was the young King's first experience of Party politics, as
Party politics were then understood. The effect upon his
mind was what might have been anticipated. His reading
and education had taught him much of the evils of Party.
His first entrance into public life showed him these
in full operation. He was only two-and-twenty, and the
impression then made upon his mind was as vivid after
fifty years as when he first told Mr. Pitt that his system
of governing by the great Revolution families "would
not do."

It may be well, perhaps, before quitting this topic to
point out that there is a broad distinction between what I
have called the German system as pursued by the Whig
Party in the middle of the last century, and those alliances

* *Life of Lord Shelburne.*

with the great German Powers which we contracted at the end of it. In the reign of George the Second we had nothing to fear from France. I deny that there was any national interest whatever involved in our engagements with the German Courts. These were all undertaken for the protection of Hanover, and might all have been abandoned without the smallest danger to Great Britain. Our alliances with the Continental monarchies to resist a European Dictator who aimed at universal conquest, was a totally distinct policy. Nobody can condemn the combination against Louis the Fourteenth, or the combination against Napoleon Buonaparte. But it was one thing to incur these responsibilities for the safety of the British Empire, and another to undertake them for the security of a German province.

As there are two rival principles of foreign policy, so also are there two rival principles of domestic government to be found contending with each other at the commencement of the King's reign. In 1760 it still remained to be seen whether the theory of the Patriot King was capable of being reduced to practice on a large scale, and as a substantive and permanent polity, or whether it was only a modification of absolutism or of parliamentarianism. According to Bolingbroke's idea, the sovereign was to take a leading part in the conduct of affairs, to govern without regard to party combinations, and to select his Prime Ministers from whichever party in the State he chose. Opposed to this doctrine was the Whig conception of Revolution principles, according to which the sovereign was to reign but not govern; to assert no convictions of his own in opposition to the Cabinet, and to accept as Prime Minister whomsoever the Revolution families required him to appoint—the Tories to be rigidly excluded.

This system had been practically in operation for two reigns; for though George the First and George the Second had their own way more often than is supposed, still the Whig principle had always been acknowledged, and after five and forty years had come to be regarded as impregnable. The young King, however, had been taught a different lesson, and when he mounted the throne, lost no time in putting it to the test of experience. The experiment was exceedingly interesting; and as we meditate on the causes of its failure, among which, of course, must be reckoned the ill-success of our arms in America, we see that Bolingbroke had omitted from his calculation one element of success, to the absence of which, in the case of George the Third, the collapse of the whole plan may be attributed.

To induce the nation, after sixty years of parliamentary government, to return to any form of personal government, it was necessary that the Patriot King should be not only the most popular man in his dominions, but also among the very ablest. George the Third was a man of excellent parts, but he had not the quality of genius which supplies the defects of an imperfect education, and he had a great deal to learn at his first accession to the throne, the ignorance of which led him into fatal blunders. When he had learned it, he made no more; but his support of Bute and his rupture with Pitt were mistakes which no king would have committed who had studied the character of the people whom he was called upon to govern; and the effects of them continued to be felt long after the cause had disappeared. He had not regained his popularity when the struggle with the Colonies commenced, and the opportunity which might have restored it was so mismanaged that it very nearly ended by destroying it. A commanding mind would either have conciliated the Americans at once, or have speedily reduced them to subjection. What the genius of one man could accomplish had been shown by Chatham himself; and had the King possessed heroic qualities, it is highly probable that personal government would have triumphed. The nation was undecided ; sick of the Whigs, not particularly in love with the House of Commons, and ready to follow any new leader who promised them a healthy change.* Had the American war succeeded, the King would have been that leader : the odium which fell on its promoters would then have attached to its opponents, and it is difficult to say what limits could have been placed at that particular moment on the extension of the power of the Crown. It was not the first time that the future of the English Constitution seemed to hang on the character of one man. When James the First succeeded to the throne of England, there was no longer a disputed succession : the country was internally prosperous ; the Tudors had accustomed the people to the personal supremacy of the sovereign ; and it rested only with the Stuarts to make it permanent and absolute. Had James the First understood the situation and been equal to it, he might really have been what he tried to persuade himself that he was.

But although the experiment had failed in this extreme form, all was not lost. There was still a *via media* to be fought for, which encountered just as much opposition from the Whigs as the system of Lord North had done. The King was no longer to be his own Prime Minister.

---

* In those days the change from a self-seeking oligarchy to an honest and vigorous absolutism would have *seemed* a healthy one to many persons.

But it was still to be tried whether he was to lose the right of appointing his own Prime Minister; and in the conduct of this second struggle, the King secured the aid of a very different ally from Lord North, in the person of the young son of Chatham, the greatest of the Tories, who, with less dazzling qualities than his father, possessed greater depth of intellect, with what is not always found in combination with genius, greater common-sense and greater steadiness of character.

William Pitt was born on the 28th of May 1759, at Hayes, near Bromley in Kent. There seems to be no doubt that in his case those marks of precocious genius which are so often visible only to the eyes of relatives were recognized by all who knew him. At fourteen years of age he wrote a tragedy, declared by Lord Macaulay, to whom the MS. was shown by Lord Stanhope, to be not inferior to the tragedies of Hayley. And though he was educated at home, his progress in classical scholarship was so rapid that before he was fifteen he was considered fit for college. One part of his education has often been described. His father used to practise him in reading off the Greek and Latin authors into English, and in reciting before himself passages from the best English poets, with the appropriate gestures and elocution. By these combined means he acquired that readiness in the use of words, and those graces of voice and manner in which he was probably unrivalled. He went into residence at Pembroke Hall, Cambridge, in October 1773, and was placed under the special charge of Mr. Pretyman, afterwards Bishop Tomline, one of the College tutors, and a young man of great University distinction. He was only nine years older than the juvenile freshman, and survived him twenty-one years. Had it been the pupil

who survived the tutor, what a different tale might not
English history have had to tell !

Pitt took his degree in the summer of 1776, when he
had just completed his seventeenth year, and, as the sons
of peers passed without examination, had no opportunity
of distinguishing himself. But he continued in residence
till he was nearly one-and-twenty and pursued, with
unabated zeal, his studies in classics and mathematics.
Of the latter he is said to have known all that is usually
required of the highest wranglers.   But in scholarship he
was rather accurate than elegant, never having been
initiated into the niceties of classical composition, which,
however, I cannot agree with Lord Stanhope in thinking
"laborious inutilities."   In addition to these subjects he
read Locke, Adam Smith, and Lord Bolingbroke's political
works; and attended lectures on civil law.   During the
latter part of his university career, he mixed much in
society, and though totally free, as he continued through
life, from the irregularities characteristic of his age, was
always allowed to be a lively and amusing companion, and
a match for the readiest wits of either London or Cambridge.

During his Cambridge life he had a serious attack of
illness, for which his doctor prescribed a careful diet,
horse exercise, and plenty of port wine.   He followed
this regimen to the day of his death ; but the last-
mentioned item, though it helped to sustain his energies
under a heavy load of toil and anxiety for a term of
years, may possibly have contributed to the premature
decline of his constitution.

Pitt had entered himself at Lincoln's Inn while in residence at Cambridge, and was called to the Bar on the
12th of June 1780.   But the new scene on which he

was to achieve his world-wide reputation was now about to open itself, and after fruitlessly contesting Cambridge at the General Election of 1780, he was returned, before Parliament met, for the borough of Appleby, through the interest of Sir James Lowther.

It has so frequently happened as to have become almost a rule in English politics, that between the two main parties into which Parliament is divided there has stood a third, representing generally the followers of some great man whom special circumstances, or the bent of his genius, have made, to some extent, independent of Party. The latest example of a connection of this kind were the Peelites. Before them we had the Canningites, and the Grenvillites ; and when Pitt first entered public life the position was occupied by the followers of his own father, the Chathamites. The first Pitt had at one time been disposed to favour the theory that the nation must necessarily be supplied with Prime Ministers by the Revolution families. Before he became Lord Chatham he had abandoned this principle altogether, and gradually formed a small school of statesmen round himself, of whom Lord Shelburne was the chief, pledged to oppose it to the uttermost. These men, though on the road to Toryism of another kind, were not Tories of the school of Bute and North. But as they had either never entertained or had finally rejected the doctrine which then constituted the differential tenet of Whiggism, the distinction between themselves and the Whigs was equally essential ; and the political architect who was to make it the instrument of an entirely new Party was the young man who first took his seat in the House of Commons on the 23rd of January 1781. It is curious that Pitt's public career, extending over exactly a quarter of a century, ended on the same day as it began; for it was on the 23rd of January, just five and twenty years afterwards, that he breathed his last.

At this moment the first attempt of George the Third to carry out the scheme of Lord Bolingbroke had all but run its course, and was on the verge of explosion. The Whigs, as it seemed, had now the ball at their feet. The King had had his chance. He had tried his experiment, and personal government in that particular form had failed. He and his system had to bear all the obloquy of a disastrous and disgraceful war which the Whigs had consistently opposed. Never did a Party hold better cards than the Whigs held under Lord Rockingham in the last days of Lord North's Administration. The Chathamites were then in close alliance with them, and among the Chathamites, as a matter of course, young Pitt enrolled himself. The combined attack was too powerful for Lord North's Administration, which, after one more session of hard fighting, in which Pitt highly distinguished himself, was compelled to retire from the field, and make way for the victorious Opposition. Lord Rockingham, of course, became Prime Minister, and office was pretty fairly divided between his own supporters and the party now led by Lord Shelburne, in which, as we have said, Pitt had taken a foremost place. He himself, in accordance with a very remarkable speech which he had delivered some time after his entry into Parliament, declined more than one subordinate office which was placed at his disposal, and calmly bided his time with that confidence in his own powers which does not seem to have created any astonishment among his own contemporaries.

George the Third submitted with a good grace to the

Rockingham Administration, and what turn affairs would have taken had Lord Rockingham's life been spared only a few years longer can now be only matter of conjecture. His death, however (July 1st, 1782), little more than three months after the formation of his ministry, threw all once more into confusion, and then it was that the Whigs took the first step which showed how little they had profited by the lessons of adversity, or understood the signs of the times. Had they known how to use their victory with moderation, there seems every reason to believe that they might have recovered their ascendancy; not, indeed, upon the old terms, but upon such as would have been honourable to themselves and beneficial to the public. The newly-planted dynasty might have required the fostering protection of the Whig families. Half a century of possession had changed the situation. The dynasty was adult, and what was once a nursery had now become a prison. That the connections who were in possession of the Government when George the Third began to tug at his leading-strings, should have been shocked and startled at his conduct, was only natural. They had taken no note of the silent progress of time; the man was, in their eyes, still a boy; the monarchy was still what it was when it had been necessary to carry the Septennial Act. But that after an experience of twenty years, of which a dozen had been passed in exile, another generation of Whigs should have returned to power, only to take up the old system exactly where their fathers had dropped it, and to re-impose upon the King the very same yoke which the old race of Pelhams and Cavendishes, with all the advantage of possession and prescription on their side, had been unable to maintain, bespeaks a degree of infatuation beyond what it has been customary to attribute to either the Stuarts or the Bourbons.

The King, on Lord Rockingham's death, sent for Lord Shelburne. Fox called a meeting of the Whigs, who came to the resolution that they could not allow His Majesty to name the Prime Minister, and forthwith required him to accept their own nominee, "a great 1688 noble," the Duke of Portland. Of course, the King refused. He had resisted their pretensions from the first hour of his accession to the throne; he had resisted successfully against heavier odds when he was young and unpractised in affairs; he was not going to yield now, when, with riper powers and longer experience, he was contending against weaker foes. The difference in the position was entirely overlooked by the Whigs. On the King's refusal to accept their ultimatum, Fox and his friends resigned, and broke up the Government; and Shelburne, who became Minister, and his young lieutenant, who at twenty-three became Chancellor of the Exchequer and leader of the House of Commons, now stood irrevocably committed to the Tory theory.

But the position was critical. The King had committed the offence which the Whigs never forgave. It was the privilege of the Party to recommend a minister to the Crown; not the privilege of the Crown to recommend a minister to the Party. The King, by violating this maxim, and Shelburne, by consenting to be his instrument, had cut themselves adrift from Whig principles altogether, and no quarter was to be kept with them. We can understand and make allowance for the chagrin of the Whigs, who, after their long exclusion from power, had regained it only to lose it again in the short space of three months. It was by no means so certain as it would seem to be at the present day, that Shelburne would be unable to maintain himself. There were sources of strength belonging to Ministries under the old *régime*, to which the new one is a stranger. The support of the Crown and of the House of Lords went a long way; and George the Third himself always thought that Shelburne might have made a better fight. Under these circumstances, and regarding the position from Fox's own point of view, it was clearly the game of the Opposition to attack the new Government at once with their full strength, so as to displace it, if possible, before it had time to take root, and before the usual influences had begun to tell on the private members of the party, many of whom were old Tories, and could not have very much relished the service to which they found themselves destined. Accordingly, as soon as Parliament re-assembled, Fox opened fire on the Treasury Bench with a violence which, but for the reasons we have given, would be unintelligible. Shelburne and his friends were men " whom neither promises could bind nor principles of honour could secure ; who would abandon fifty principles for the sake of power, and forget fifty promises when no longer necessary to their ends. They were," he believed, as if this were the *ne plus ultra* of apostacy, " capable even of coalescing with Lord North ! "

If this was a crime, the time arrived when not only Lord Shelburne but Fox himself was ready to commit it. Parliament was prorogued on the 11th of July, and the attention of Ministers during the recess seems to have been equally divided between negotiations with the belligerents abroad, and negotiations with the Opposition at home. It was necessary for them to obtain a vote in favour of the peace. Could Fox be induced to join the

Government ? Could Lord North be persuaded to support it ? Shelburne inclined to an understanding with
Lord North ; Pitt to a junction with Fox. The former,
no doubt, was the more natural alliance of the two ; for,
although Shelburne had opposed the American War, and
had made himself obnoxious to the Court in many ways
during Lord North's Administration, that was all over
now, and both alike represented the only real principle
on which at that time the Tories differed from the
Whigs, namely, the independence of the Sovereign, and
his right to select his own Ministers. And it is clear
that at one time Lord North would have preferred this
connection to any other. His own party in the House
of Commons, which numbered a hundred and twenty
members, would have followed him to the camp of Shelburne, at least as readily as they followed him to the camp
of Fox. And he, himself, must have been conscious that
such was the course most consistent with his previous
conduct, and with the dictates of gratitude and generosity.

But powerful counter influences were brought to
bear upon him. Lord Loughborough, himself notorious
for laxity of principles, and who played such a sinister
part afterwards on the Roman Catholic question, and
Mr. Eden, the first Lord Auckland, besieged North with
solicitations on behalf of Fox, chiefly, it would seem,
from personal dislike of Shelburne. But North was a
long time before he yielded. Even so late as the beginning of February, Loughborough wrote to Eden that
North meant to join Lord Shelburne. In a fatal moment
for himself he took an opposite determination. But it
is to be borne in mind that his accession to the Ministry
would have been purchased at a heavy price after all;
for as Fox was determined not to act with Shelburne,

Pitt was equally determined not to act with Lord North ; whether because he really dreaded the re-establishment of the old system, under which he, himself, must have been condemned for many years to a subordinate position, or because he still retained so holy a horror of the American War and its author that he could not bring himself to take his hand, it is impossible to determine. Considerations of the latter kind are more powerful at twenty-three than they are at a more mature age, and we have no right to doubt his sincerity on this occasion, whose whole life unfolds a picture of unsullied integrity. His aversion, however, did not extend itself to Lord North's friends ; and places would have been found for some of them had his lordship been willing to give an independent support to the Administration.

He certainly did not turn a deaf ear to the overtures that were made to him ; and it was believed by competent judges that he was on the point of acceding to them, when the negotiations were suddenly broken off by a premature communication from his friend, Mr. Adam, informing him that Shelburne was contemplating resignation before the meeting of Parliament, in which case a Government would be formed between Pitt and Fox to the exclusion of himself. North was told this under the belief that it would quicken his movements, and make him anxious at once to prevent the resignation of Shelburne by offering him the support he required. It had just the opposite effect ; and drove him to see the necessity of making terms with Fox while the way to it was still open to him. When, a little while afterwards, the veteran go-between, Rigby, made a final application to him on behalf of Shelburne, North replied, " It is too late."

2 *

Thus it is quite impossible to father North's accession to the coalition on any deep disapproval of the Peace : and if any further evidence were wanting, it is to be found in the conversation between himself and the King, which the latter repeated to Lord Ashburton, and which is published by Lord E. Fitzmaurice, in his *Life of Shelburne.* He must have known that no better terms could be obtained ; and that a man like Lord North should have been driven either by a fit of indignation, to which he was usually a stranger, or by the love of office, to which he was known to be indifferent, into so unprincipled and mischievous a compact as that which, by common consent, has been damned to everlasting fame, is one of the riddles of human nature of which no explanation can be given. I should prefer to believe that North yielded to neither of these two motives, but was over-ruled by the influence of associates, who prevented him from taking the step to which his own better judgment would have led him. We have seen a similar influence prevail against a similar bias, even within our own times ; and it is one against which all public men cannot be too strongly on their guard.

What, then, was the case with Fox ? The alternative plan, as we have seen, was Pitt's—to take Fox into the Cabinet ; and Pitt accordingly sought an interview with Fox to talk it over. This was as late as February 1783, when the terms of the Peace must have been known : and what was Fox's answer ? It was based directly on the Whig doctrine, which has been already mentioned, concerning the manner of appointing the Prime Minister. Shelburne had been appointed in defiance of this doctrine, and, therefore, must be deposed before the proposal could be entertained. Fox referred to no questions of policy or measures of reform ; he only asked if it was meant that Shelburne was to continue Prime Minister. On being answered in the affirmative, he said he could join no Government of which Lord Shelburne was the head. "I did not come here to betray Lord Shelburne," said Pitt, haughtily. The discussion was at once concluded, and Pitt and Fox, it is said, never met again in private. Now, as Fox knew perfectly well that his assistance was required by the Government to avert a vote of censure on the Peace, is it credible that if his repugnance to that settlement had been as deep as he afterwards declared, he could have been willing to entertain, even for a moment, the question of a union with its author? If his disapproval of their policy was strong enough to justify him in expelling the Ministry, even by such dubious means as the coalition with Lord North, it must have been enough to prevent him from ever dreaming of combining with them for the express purpose of defending it.

The preliminaries of a general peace were signed in January 1783. Parliament met in February, and the debate on the Address took place on the 17th, when an amendment adverse to the Peace, moved in the House of Lords by Lord Carlisle, was defeated by a majority of thirteen, and one proposed by Lord J. Cavendish in the House of Commons, carried by a majority of sixteen. A further motion was carried against Government on the 21st, and on that Shelburne resigned. We need not repeat the arguments for and against the Peace; it seems generally to be allowed that it was the best that could be obtained under the circumstances. That no better was obtainable was the fault of anyone rather than of Shelburne; of Fox and his party, who had encouraged the Americans to resist; of North and his colleagues, who

had so managed our military operations as to expose us
to ultimate defeat.

But whether we look to the responsibility of Fox and
North for the triumph of America, or to the actual
terms of peace which were secured by Lord Shelburne,
the conduct of the two first-mentioned statesmen will
appear equally indefensible. There should have been
something monstrous in the treaty to justify so monstrous
a union as the alliance by which it was condemned.
There was no proportion at all between the means and
the end. The Peace might be open to objections, but
they were of an ordinary kind, and not such as to call
for the suspension of all party ties in order to enforce
them. When the Ministry of Lord Aberdeen was overthrown by a concurrence of parties, not ordinarily
acting together, the Opposition represented the opinion
of nearly the whole country, expressed through a thousand different channels, on mismanagement of the grossest
character, resulting in great public calamities. But nobody could say that the Treaty of Versailles was open
to any such description; and even if it had been, the
author of the mismanagement, which had made the
Treaty necessary, was North himself. Had a coalition
been directed against him, there might have been more
excuse for it. But Lord Shelburne was innocent of
the whole affair; he had to do the best he could with
the situation he found in existence, and Fox must have
been perfectly conscious that he could have done no
better with it himself. This is all so evident that the
conclusion hardly requires to be enforced. The cabal of
1783, in short, was just the cabal of 1763 over again:
a factious combination against a particular individual
disguised under an affected solicitude for the public

welfare. The vote of censure was not really aimed at the Peace, but at Lord Shelburne. The coalition was directed against the one man who had made himself obnoxious to the conspirators.

"I repeat, then," said Pitt, "that it is not the Treaty, it is the Earl of Shelburne alone, whom the movers of this question are desirous to wound. This is the object which has raised this storm of faction. This is the aim of the unnatural coalition to which I have alluded. If, however, the baneful alliance is not already formed, is not already solemnized, I know a just and lawful impediment, and in the name of the public safety, I here forbid the banns."

It must be allowed, of course, that Shelburne's personal unpopularity had a good deal to do with it. Both the Whigs and the Tories had something against him. By the Whigs he was remembered as one of the earliest supporters of the King in his efforts at Emancipation ; by a certain section of the Tory Party he was regarded with suspicion and dislike, as the author of reforms injurious to themselves and distasteful to the King. It is said that some of them asked him the price of their support, and, on being told that there was no price, voted against him in a body. And we are even required to believe that this was done with the connivance of the King, notwithstanding his well-known anxiety to keep Shelburne in office. Shelburne, we are told, fancied so himself ; but the supposition is hardly reconcileable with the other circumstances of the case, and may be dismissed, we think, as entirely groundless. But over and above all these considerations was the fact—a fact sufficiently attested by all Shelburne's contemporaries—that he was not as other men. His abilities were recognized and feared ; but he was reserved, and supposed to be "peculiar." He was neither a Whig nor a Tory, and differed with both on some of their most cherished tenets. He was the enemy of the Revolution families, and suspected by the King's friends ; and, between the open hostility of the one and the lukewarm friendship of the other, he fell to the ground.

Fox and North did not agree even about the Peace. Fox would have made peace with America and have continued the war with the Bourbons. North would have made peace with the Bourbons, and have continued the war with America. But they agreed on one point, and that was that Shelburne must be got out. For this purpose they determined—to use a gentle euphemism— " to sink their former differences," and to combine against the hated individual.

The combination succeeded. But George the Third made desperate efforts to avert the consequences. For nearly six weeks the struggle continued ; and for that time the country was virtually without a Government. The most violent and peremptory resolutions were carried in the House of Commons, calling on the King to form a Government, but down to quite the end of March the issue was uncertain. It was proposed that Pitt should be Prime Minister, on the understanding that Lord North and a section of the Whigs would give him an independent support. But could he have waived the obvious objection to allying himself with any section of the coalition, the young statesman was at once too wise and too proud to grasp the shadow for the substance ; for he could only have been Minister upon sufferance, with the half-contemptuous toleration of his former opponents, who were not yet sufficiently unpopular to justify a *coup d'état*. Pitt, who was precocious in everything, and had an insight into public opinion beyond his years, was, perhaps, not without some presentiment of the great career that was

in store for him if he only bided his time and preserved
his independence. If he once consented to lean on the
support of the Whigs, or place himself in their hands,
he might say farewell at once to any dreams of future
greatness in which he had allowed himself to indulge.
"Apply to Mr. Thomas Pitt, or Mr. Thomas Anybody,"
said the unhappy monarch, when that gentleman's name
was suggested to him. But it was all in vain. He was
compelled to submit, though not on this occasion to dis-
semble. On the 1st of April he announced to the Duke
of Portland his readiness to accept his terms, and on
the following day the seven Ministers named by him kissed
hands, and took possession of the fortress they had
stormed. One can hardly help noticing that the birthday
of a Ministry expected to live for many years, and doomed
to die in less than one, is the day which popular tradition has so long consecrated to the mortification of
shortsighted credulity and the disappointment of ill-
founded hopes.

England has reason not to love coalitions, for they
have seldom done her anything but harm. The coalition which came into power on the 1st of April, 1783,
was certainly no exception. It is by no means improbable
that if Shelburne had remained Prime Minister, the war
of '93 might have been avoided ; just as, had Lord
Derby remained Prime Minister in 1852, the Crimean
War might have been avoided. The coalition of Fox and
North, at all events, robbed England of the chance, and
without having anything to show for it. Nor is this all.
Had it not been that in Mr. Pitt both the King and the
country found a Minister exceptionally well qualified to
deal with this peculiar crisis, the probability is that
personal government would have again entered into our

Constitution, and that its second state would have been worse than its first. The coalition of '83 provoked a reaction in the public mind, of which, under a weaker Minister than Pitt, the King would have reaped the whole advantage. It is hardly likely that the country gentlemen would have remained faithful to the Coalition, and, if there had been no Mr. Pitt, the King would have found another Lord North : the country, utterly disgusted with past tactics, would have contentedly acquiesced in the system ; and, with the French Revolution to intensify the loyalty of the nation, the Crown might have acquired powers which, after a quarter of a century, it would have been extremely difficult to abolish. In that case, the time might have come when we should have had to choose between a Monarchy and a Republic. Thanks to Mr. Pitt, the danger was averted. But how real, and how great it was, has hardly, perhaps, been fully understood. Even as it was, and in spite of the determination of Mr. Pitt not to serve after the fashion of Lord North, the reaction against the Whigs, by destroying all the moral power of the Opposition, had made the King so strong that he was able to have his own way on the only question which he cared about. We owe it to the Coalition that he was able to beat Mr. Pitt on the Roman Catholic question, and it is hardly an exaggeration to say that all the subsequent troubles of Ireland are traceable to the same source. The division of the Tory Party into two camps, and the delay of Roman Catholic Emancipation and Parliamentary Reform, till it had been almost as dangerous to concede as to refuse them, *hinc causas habuere*. We are still, even now, paying the penalty of an error which a hundred years have not expiated.

Of the blame attaching to the two authors of the Coalition, by far the larger share must rest on the shoulders of Lord North. Fox, after all, was only maintaining the cardinal principle of his party, and if the Tory leader chose, for ends of his own, to take it up, he might. But North had all his life been the representative and champion of the contrary principle. He had enjoyed the entire confidence of the King in that capacity. The majority of the public, who knew little of the Constitutional question at issue, revered " King George " as a true English King, respected his prerogative, and sympathised with him heart and soul in his struggle with America. They saw in Lord North, or supposed themselves to see, his loyal and sincere servant. They supported him for thirteen years on this express understanding ; and Lord North had no moral right to turn round in a moment, and not only belie all his former ˉprofessions, but use the majority who still obeyed him for destroying all which he . had upheld. That he had all along had his doubts of the system he was supporting, and of the justice of the war which he was prosecuting, seems only to aggravate his offence. To continue from year to year to appear as the advocate of a policy which he was secretly prepared to abandon; to accept the confidence and support of his Sovereign and his countrymen, on the faith of his unfeigned devotion to the principles they were known to entertain ; yet, as soon as it suited his convenience to declare that he had always disapproved of them, and join heart and soul with their opponents—is conduct which only the amiable private character of Lord North has rescued from the obloquy it deserves.

It is useless to say that his private friends were made

aware of his sentiments. An English statesman has others to look to beyond the inner circle of his friends. The public could only judge of his opinions by his conduct, and it may be taken for certain that could they have foreseen, three years before, what his conduct was to be three years afterwards, he would never have had the majority which was sent up for him at the General Election of 1780. Ministers, like other men, have a right to change their opinions; but, when they do, a decent interval, at least, should be allowed—a short period for retirement and meditation—before their appearance under different colours to lead the attack upon their former friends.

The compromise offered to Pitt had been a tempting one. But, with that amazing self-reliance which distinguished both himself and his father, he only took a day to reject it. He would play the more arduous, but, if successful, more effective game, and strike the visor, not the shield, of his opponent. So he turned his back upon the Coalition, and left them to their own devices, pretty certain, perhaps, from his knowledge of the men, that if they were allowed rope enough they would hang themselves. They were allowed rope enough, and they did hang themselves. Their nominee, the Duke of Portland, was Prime Minister. Their majority in the House of Commons seemed invincible. Now or never, if I may be allowed to use such an expression, seemed the time "to plunge," to back their luck, that is, and bring in some measure which would have the effect of neutralizing the influence of the Crown, and secure themselves a monopoly of office for perhaps a generation. Accordingly, when Parliament reassembled on the 11th of November, Fox gave notice that on that day week he should introduce a Bill to provide for the better government of India. Few who heard the announcement, perhaps none, could have the faintest idea of the mighty issues involved in it. But as soon as the measure was laid on the table of the House it very soon appeared that the language in which another famous measure has recently been described was strictly applicable to it, and that, while recommended by its authors in the interests of justice, it was also well calculated " to develop and support the party to which they belonged."

The Bill handed over the entire administration of India, and with it the entire patronage, to a Board of seven persons, to be nominated in committee, and to be immovable for four years. This patronage, according to the very lowest estimate worth £300,000 a year, and according to the highest exceeding two millions, would, it was thought, enable the party which dispensed it to maintain itself in power against all odds, and this instrument of corruption was instantly to be placed in the hands of Charles Fox. The Bill confiscated by a stroke of the pen all the real property, charters, and title-deeds of the East India Company, and transferred them, not to the Crown, to whom they ought properly to have reverted, but to a Board appointed by the House of Commons. Thus the Bill combined in itself a gross violation of the rights of property, a direct infringement of the Royal Prerogative, and an ill-concealed project for securing the ascendancy of a party. Pitt saw at once that it must either make or mar the Coalition, and Fox seems to have held the same opinion. Which of the two was the more probable consummation did not long remain in doubt. The Whigs had pushed their victory too far. The odium

of the Coalition, if followed by a measure of a moderate
and independent character, might in time have died away.
The India Bill trebled it at once. The Bill passed through
the House of Commons by majorities which it was useless to resist. But the King saw that his hour had
arrived, and that in the then state of public opinion he
might use his influence to defeat it in the House of
Lords with perfect safety. Pitt, it is believed, was
wholly ignorant of the means to be employed for this
purpose, but Lord Temple was commissioned to say
that the King would regard every Peer as his enemy who
supported the second reading of the Bill. This stroke
was decisive. On the 17th of December the Bill was
thrown out by the House of Lords, and on the 18th the
Ministry was dismissed. Pitt hesitated no longer; he at
once accepted the Treasury, which the King at once
offered him, and both the Sovereign and his servant
might now rise in their stirrups and cry "Farewell,
Portugal."

The fighting, however, was not over yet. Pitt had re-
captured the heights, and once more planted the royal
standard on the ground which Shelburne had surrendered.
But the unbroken masses of the enemy were collecting all
round him, and scarce anyone believed that he would hold
the point which he had won. Pitt, indeed, was a host
in himself; but he was a mere boy, fresh from college,
and with only six months' experience of office. How could
he compete against a powerful majority, led by the first
orator and most experienced statesman of the age ? The
opinion of " society " was the opinion of Mrs. Crewe, that
it would be only a mince-pie administration. And so
possibly it might have been, but for one circumstance,
which seems strangely to have escaped attention. The

immediate followers of Lord North in the House of Commons were, according to the computation of Gibbon, a hundred and twenty. But these men were all Tories, all part of that Tory majority returned in 1780 in defence of the Royal Prerogative, and bitterly hostile to the Whigs : the sons of those country gentlemen who, on the accession of George the Third, once more flocked to Court, delighted to think that the reign of exclusion was at an end. How is it to be believed that these men could enter into the new coalition with any real zeal or approbation : and even the personal popularity of Lord North only drew the number we have mentioned. The rest made part of the hundred and forty which had supported Lord Shelburne, and were now ready to support Pitt. Must not the Tory squires and baronets who sat upon the Speaker's left have often secretly felt that their proper place was elsewhere—at the back of His Majesty's servant who was doing battle so manfully for the very principles which they had always supported ? Pitt had at one time attacked Lord North very bitterly, and had North agreed to act with Shelburne, Pitt would have refused. These circumstances explain the early hostility of the Tories to their future chief. But they must have felt, ere the Coalition was a week old, that Pitt and North had now changed places, and that they could no longer be loyal both to the King and his former Minister at once.

In addition to their other blunders the Whigs committed the extraordinary mistake of trying to prevent a dissolution, when it ought to have been their first object to enforce one. Whenever either the Crown or the House of Lords sets itself in opposition to the majority of the House of Commons, its only justification is that the existing House of Commons is out of harmony with the

opinion of the public. " The House of Lords," says the
Liberal historian, Mr. Lecky,* " is exercising not only a
legitimate but a most useful function when it throws out
measures of the House of Commons which it believes to
be contrary to the wishes of the people, and thus compels
Ministers either to abandon them or to give the people
an opportunity of expressing their opinion at an election."
But when the majority of the House of Commons itself
protests against any such appeal, the leaders of the
minority may very well assume that they have got their
answer; the litigant who declines a jury anticipates the
verdict.   The Whigs, in fact, cut their own throats.
Had they forced a dissolution while the King's interposition was still fresh in the public mind, they would
have had a very good cry, and might possibly have secured
a majority.   But every day that passed served to weaken
its effect, and at the same time to strengthen the counter
feeling in favour of the Government, partly excited by
the overbearing conduct of the Opposition, partly the
result of sympathy with the young Prime Minister in his
struggle against such crushing odds.

This last mistake sealed the doom of the Whigs.   They
had once had the game in their hands.   Had they played
it with due regard to the altered circumstances of the
time, avoiding the rock on which the older " connections "
had split at the beginning of the reign, they might have
governed the country for another fifty years instead of
the Tories.   But in place of doing this, they steered
straight upon the breakers.   Their conduct, first of all,
in trying to force their nominee upon the King after the
death of Lord Rockingham; secondly, in opposing the

---

* *History of the Eighteenth Century.*

Peace; and, thirdly, in denying the right of His Majesty to dissolve Parliament when the opinion of the House of Commons was against him, plainly showed that they were unprepared to forego any one of their most cherished pretensions, and that it was useless to attempt to make terms with them. The original Coalition had not disposed the public mind to take an indulgent view of these proceedings. The junction of Fox and North had, no doubt, created the impression attributed to it by Bishop Watson, that " patriotism is a scandalous game played by public men for private ends, and frequently little better than a selfish struggle for power." But this, under the exercise of common prudence and forbearance on the part of the Whigs, might possibly have worn off. It was burnt into the public mind in characters which a hundred years have not effaced, by what they actually did. Nor ought it to be overlooked that it was only the conduct of the Whigs which brought Mr. Pitt to the front. But for this he might long have continued to play a very different part in public affairs, or have confined his ambition to the woolsack. The desperate nature of the crisis revealed the only man who could cope with it, and the same hand which wrought the toils evoked the spirit who was to cut them.

That by the judgment, the courage, the eloquence, and the great Parliamentary ability, something distinct from all three, which he displayed in the last great battle of this long and fluctuating campaign, Pitt won over to his side a good many members who were at first strongly opposed to him is clear. The " Cave " of that day, oddly enough headed by a Grosvenor, consisted of about fifty members, who tried to mediate between Pitt and the Opposition, but most of whom ended by becoming supporters of the Government. Two of the most active among them were Mr. Powys, the Member for Northamptonshire, and Mr. James Lowther, both of whom became afterwards staunch supporters of Mr. Pitt. The "Cave," or "independents," as they were then called, met at the "St. Alban's Tavern," on the 26th of January, and passed a resolution inviting Mr. Pitt and the Duke of Portland to communicate with each other. But compromise was obviously impossible. There is no middle course between two contradictories. The Whigs required that Mr. Pitt should resign, and the King's right to name his own Minister be thus formally renounced, before they would listen to proposals. Pitt was equally firm upon the other side, and though the Cave continued to move resolutions in the House of Commons they produced no effect. Two months afterwards Parliament was dissolved, and most of these gentlemen, finding that public opinion, after all, had been on Pitt's side, became avowed Tories. On the 2nd April 1783 the Coalition Ministry had kissed hands; by the 2nd April 1784 their Party was scattered to the winds. Pitt returned to Downing Street with two-thirds of the House of Commons at his back, and the entire English nation became the "King's friends."

Fox, like Lord North, is said to have been a good-natured man. He boasted of it himself. He liked, he said, to forget his enmities, and was constant only in his friendships. But, be this as it may, the iron entered into his soul in 1784, and we know it was with difficulty that he could speak of Mr. Pitt in terms of ordinary civility. In Lord Malmesbury's diary the reader may learn what epithets he applied to him in private. If he did not call his conduct "fiendish," or say that he was "hateful to God"—expressions which have been reserved for the more righteous politicians of our own day—he spoke of him in language equally at variance with the best known and most conspicuous features of Pitt's character. But Pitt could afford to forgive him. As no man ever fell so completely and rapidly as Fox, none ever rose so swiftly and so surely as Pitt. The reward of his loyalty and moral courage came at once, and for his life. For twenty-three years he continued, without doubt, the most powerful subject in the kingdom. Others not less deserving, perhaps, than Pitt, have climbed their way to eminence by long and painful routes, and have reached it only when they were too old to reap the full advantage of it, when they were " solitary and could not impart it." But to Pitt it came in the full flush of youth and energy, without stint or drawback. He had scaled the heights, almost like a hero of romance, without a word or a deed which could prick the most sensitive of consciences. Amid all the trials and temptations of that reckless age, he had remained faithful alike to his creed, his colleagues, and his master. And in the unexpected triumph which awaited him, the unbroken authority which he wielded for nearly a quarter of a century, and the veneration with which he never ceased to be regarded by the great body of the English nation, from the highest to the lowest, we see a truly wonderful illustration of the glory which even in this world is occasionally the prize of virtue.

The new Cabinet consisted of Pitt as First Lord of the Treasury and Chancellor of the Exchequer, Lord Sydney and Lord Carmarthen as Home and Foreign Secretaries respectively, Lord Howe at the Admiralty, Lord Thurlow as Lord Chancellor, Lord Gower President of the Council, and the Duke of Rutland Lord Privy Seal. Lord Temple, who had accepted the Foreign Office on the 19th, resigned

3 *

it on the 21st, because the King refused him a Duke-
dom. But William Grenville, destined to be Pitt's right
hand in the great revolutionary struggle, adhered to the
Minister, and was joint Paymaster of the Forces.

We need consider no further either the morality of
the Coalition, or the nature of the means which the
King employed to overthrow it. But this seems to be
the proper place for referring to a question which was
the source of great perplexity to Lord Beaconsfield, who,
indeed, was the first public writer to take notice of it, and
that is, where, all this time, was the Earl of Shelburne?
Lord Beaconsfield wonders why the King did not give
the Treasury to Shelburne, with Pitt to lead the House of
Commons under him. His knowledge of foreign affairs
was greater than that of any other living statesman.
He was a master of political economy. He was the
acknowledged head of the Party to which Pitt himself
belonged ; and always stood up for that " real " monarchy
which the King was determined to establish. It seemed
when the Coalition fell that he must necessarily be the
new Minister. But it was not so. As far as I can ascertain, he was not even consulted. Lord Beaconsfield
thought that if Lord Shelburne had been at the head of
affairs when the French Revolution broke out, his knowledge of Continental politics would have saved us from
some serious errors. But I think that the King had
really no alternative. Some of the difficulties in the way
of Shelburne's appointment might, perhaps, have been
surmounted. The King thought that he had capitulated
too easily on the last occasion, and was not the man to take
the lead in a fresh crisis, which promised to be infinitely
more severe than the one which had already proved too
much for him. Mr. Pitt said that for all the political

sins he had ever committed, it was sufficient atonement
to have sat for a single year in the same Cabinet with
Lord Shelburne. The fact seems that neither Shelburne
nor Pitt was willing to serve under the other. These
objections, however, might possibly have given way before
the various considerations which dictated the selection
of Lord Shelburne. But there were two which have
always seemed to myself insuperable. One is mentioned
by Lord Edmond Fitzmaurice, and is the one on which
Pitt himself always laid the greatest stress. The other, I
think, has not been generally observed.

With the dismissal of the Coalition and the appointment
of Mr. Pitt, a new chapter of our political history had
begun. George the Third had beaten the Whigs. But
heaven only knew "by what bye-paths and indirect
crooked ways" he had gained his ends. With all these
Shelburne had been mixed up, and as long as he remained
about the King they could not be forgotten. Nearly a
quarter of a century had elapsed since he entered public
life as the colleague of Lord Bute, and he was still associated in the public mind with all the mysterious machi-
nations which popular prejudice imputed to the detested
favourite. From all this past history Pitt stood entirely
free. He marked a new beginning—a new formation of
parties, a new generation, a new policy—and it was desirable above all things that it should be as free as possible
from all taint or connection with the old. To have
placed Shelburne over his head would have been to destroy
the whole effect of this distinction. All·the soil of the
achievement had disappeared with its original instruments,
and Pitt stood before the world the representative of both
loyalty and purity—the youthful conqueror who had
beaten the veterans of faction with their trained legions,

and who at once assumed a place in the popular imagination which the King with his peculiar instinct may have
divined from the first that Shelburne could never hope
to fill. With Pitt an altogether new scene would open
on the nation ; new men, new methods, new ideas, before
which it was hoped, as did actually happen, that the
memory of the past would be swept out of the public
mind. Whether to ensure this result it was absolutely
necessary to sacrifice Lord Shelburne is, perhaps, an
open question. But it is clear enough that Pitt thought
so ; and we may take it for granted that the King thought
so too.

There remains, however, what, in my own opinion, must
have determined the King's choice, had there been no
other cause in operation. From the moment of Lord
Shelburne's resignation in February 1783, Pitt became
at once the acting head of the Party. It was he who
fought the Coalition in the House of Commons, and it
was on Pitt that every eye was fixed when Parliament
reassembled in the autumn. Lord Shelburne had retired
to Bowood, and took no further part in the business of
the year. The figure of William Pitt towered high above
all others ; and the King must have felt instinctively that
his was the name to conjure with, if he was again to
appeal to the country with any hope of permanent success. Lord Beaconsfield says, " Perhaps he was prescient
of the power of youth to touch the heart of a nation."
No doubt Pitt's youth was a potent element in his
favour ; but it was because he stood out before the people
as the hero of the hour, who had borne the burden and
heat of the day, and ridden in the van of the battle till
the field was won, that public opinion singled him out
as the only possible successor to the Duke of Portland

who would have a chance of maintaining himself in
power.

Of the new Toryism which now emerged from the long
struggle between Whiggery and Regality, the differential
feature was a Constitutional principle, and not a particular policy.   The Revolution of 1688, like most other
revolutions, tended to place power in the hands of ultra-
partizans, and instead of settling down after the manner
which had been contemplated by the more disinterested
among the Whigs and the more reasonable among the
Tories, the Constitution for a long time continued to
oscillate between the two extremes of personal government and pure oligarchy.   Unless we remember that the
new Toryism inaugurated by Mr. Pitt marks the precise
point at which this oscillation ceases, and the Constitution regains its equilibrium, we shall never rightly understand either its past or its future.   The Whigs would have
governed by party to the extinction of prerogative.   The
King would have governed by prerogative to the extinction
of party.   Pitt combined both.   Government by Party, in
the sense in which the Whigs understood it, meant handing over the country for a long term of years to the domi-
nion of a few great families, and the renewal of the system
of proscription which George the Third endeavoured to
abolish.   It meant the virtual exclusion from the Court,
from public business, from all share in the privileges and
emoluments of office, of the great body of the country
gentlemen ; and the exclusion from the highest offices of
the Church of the great body of the country clergy.   But
the country clergy and the country gentry at that time
were the two most popular classes in the nation; and it
was mainly owing to their influence that the French

Revolution passed over us as harmlessly as it did. What would have happened had that terrible tempest found these classes disaffected, and England still under the rule of an unpopular oligarchy, without a trace left of that pristine public virtue by which it was once supposed to be distinguished, steeped to the chin in jobbery and nepotism, and governing in defiance of public opinion, by means of the enormous patronage of which they had robbed the rightful owners, it is difficult to say. But that the crisis would have terminated without some kind of political or social convulsion, it is impossible to believe. It might have ended in Absolutism, or it might have ended in Republicanism, and either would have been a great curse.

Government, on the other hand, without Party, such as Bolingbroke recommended, and George the Third, with the help of Lord North, did for a short time succeed in establishing, though the natural reaction against the Whig system of the previous fifty years, would have brought us, only by a different path, to the same goal. Under the first weak Minister, it must have ended in personal government of a more pronounced type than had existed during the American war, which, under the first great strain of public discontent, must have ended in revolution.

It was this reconciliation of prerogative with party, this vindication of the monarchical principle combined with the full recognition of the Parliamentary system to which the people had so long been accustomed, which was the work of the Toryism inaugurated by William Pitt. Like many other compromises, it is difficult to describe in words. It was an understanding. The King's will was to be an element of government. His opinion on public questions was to count. His right to appoint and to dismiss his own

Ministers was established. If any difference arose between the Crown and the Cabinet, sometimes one and sometimes the other would give way. But the King was not to dictate the policy of the country, or to reduce the heads of departments to the level of administrative clerks, as had been the case under the Government of Lord North.

It is, indeed, essential to this form of government, that the Minister should be supreme in his own Cabinet, and that when he and the Sovereign have agreed on a certain course of action, it should be accepted as a matter of course by the rest of the Ministers; and as these conditions cannot always be ensured, the efficiency of the system will vary with the varying degrees of force of character possessed respectively by the Premier and his colleagues. But no form of government has yet been devised which may not work well or ill according to the character of those who administer it. Absolutism, constitutional monarchy, republics, pure democracies, are all more or less dependent on the virtues and abilities of individuals; and as dulness and wickedness predominate so greatly in this world over genius and goodness, that is the best and safest polity under which the action of individuals is fenced round with the most numerous securities, without unduly hampering at the same time the energies of the executive authority. Now, I think that in that interpretation of the Revolution monarchy which was finally adopted both by George the Third and Mr. Pitt, we have a nearer approach to the realisation of this ideal than in any other phase through which our Constitution has passed. The Ministers of the Crown were strong enough to carry out, for a long term of years, both at home and abroad, a definite and consistent theory. But they were surrounded by powerful influences. The same aristocracy which supported them was able also to control them; and thus, while our policy was in no danger of fickleness, Parliament was in no danger of a dictator. The nominee members represented an outside opinion which was at the same time a thoroughly well-informed and educated opinion, and the opinion of a class capable of opposing the Minister, on public grounds, though the leader of their own party. One result of this system was that a single adverse vote of the House of Commons did not necessarily involve the resignation of the Ministry, and, consequently, that private members were often able to act independently without the fear of a " Ministerial crisis " to damp their resolution. At the present day the First Minister of the Crown has little beyond his own personal popularity and authority to rely upon, and cannot afford the loss of prestige which is inflicted by Parliamentary defeats. Then he had a force at his back on which they often made but little impression, since it was known that they were due to interests which, though they might thwart him on occasion, were pledged to his permanent support. His power was less absolute than that of a modern Minister with a large majority, but it was more solid. The one is built upon the sand, the other was founded on a rock.

Nor were the aristocracy in those days less alive to the wants and wishes of the people than were the middle classes after the Reform Bill. I say this on excellent authority,* while above both the aristocracy and the Ministry stood the august figure of the Sovereign, once more a real living power, with sufficient personal authority to make loyalty an active principle, and sufficient hereditary right to satisfy the national imagination; the best guarantee that can be found for the stability of political

* Mr. Gladstone, in *Nineteenth Century*, vol. ii. pp. 540, 541.

systems; stronger than prosperity, stronger than liberty, stronger even than the love of social order, which is commonly supposed to be the strongest.

If good government be the end of all constitutions, I know none better suited to ensure it than the monarchy which ruled in England during the first half of the period which I have undertaken to illustrate. Had Mr. Pitt been spared, we might have been living under it still. He would certainly have settled during his lifetime the three great questions on which the modern Tory Party has been wrecked—the Roman Catholic Claims, Parliamentary Reform, and Free Trade. Pitt would have satisfied the first before satisfaction was extorted. He would have so settled the second as to have removed the worst anomalies of the old *régime* without breaking its backbone. And he would probably never have consented to the imposition of the Corn Laws, or if he had, would have taken advantage of the first gleam of returning prosperity to repeal them.

A hundred years ago neither party had tied its hands by pledges on subordinate questions. No man was either a Tory or a Whig in virtue of his views on Free Trade, or Parliamentary Reform, or Religious Disabilities. Lord Macaulay, with his customary audacity, tries to make out that, because of his opinions on these subjects, Mr. Pitt was a Whig. It would be truer to say that, because of their opinions on these points, Lord Grey and Lord John Russell were Tories. Free Trade, which had many more adherents in the House of Commons among the Tories than among the Whigs, was introduced by Mr. Pitt and violently opposed, on principle, by Mr. Fox. Parliamentary Reform was the natural resource of the Tory Party when the great borough-mongers were the Whigs, as it was the natural resource of the Whigs when the great borough-mongers were Tories. On the question of Religious Disabilities the Tory Party was evenly divided—the Pittite section, led by Mr. Canning, taking one side, and the Addington section, led by Mr. Peel, the other. The effect of the French Revolution was to transfer the Reform question into Whig hands, a result for which the Tory leaders of a later epoch have been severely blamed. But we shall see, as we approach the period, that whether the Whigs or the Tories were to be the Party to carry a Reform Bill was a question which at one time hung very evenly in the balance.

Finally, we may say this much of the character and policy of George the Third : that if, as was almost certain to be the case, a reaction was to come against the Revolution oligarchy, we may thank Providence that it came under a king like George the Third. With the same abilities, had he been less virtuous, he might have established despotism. With the same virtues, had he been less able, he might have destroyed the monarchy.

With the Session which opened in January 1785 Pitt introduced the question of Parliamentary Reform, with all the authority and influence of the most powerful Prime Minister which England had ever yet seen. But it was all in vain. He proposed to establish a fund for compensating borough proprietors, by means of which thirty-six boroughs might be disfranchised at once; and others in succession as they gradually declined in population and importance. The seats thus gained were to be distributed amongst the counties and the large unenfranchised towns. The only feature in the Bill to which we are unaccustomed was the compensation of proprietors and the voluntary surrender of the franchise. It was not assailed, however, on these grounds, but on much more general ones; Burke and North alike declaring, as the Duke of Wellington did more than forty years afterwards, that our representative system was incapable of improvement, and that if one stone of it was touched the whole fabric would probably come down. Pitt's speech was a very able one, showing that he only proposed to do with the sanction of Parliament what the Crown had been used to do without it. He was mistaken, however, in supposing that the borough-mongers would rise to the bait. The Bill was rejected by a majority of seventy-four; and it is worthy of notice that neither on this nor on other occasions when measures were rejected which the Minister had set his heart on carrying, did it ever seem to occur, either to himself or to anybody else, that the Government was called on to resign. This was another peculiarity of the old *régime* to which we have already called attention. Pitt, we are told, accepted the result as decisive of the question for that Parliament; and before the return of a new one gave him an opportunity of reviving it, events had already taken place which made the very name of Reform stink in the nostrils of the nation. It is curious enough that as one French Revolution was fatal to Parliamentary Reform in this country, another gave it new life and was the main cause of its success.

The Bill was supported by Fox because he could not vote against the principle, but he strongly disapproved of its details. It was, in fact, a genuine Tory Bill—a Bill for increasing the political power of the most inde-pendent class of the community, which then was, and undoubtedly still is, the country gentry. Its members

want nothing from the Government and want nothing
from the mob, neither places from the one nor plaudits
from the other. On their own estates they are already
surrounded with most of those circumstances which
dignify and ennoble life, and are under little temptation
to court either power or popularity. Hence it results
that they are far less active politicians than the inhabitants of towns, and hence it is that in all our political
contests of recent years they have usually been worsted.
But there was another feature in the English counties
at that time to recommend them to Parliamentary
Reformers. They not only produced the most independent members ; they possessed the most independent
constituencies. The freeholders below the rank of
gentry, from the owner of a forty-shilling plot to the
yeoman of three hundred acres, were then a much more
numerous class than they have since become ; and though
always willing to be led, were not to be driven by the
county families. They were incapable of being bought
and sold, and acted independently at more than one
great crisis of the eighteenth century.

Baffled in his attempts to reform the representation,
Pitt in the same Session introduced his " Irish propositions," the object of which was to place England and
Ireland on a footing of commercial equality. Ireland
was offered free trade with all the English colonies
except those east of the Cape of Good Hope, excluded
by the charter of the East India Company. She was
admitted to an equal share of the carrying trade with
Great Britain. The duties on Irish goods imported into
England were to be the same as those on goods imported
into Ireland, and both very low. Irish linens were
still to be protected in the English markets by pro-

hibitive duties on the linens of Germany and Russia; and in return for these concessions Ireland was asked to contribute a small annual sum, when the Revenue exceeded a certain amount, to the expenses of the English navy. But the " tributary clauses," as they were called, were at once assailed fiercely by the Irish patriots, and Yorkshire and Lancashire rose as one man against the free trade clauses. Mr. Fox and the Whigs first took part with the Protectionists, and denounced the measure as unjust to England; and then, as soon as it was modified in conformity with their own representations, immediately turned round and denounced it as unjust to Ireland. Here, then, the Whig party, under its regular leaders, Fox and Burke, stood forward openly as the enemies of Free Trade, and the champions of Protection; at the same time taking advantage of Irish prejudices and antipathies to embarrass the Government of Great Britain. Pitt and the Tories, on the other hand, appear as the supporters of commercial freedom, and the bearers of a measure of peace and good-will to Ireland, which interested demagogues on one side of the channel, and the bitterness of Party spirit on the other, combined to baffle. Had Toryism prevailed, and Whiggism been defeated a hundred years ago, we might have been spared the Irish question of to-day.

Lord John Russell tries to show that Pitt fell to the ground between two stools; and that by retaining any part of the protective system he disabled himself from answering those who were in favour of the whole. He is also of opinion that the clauses binding Ireland to the commercial policy of England, as well as what was called the tributary clause, however beneficial the one or equitable the other, could not have been expected to satisfy the Irish patriots, elated as they were by their newly-won legislative independence : and that thus the commercial jealousy of England and the national jealousy of Ireland were both arrayed against the scheme. But it seems perfectly certain that Pitt could not have ventured to go farther in the direction of Free Trade than he did, without making it impossible to carry his proposition through the English House of Commons. His position might, perhaps, have been more logical had he done so; but that would have availed him nothing. Had the English manufacturers been amenable to logic, they would not have acted as they did. And Pitt would only have doubled the agitation against himself without gaining anything in return. For the Irish, be it remembered, were quite satisfied with the share of Free Trade accorded to them. They desired protection for their linen goods; and unlimited Free Trade would have been by no means regarded as a boon. That the very slight equivalent which Pitt required in exchange was a cheap price to pay for these substantial benefits, would have been apparent at a glance to anyone but an "Irish Patriot."

Pitt's second adventure in the region of commercial legislation was carried to a more prosperous issue, though it places the difference between the two Parties in a still stronger light than the first. The principle of the French Commercial Treaty was what is now generally accepted as an axiom of fiscal economy, but which in those days it was a proof of genius to appreciate, and of great moral courage to profess. "Increase of revenue by reduction of duty," said Pitt, "was once thought a paradox, but experience has assured us that it is more than practicable." The Convention was signed on the

15th of January 1787, and as soon as Parliament met
was violently attacked by the Opposition. The objections put forward by the Whigs on this occasion were,
however, rather political than economical. They had
declared themselves rigid Protectionists in the debates
on the Irish propositions. They were now to come
forward as the fomenters of an hereditary international
feud which neither time nor circumstance was to be
allowed to mitigate. Burke, Sheridan, and Grey, then
heard for the first time, all thundered against the
Treaty on this ground : as one that sold us to our
natural enemy, who would take advantage of its provisions to exclude us from all other alliances. Pitt
aughed at these ideas, and called them childish; and,
in fact, they were very far from being entertained so
generally in England a hundred years ago as they have
been since. The doctrine was essentially a Whiggish
one, founded on the foreign policy of the Revolution,
which was perpetually embroiling us with France. Then,
as now, there was a German interest and a French
interest in Europe, and whatever made us the allies of
the one necessarily made us the enemies of the other.
But, in spite of Louis the Fourteenth at one period,
and the Family Compact at another, there was, among
Englishmen in general, no deeply-rooted antipathy to
France before the Revolutionary war. It was not the
popular sentiment. The traditional enemy of England
was Spain. The hostile attitude of Spain every Englishman could understand. From the days of the Armada
downwards she had been our great naval and commercial rival; and our navy and our commerce were much
more interesting to an Englishman of George the
Second's time than the balance of power on the Con-

tinent, with which he firmly believed that we had nothing in the world to do. The Whigs accordingly found out, to their mortification, that they could not excite any class against the French Alliance, as they had done against the Irish propositions. Popular feeling was with the Tories, and the Commercial Treaty was ratified by immense majorities.

We now come to the question of Religious Disabilities, the third test-question by which it is usually decided whether any given statesman is a Whig or a Tory. I have already pointed out the unfairness of doing so, because, from Pitt's time at all events, the Tory Party had been divided on the question. But I willingly admit that the maintenance of the Church of England in the full enjoyment of all her dignities and possessions, and opposition to all reforms which were thought likely to endanger them, was not only a Tory but a highly popular doctrine down even to 1829. Sir Robert Walpole, in 1735, had found the national feeling on the subject too strong to permit of his rewarding the Dissenters for their support at the General Election of 1734 by the repeal of the Test Act. Pitt, who, without any understanding of any kind, had also been supported by the Dissenters, thought it his duty, when the question was brought forward, to consult the Bishops. This was in 1787 ; and of fourteen who assembled, including the Archbishop of Canterbury, only two were in favour of the measure.

This decided Pitt, who said in his speech that the loyal and peaceable Dissenters were unavoidably suffering for the faults of the more turbulent and aggressive, and that there was no means of excluding the one and admitting the other. The general question of religious exclusiveness

turns on broader considerations than were present to the
mind of Pitt, who, in common with ninety-nine Englishmen
out of every hundred at that time, had never probably
given a thought to the true nature of the Anglican
theory. But there can be no doubt that he spoke the
popular feeling in describing the emancipation of Dissenters as dangerous to the established Constitution ; and
to those who doubt whether he did so or not, I would
recommend a very striking passage on this subject in one
of Mr. Froude's essays.*

Subsequent attempts were made to procure the repeal
of the Test Act ; but, as in the case of Parliamentary
Reform, the movement had lost ground with the progress
of events in France ; and in 1790, when a resolution
introduced by Fox was thrown out by a majority of
three to one, Burke declared himself against it, though
ten years before he said he should decidedly have supported it. I think it ought to be remembered that
what a Tory Government declined to do in 1790, a
Whig Government had declined to do, under far more
favourable circumstances, more than fifty years before ;
and that if the Whigs had been in office again in the
last decade of the eighteenth century, Fox would have
had no alternative but to answer the claims of the
Dissenters in the words of Walpole. The character of
our domestic policy between 1780 and 1830, though associated with a Tory Government, was stamped on it by the
English people.

I have now surveyed briefly, but, for our present
purpose, I hope, adequately, the position of Mr. Pitt ;
first with regard to the Royal Prerogative, and, secondly
with regard to the three great principles of Parlia-

* *Short Studies on Great Subjects*, vol. ii. p. 259.

mentary representation, commercial freedom, and religious tests. Pitt, and the younger school of Tories whom his example had created, were in favour, generally speaking, of a liberal policy. On Parliamentary Reform they were opposed by the high-and-dry Tories of whom Lord North was the representative, and a considerable section of the Whigs who followed the lead of Mr. Burke. On the commercial principle they were opposed by the whole body of the Whigs led on by all their leaders, Fox, Burke, Sheridan, and Grey. On the religious question they acted for a time with the high-and-dry school, but ultimately reverted to the principles to which Pitt had always been inclined, and which, handed on by Mr. Canning, Lord Castlereagh, and Lord Grenville, were finally adopted by the other section of the Tory Party twenty-three years after Pitt's death.

Before passing on to the foreign policy of Mr. Pitt, and his character as a War Minister, it will be necessary to refer very briefly to the question of the Regency, which arose in 1788, as what occurred then had a most important bearing on the fortunes of the two Parties a quarter of a century afterwards. It was in November 1788 that George the Third first showed some signs of that mental disorder which, lasting through the whole winter, finally disappeared in the month of April. Nearly the whole of this interval was taken up with debates on the Regency Bill, and the position assumed by Mr. Pitt was what might have been expected from one who had fought the good fight of 1783-4. His contention was that the Regent could only be the King's deputy, not his substitute; and exercise only such powers as were absolutely necessary for the conduct of the administration, and not those prerogatives which were part of the King's personal authority. Fox, on the other hand, practically maintained the doctrine that the Prince of Wales was as much heir-apparent to the Regency as he was to the Throne, and had a right to step at once into the place of the Sovereign when the latter was incapacitated, without any other restrictions on his authority than were imposed on the Sovereign himself. Pitt regarded the King's illness as creating a temporary vacancy which it was for Parliament to fill up, as James the Second's flight had created a permanent vacancy which it was for Parliament to fill up; and Fox, by contesting this position and setting up an indefeasible *à priori* right of the Prince of Wales to succeed to the Regency, laid himself open to the charge of contradicting the principles of the Revolution.

It might be argued, perhaps, with some show of plausibility, that as the greater includes the less, if the Prince's right of succession to the Crown did not require to be declared by Act of Parliament, neither did his right to assume its functions in the absence of the actual wearer. The point, I think, is not very clear. But the violence of the Whigs gave Pitt an advantage over them in public opinion, which enabled him to hold his ground triumphantly during the whole of that trying winter, though fighting against difficulties second only to those which he had encountered in his great battle with the Coalition. But he was true to the principle which I have already described as constituting the differential feature of his Toryism. "He stood forward," says Mr. Massey, "at once to defend the rights of the Crown, no longer in a condition to defend itself, and to vindicate the supreme authority of Parliament assailed by those who had always assumed to be its champions."

Here we see again the natural fruits of that reconciliation of the Parliamentary principle with the monarchical principle of which Pitt was the representative.
He was still the King's servant, and would oppose any
delegation of his prerogatives, except such as were
absolutely indispensable, to those who might exercise
them in a manner prejudicial to his master's authority, and likely to excite his indignation on the recovery
of his health.   At the same time he was upholding
the rights of Parliament, which the Whigs in their turn
were assailing.   " I will un-Whig the gentleman for life,"
said Pitt, slapping his thigh in great triumph, when
Fox first propounded, in the House of Commons, his
doctrine of inherent right.

Of Pitt's restrictions on the Regency, the one which
gave the greatest offence, and the only one which it is
necessary to notice, was the conveyance to the Queen
of the sole right of filling up the Royal Household.   The
Regent could, of course, appoint his own ministers, and
dismiss Pitt.   But those who remember what a thorn in
the side of an administration an unfriendly Household
was thought capable of becoming so recently as 1839,
will not, perhaps, be of opinion that the wrath of the
Whigs was inexcusable.   It has been imputed to Pitt
that he insisted on this condition, not for the King's
sake, but for his own, and with the view of making
Fox's position intolerable should he actually become
Minister.   With the whole patronage of the Household
at his back, he could, so it is said, have secured a party
for himself which would have made him virtually master
of the situation; and was, in fact, contemplating precisely the same manœuvre as Fox had contemplated in
his India Bill.   It will occur to some people to ask,

perhaps, where was the necessity for doing this? Where would have been the freeholders of Yorkshire all this time? Where the constituencies who had given Pitt his triumphant majority five years before? And must he not have come back again as strong as ever at the first General Election that ensued, with or without the House-hold patronage to help him?

Turning now to Pitt's foreign policy, we find that, though emphatically a peace minister, and naturally anxious not to arrest the tide of that internal prosperity which he himself had set flowing, he never hesitated, when the interests of England were at stake, to assume a resolute attitude, even at the risk of war, and to turn back danger by looking it boldly in the face. At this time, *i.e.* in 1787, a revolution had occurred in Holland, by which the Stadholder and the Prince of Orange, who was married to a Prussian princess, had been driven from the Hague, and the whole power of the State aban-doned to the Democratic Party, who were the mere tools of France. To the French announcement that they intended to assist the Democrats, if necessary, by force of arms, Pitt replied by a close alliance with Prussia to resist the threatened intervention. This decisive step was crowned with complete success. France drew back directly, and a league was formed between England, Holland, and Prussia, which was attended with the happiest results. "The part played by England in these affairs," said the Russian Ambassador in a letter to St. Petersburg, "has been brilliant and courageous, and exactly what Lord Chatham would have done under similar circumstances."

In a difference with his own Court, however, which occurred immediately afterwards, the Ambassador found

the Tory country gentlemen as much attached to peace
as they had been either in 1713 or 1763. A jealousy
of French encroachments in India was always soon
awakened in England; and on the present occasion, in
a difference between the two countries relative to the
Indian trade of France, the Dutch States, in which the
Democrats were predominant, had espoused the French
side. Pitt, therefore, found no opposition to his spirited
policy in Holland. But the Tories had not yet learned
to be equally suspicious of Russia, though Pitt's far-
seeing eye showed him the nascent troubles of our
Eastern question ninety-seven years ago. A scheme for
the partition of the Ottoman Empire had even then been
entered into between the Emperor Joseph the Second
and Catherine of Russia; and on war breaking out
between Russia and Turkey, in 1787, Austria at once
struck in and invaded the Turkish dominions at the
head of 200,000 men. Pitt's good understanding with
the Dutch and Prussian Governments enabled him to
break up this alliance, and other minor ones connected
with it. But his efforts to make Russia disgorge part
of her booty were less successful. He would have treated
her as he had treated France, Austria, and Denmark;
and when she refused to give up the frontier fortress
of Ockzacow would have considered it a *casus belli*. He
had little doubt that when she saw England was in
earnest she would give way, as Austria had given way,
and as Denmark had given way. A fleet which came
to be known as the Russian Armament, was ordered to
be got ready with all despatch. But when the King's
message was brought down to the House, though Ministers
at first maintained their majority, it was soon found
out that the general feeling was against it. Out of doors

the popular feeling was still more unmistakable. Russia was a long way off. The necessary expenditure would knock at every man's door. The necessity of arresting the progress of Russia on the west coast of the Black Sea was understood only by a very few. The King himself was averse to war; and Pitt's scheme, which would have put the coping-stone on that period of his foreign policy, was obliged to be abandoned. But, being obliged to give way, Pitt had the excellent sense to give way in good time, before any ultimatum had been presented to the Court at St. Petersburg, and when England had not gone so far that a halt would look like a retreat.

Lord Stanhope speaks of the abandonment of the Russian Armament as Pitt's first failure, the first event which cast a momentary shade on his reputation. The justice or injustice of this criticism will depend, it seems to me, on how far Pitt was in the right. He had been obliged to withdraw his Irish propositions; he had abandoned Parliamentary Reform; but Lord Stanhope does not say that these were any signs of weakness. If he were as much in the right in wishing to keep Russia from the Euxine as in wishing to set free the trade of Ireland, or to diminish the power of the borough-mongers, it does not seem to me that his failure to do the first was any greater blow to his prestige than his failure to do the second or the third. Pitt himself, in his heart of hearts, probably attached even greater importance to Parliamentary Reform and Free Trade than he did to the arrest of Russia; but, however this may be, especial attention should be given to the one fact that the most powerful of all the Ministers who governed England before the Reform Bill, "more powerful than his father,

more powerful than Walpole, more powerful than Marlborough," was, during the first eight years of his administration, obliged to abandon three measures of first-class
importance in deference to the opinion which, in spite of
his large majority, it was possible to bring to bear on
him in Parliament. Whether Pitt's Reform Bill or Free
Trade Bill, or his Russian Armament were good or bad
things in themselves is nothing to the purpose. He had
set his heart on all three, and he was obliged to
relinquish them all. A modern Minister would probably
have insisted upon going on with them; and no more
interesting question will encounter us in the course of
these articles than how far the old checks on the power
of individuals, which existed down to 1832, were for good
or for evil. It is perfectly clear that in those days
public opinion had no difficulty in making itself felt.
This was proved by the General Election of 1784. It
was proved by the rejection of the Irish propositions;
and it was proved by the withdrawal of the Russian
Armament. Yet, at the same time, Governments and
political systems were infinitely more durable, more consistent, and therefore more influential with foreign Powers,
under the old *régime*, than they have been under the
new. The majority of the moment in the House of
Commons is now all-powerful. A hundred years ago no
Minister could have persevered in a policy so utterly
condemned by the public opinion of the country as the
Egyptian policy of Mr. Gladstone. Yet we delude ourselves into the belief that public opinion is now everything,
and was then nothing.

We now come to what is often regarded as a turning-
point in Mr. Pitt's career : the event which has always
been considered the best test of his character and policy.

Of Pitt before the French Revolution little is really known,
except to professed students. In connection with subsequent events his name is as familiar to us as that of
Nelson, Wellington, or Napoleon. It is not, however,
my own opinion that the latter part of his history is
so instructive as the former, while, on the other hand,
the ground has been almost completely exhausted by
previous investigators. I do not propose, therefore, to
examine Pitt's Continental policy in any detail. There
are, I think, only two questions in connection with it
on which, at this distance of time, it is necessary to
pause; and these are the beginning of the war with
France in 1793, and the system on which it was conducted down to Pitt's retirement from office in 1801.

It is certainly surprising that contemporary politicians,
occupying positions of great eminence, and conscious
that every word that they utter in public is sure to be
vigilantly scrutinized, should continue to make assertions
with regard to the origin of the war which are capable
of such easy refutation. Mr. Bright himself has often
said that the French war was provoked by the policy
of Mr. Pitt, and has founded long tirades against historical
Toryism on that very circumstance. The facts are these.
It was in July 1792 that the famous proclamation of
the Duke of Brunswick was issued from Coblentz, which
was followed by the formal deposition of Louis XVI. on
the 10th August. Our ambassador was recalled from
Paris, but the French ambassador was allowed to remain
in London, and no thought of hostilities was as yet entertained by our Government. In September virtually began
the Reign of Terror, and those " atrocities which," says
Lord Stanhope, " even amid the many evil deeds of the
first French Revolution have attained a pre-eminence

of shame." These, then, at all events, were not owing to the English "invasion," however the horrors of a subsequent period may have been. On the 6th of September was fought the battle of Jemappes, which was followed immediately by the French conquest of Flanders; and instructions were issued to the French General to throw open the navigation of the Scheldt and the Meuse, the control of which had been guaranteed to Holland by the Treaty of Munster in 1648, and all subsequent treaties, and was an unquestioned and most important part of the public law of Europe. France now declared this guarantee to be "contrary to the rights of man," and prepared to annul it. Still, though Mr. Pitt and Lord Grenville did not see their way to avoid hostilities should France persevere in this intention, and Holland be actually invaded, they did not despair of a peaceful settlement of the question. "Perhaps," says Pitt, in a letter to Lord Stafford, "some opening may arise which may enable us to contribute to the termination of the war between the different Powers in Europe, leaving France (which, I believe, is the best way) to arrange its own internal affairs as it can." But six days after this letter was written appeared the extraordinary decree of the French Convention, exhorting all nations to rise against their established Governments, and promising to all who should do so the assistance of the French people. As it was known that English seditious societies were in communication with the French Government, and as Mons. de Chauvelin, the French representative, would not deny, when appealed to, that the invitation might apply to England, it is difficult to see by what degree of casuistry the celebrated document falls short of Louis the Fourteenth's recognition of James the Third. At all events, it formed a strange comment on our remonstrance addressed to the French Government against its proposed aggression upon Holland.

To sum up : in the month of September the atrocities perpetrated in Paris, wholly unprovoked by anything which this country had done, had excited the strongest feelings of indignation in England. In the following November the same Government which was responsible for these atrocities had been guilty of a glaring breach of international obligations, to the maintenance of which England, as well as France herself, was solemnly pledged. And, finally, on the heels of the English protest against this act of violence, came a decree of the French Government inviting all the nations of Europe to rise against their rulers, and promising them French assistance. This accumulation of provocation constituted as reasonable a *casus belli* as almost any which history records. It may be very foolish to go to war at all ; but, on the principles by which mankind in general are guided—on the principles of ordinary common-sense as applied to international relations—we cannot condemn Mr. Pitt without condemning almost every other war in which this country has been engaged. The whole world knows the frenzy created in the country by, first, the Reign of Terror ; secondly, the November decree ; and, thirdly, by the execution of the King. Whether this passion of indignation, with Burke to fan it into fury, would not in time have carried any Minister before it, is extremely doubtful. Pitt had this tremendous force to reckon with, as well as his own convictions. But the war of 1793 was no war against the French Republic as far as respected the rights of other people. It was a war against the armed propagandism of anarchy, and against the claims of France to impose her own peculiar ideas on all other nations ; but it was no war against the principles of the Revolution in any sense in which an English Liberal could defend them.

With regard to Pitt's conduct of the war, we all know the criticism of Lord Macaulay. Pitt should either have done nothing at all, or have accepted the counsels of Mr. Burke and joined in a grand continental crusade against Revolutionary principles. Lord Stanhope's answer to this is good, as far as it goes; but has never seemed to me to take sufficient account of the essential element in the controversy. It cannot too often be repeated that Mr. Pitt was a Tory; and that to confine our wars as much as possible to naval and colonial operations was a standing tradition of Toryism. It was against Pitt's better judgment that he embarked on the campaign in Holland; and although, when our independence was directly threatened by the first Napoleon, Pitt would have recognized the necessity of carrying the war into the enemy's country, and of fighting him in the Peninsula to save ourselves from fighting him in England, he did not, at the first outset of the matter, at all relish the prospect of joining in a German confederacy, as we had done on several previous occasions, for the maintenance of dynastic claims. That the Navy was the true defence of England, and that in the extension of our colonies and our commerce lay the true interest of England, were old Tory doctrines to which Pitt most heartily subscribed. In requiting the insolence of the Convention by the destruction of French commerce and seizure of French colonies, Pitt was killing two birds with one stone. The fortresses which he might capture in the Low Countries we could not keep; the sugar or coffee plantations which we might capture in the West Indies we could. Right or wrong in his conduct of the war with France, Pitt was essentially a Tory.

He did not escape the ordeal which almost every public man of any mark was doomed to undergo in those days at some period of his career. In May 1798 he introduced a Bill for the more effective manning of the Navy, and, pleading urgency, pressed the House to pass it through all its stages in a single day. Mr. Tierney, while allowing that it was a necessary measure, and that unless passed at once its immediate object would be frustrated, nevertheless opposed it on the ground that longer notice ought to have been given. Pitt, provoked by what seemed vexatious opposition, replied that coupling the right hon. gentleman's motion with the admissions which he had made simultaneously, he could only suppose that his object was to obstruct the defences of the country. Tierney declared that this was not Parliamentary language, and appealed to the Chair. Addington, then Speaker, ruled that whatever tended to cast a personal imputation for words spoken in debate was certainly disorderly and un-parliamentary, and called on Pitt for an explanation. He declined either to explain or retract ; and a duel on Putney Heath, which luckily terminated without bloodshed, was the necessary consequence. Now that hon. members no longer have the consolation of single combat to resort to, it is difficult to see what a man in Mr. Tierney's position could do ; for, however the House might punish a member in such a case, it would be for contumacy towards the Speaker, and not for the words spoken ; so that the injured individual would get no salve for his honour. Even then, however, the duel excited some dissatisfaction. The King spoke gravely of it, and Wilberforce was with difficulty withheld from giving notice of a motion condemnatory of the practice of duelling. Pitt told him at once that the inevitable result of such a motion being carried would be his own retirement from office.

It may cause some surprise, perhaps, that I have said nothing of Mr. Pitt's financial policy, and his celebrated " Sinking Fund." But these are hardly subjects of controversy at the present day. That Pitt was a master of finance is not disputed. That his idea of a Sinking Fund was based on calculations not unlike those which inspired Mr. Gladstone's financial measures from 1860 to 1864, will be allowed with almost equal unanimity. Continued peace, and ever-growing material prosperity, were essential to the success of both ; and we have been taught by long experience that it is impossible to rely on either. At the end of the last century, however, men thought differently. Even on the eve of the French Revolution, philosophers were hailing the dawn of an era of peace and goodwill, of scientific discovery, and national progress ; and if Pitt, at four-and-twenty, was under the influence of this general delusion it is the worst that can be said of him.*

Of this branch of Mr. Pitt's administration I shall here quote the very concise summary to be found in the pages of a highly competent authority, and at the same time no very willing witness :—

Mr. Pitt's financial and commercial administration was remarkable certainly for directness of aim, boldness of action, and firmness of grasp Realising to the full the paramount obligation of a man placed at the helm

---

* " His policy was founded on the continuance of peace. We have reason to know that he, an early disciple of Adam Smith, contemplated at this time a larger measure of free trade than the National Debt, accumulated during the subsequent war, now permits ; we mean an abolition of all custom duties, and a limitation of the national income to internal taxation."—Sir George Cornewall Lewis's *Administrations of Great Britain*, p. 134.

of the State to secure its internal and external safety at all hazards, he left no stone unturned to achieve that end. So long as peace lasted, he strained every nerve to bring about an equilibrium in the budget by equalizing the revenue with the expenditure. Immediately war commenced he threw aside every other consideration, and placed the safety of the State first and foremost over everything else. But, after all, what poor results, in an economic aspect, have come from an administration otherwise most brilliant.*

The Professor does not see that the first part of this statement answers the last. It is admitted by everybody, Lord Macaulay among the number, that Pitt's administration from 1784 to 1793 was economically brilliant. It is admitted by the Professor that his change of system after 1793 was a work of necessity; and if the later policy thus forced upon him was as brilliant in one way as the earlier had been in another, I think it will be generally agreed that little room is left for censure. Had Pitt preferred economical considerations to imperial, we should have undergone all the horrors of a French invasion, our army and navy would have been annihilated, our commerce would have been destroyed, our colonies would have been lost to us for ever; and we should have been reduced to the level of a fourth-class Power, with no more voice in the affairs of Europe than Sweden or Portugal. It is the glory of Pitt that, deeply interested as he was in the maintenance of peace, devoted as he was to the cause of retrenchment and reform, and feeling as he did that these were the spheres of policy most congenial to his own powers, he knew, nevertheless, that there was something greater even than these; and that he did not hesitate for a moment to sacrifice all his darling projects and, as he probably thought, his most assured road to fame, when the inheritance of our fathers was at stake.

* *History of British Commerce*, by Prof. Leonine Levi, 2nd edition, 1880.

5

We have seen what was Pitt's first idea of a union with Ireland, a union founded on identity of interests and complete commercial equality. This being rejected, he was driven to consider the possibility of an amalgamation of the two Legislatures, with a view to neutralizing the effects of that national jealousy which, in an Irish Parliament, was fatal to every overture from England. That the Act of Union was the direct result of the rejection of the Irish propositions, and would certainly have been proposed had no rebellion occurred in '98, must be plain to everyone who reads the history of the two transactions consecutively. It was Lord Cornwallis's conviction, who was then Lord-Lieutenant of Ireland, that the removal of Roman Catholic disabilities should have formed an integral part of the Act of Union. Pitt seems to have thought it would be easier to pass the two Acts separately. But it is evident now that many who would have acquiesced in emancipation as the price of the Union, changed their minds when the Union had been passed without it. The King, of course, might have stood out against it in any form. But he would have been less likely to do so, perhaps, had it been originally wrapped up with the other provisions of the Act, and represented to him as an essential element of one comprehensive measure which could not survive the excision of it. I am disposed to think that this is the one great error of judgment with which Mr. Pitt is chargeable. The intrigues of Lord Loughborough and Lord Auckland made that impossible which would otherwise have been only difficult, and have often been considered the real cause of the miscarriage. But, had Pitt taken the advice of Lord Cornwallis, he would probably have been beforehand with both of them.

As the Irish Roman Catholics had supported the Union

on the understanding that it was a stepping-stone to the removal of their religious disabilities, Pitt, when he found that he could not fulfil his engagements, felt it incumbent upon him at once to give some signal proof of his sincerity, and resigned office. His enemies said it was only a good excuse for devolving upon somebody else the responsibility of making peace with France. This insinuation was made by Lord Auckland, and indignantly repelled by Pitt himself in the House of Commons, who said, with justice, that he had lived to very little purpose during the last seventeen years if it was not clear that a disposition to shrink from responsibilities was not among his faults. It was on the 5th of February 1801 that the King very reluctantly accepted Mr. Pitt's resignation, and charged Mr. Addington, then Speaker of the House of Commons, with the formation of a new Government. But, before the new arrangements could be completed, the King fell ill of his old complaint, and for a time his life was despaired of. The situation was extraordinary. There was no regular Government, and no acting Sovereign. And the conditions of a Regency had to be discussed with one Minister who had no authority, and another who had no Cabinet. However, the recovery of the King once more restored order, and Mr. Addington's Administration was completed. But during His Majesty's illness, alarmed by the evidence which it gave of the depth of his feelings on the subject, Mr. Pitt sent a message to his Sovereign promising never to revive the subject, either in or out of office, during his lifetime. " Now," said George III., " my mind will be at ease "; and, in fact, his recovery set in from that moment. Under these altered circumstances Pitt, it appears, would have been willing to retract his resignation could Addington's claim have been amicably and

5 *

honourably disposed of. This, however, was just what it was impossible to do. Some of Pitt's friends, without his knowledge, actually proposed to Addington that he should recommend the King to recall Mr. Pitt. Addington, however, strange to say, declined to lay his head upon the block, as these gentlemen suggested; and the matter fell through, Pitt declaring "that he meant to give his strenuous support to the new Administration, and expected his friends to do the same." The King had chosen his Minister, and Pitt was bound to support him till circumstances should reveal his incapacity.

Finally, it is very clear that both the charges brought against Pitt with regard to his conduct in this affair cannot be true. They destroy each other. If he was anxious to resign to throw on Addington the burden of the peace, he could hardly have been anxious to come back before the peace was made. And if he was really as willing to come back as we are told he was, he could not have been actuated by any dread of the responsibility of office.

Addington's Ministry lasted from March 1801 to May 1804, and throughout the whole period there seems to have been a general belief that Pitt would sooner or later come back again, either at the head of his former colleagues, or in company, perhaps, with some members of the Opposition. Negotiations were constantly going on, having for their object one or other of these consummations, and many amusing stories are told of the efforts to seduce Mr. Pitt into a coalition with the Doctor. Pitt, at this time, was residing principally at Walmer Castle, where various emissaries visited him from time to time with the above object. His great friend Dundas was one of them, who was probably more intimate with Pitt than any other man alive. But even he, when charged with the suggestion that Pitt and Addington should serve together on a footing of equality under some nominal Prime Minister, was afraid to open his commission till they had reached the second bottle of port. Then, it is said, Pitt stopped him with a single look, and Dundas returned to town without the scheme having been so much as talked over. According to another anecdote, attributed to Pitt himself, when the suggestion was first broached to him he really had not the curiosity to inquire what place was destined for himself. At all events, whatever the cause, whether it was the interference, at a critical moment, of Lord Grenville, who perhaps wished to keep the schism in the Tory Party open, or whether Mr. Pitt himself was disappointed at not being called for more loudly by the public voice, nothing came of such attempts. Perhaps they had been hopeless from the first. Pitt would not endure an equal, nor Addington a superior. Nor were Addington's feelings towards Pitt rendered more amicable by the suspicion instilled into him by his friends, that Pitt had been using him as a warming-pan. Nobody, however, can with justice blame Mr. Pitt for refusing to accept the situation which Mr. Addington was offering to him. There is something almost ludicrous in it when one comes to consider it dispassionately; nor is it necessary, at the present day, I think, to defend Pitt's conduct any further.

Not so, however, with another negotiation which immediately preceded Pitt's return to power. When Addington's retirement was seen to be inevitable, we were again at war with France, and a picked army of two hundred thousand men was encamped at Boulogne waiting only a favourable opportunity to invade our shores. This was no time for party jealousies and personal antipathies, and Pitt at once recognized the propriety of endeavouring to form an Administration which should represent all parties in the country. Communications were at once opened with the leaders of the Opposition, which now included not only the regular Whigs, but some of Mr. Pitt's former supporters as well, who acknowledged Lord Grenville as their leader. No difficulty was made in the first instance by any of the gentlemen in question, though there was some little show of *nolo episcopari* about Fox himself which probably meant nothing, and, even if it did, would not have prevented him recommending the alliance to his friends. His own words upon the subject not only show what he thought about it, but are a curious illustration of the manners and language of our forefathers. " The plan ought to succeed," he said, " it must succeed, it was so damned right." It was doomed to failure for all this. When Fox's name was mentioned to the King, George the Third at once refused to have anything to say to that statesman, and when the rest of the Opposition heard of this they refused at once to have anything to say to Mr. Pitt. Lord Grenville, in particular, made the admission of Mr. Fox an indispensable condition of his own accession to the Ministry. " I will teach that proud man that I can do without him," said Mr. Pitt, " if it cost me my life." He taught him the lesson, and he paid the price.

That the mortifications and disappointments which he experienced on this occasion hastened the decline of Mr. Pitt's health, which was even then in a precarious state, there can be no manner of doubt ; and what justification there was for Lord Grenville's conduct I have never been able to discover. For fifteen years he had been Pitt's ablest colleague, and Fox's ablest opponent. The whole policy of the war, down to 1801, which had been conducted by Lord Grenville, had been unsparingly condemned by the Whig leader. They had hardly an opinion in common, except the conviction that Addington was unfit to be Prime Minister. However much Lord Grenville might agree with Mr. Pitt in the wisdom of letting bygones be bygones, that he should have refused to join the Minister with whom he had acted for nearly twenty years, for no other reason than that another statesman was excluded from the Cabinet who had been in opposition to that Minister for twenty years, and with whom he himself had been on friendly terms for only three, is what no advocate would ask any jury to believe. Lord Malmesbury's explanation is more probable ; namely, that Lord Grenville had been anxious for some years to throw off the authority of Mr. Pitt, and to set up in politics for himself.

But it is said that Mr. Pitt, if he had been firm, could have forced the King to accept Mr. Fox. If he had refused to form a Government except on that condition, the King, it is thought, must have given way. Those who say so forget, perhaps, that the Addington Ministry could still command a majority in the House of Commons; not such majorities as Mr. Pitt's, but as large as many Ministers have commanded whom George the Third had been able to maintain. Addington was personally popular ; he was fond of describing himself in after life as " the last of the port-wine faction "; he represented the Protestant interest ; and if the King had chosen to dissolve, it is by no means certain that his majority would not have been increased. It is, at all events, quite certain that George the Third would have tried the experiment before yielding to dictation. But what has been still more completely forgotten is the fact that Mr. Pitt could *not* have pressed Fox upon the King; it was morally impossible. Mr. Pitt had come into power as the direct champion and representative of the Royal Prerogative in this very particular. The freedom of the Crown to choose its own Ministers was the great principle for which he had fought and conquered, and the key-stone of the new Toryism which he had inaugurated. To have flown in the face of it now, and to have insisted on the right of a political party to dictate a Minister to the Crown, would have given the lie to his whole career. Had he done this, then, indeed, with some justice might Lord Macaulay have claimed him as a Whig.

Mr. Pitt's second Administration lasted from May 1804 to January 1806. But, short as it was, it witnessed two of the greatest events of the Revolutionary war—the battles of Trafalgar and Austerlitz. The one annihilated the French and Spanish fleets, and left England mistress of the ocean; the other annihilated the coalition which Pitt had formed against Napoleon, and left France mistress of the Continent. We can see at this distance of time that Trafalgar was more important than Austerlitz, because, even after the defeat of the Austrian and Russian armies, there were plenty of materials left for fresh combinations against France, which were, in fact, renewed over and over again till the fighting power of the French was exhausted. But Trafalgar cut the naval power of our enemies down to the ground, so that a generation had to pass away before it could again become formidable. Trafalgar, therefore, struck a far heavier blow at Napoleon than Austerlitz struck at his opponents, while England herself was relieved by it from all dread of invasion during the remainder of the war. But it was natural that Mr. Pitt himself should not view the two events precisely from this point of view. The alliance against France, which ended with the battle of Austerlitz, was his own special work. He expected immense results from it. " England," he said, at the Lord Mayor's dinner, only three weeks before the battle was fought, " has saved herself by her exertions, and will, I trust, save Europe by her example." This was his whole speech, and it was the last he ever made in public. The sudden destruction of all his hopes proved too much for his already shattered constitution, and he died at Putney the 23rd of January following, with almost the same words on his lips as the imagination of Pope has assigned to the death-bed of Cobham.

A few words remain to be added on the personal character and private life of Mr. Pitt, which have both been much misrepresented. And even now, though many wrong impressions have been effaced by time, others still linger, of which political prejudice will always, perhaps, prevent the complete eradication. Mr. Pitt, for instance, has been charged with insincerity. Evidence of this is to be found, we are told, in his treatment of Parliamentary Reform ; in his change of front with regard to the impeachment of Warren Hastings, in his conduct of the Regency Bill in 1788, in his own retirement from office in 1801, and in his consent to the exclusion of Fox in 1804. On the first of these questions it is enough, I think, to quote what has been said by Lord Beaconsfield: " Pitt not sincere! why, he was fighting for his life." The charge against him in regard to Warren Hastings is a pure assumption, and shows rather, in my opinion, of what those were capable who made it,

than of what Mr. Pitt was capable. It is said that he
abandoned Hastings to the Whigs, to divert their fire
from himself. The simple answer to this is, that till the
night before the debate, in which he announced his intention of not opposing the inquiry, he had never gone
through the evidence, and though he approached it with
a mind decidedly favourable to Hastings, he rose from
it with a different impression. This explanation of his
conduct rests on the positive statements of Mr. Pitt's own
friends who were in constant intercourse with him at
the time, while for the other interpretation we have only
the unfounded surmises of his political opponents, who
seem, as we have already hinted, to have judged of Mr.
Pitt by themselves.

Of his conduct in the Regency, in the crisis of 1801,
and again in 1804, we have already spoken. It may
readily be allowed that Pitt was not absolutely anxious
to sit in the same Cabinet with Mr. Fox though he
himself were Prime Minister. He understood the good
effect that would be produced upon the Continent by the
spectacle of a general union and a combination of the
Leaders of all parties, dropping all minor differences of
opinion, against the common enemy. For this great object
he was willing to run considerable risks both public and
private : public, because the chances that Mr. Fox would
continue to act harmoniously with himself were exceedingly slender, and a rupture with him afterwards
would be more injurious to the public interests than never
to have joined him at all; private, because he could
not but be sensible that in Fox he would have no tract-
able subordinate, but a very troublesome and ambitious
equal. But he was clearly not bound to press Fox upon
the King beyond a certain point. Mr. Pitt was as proud

a man in his way as Lord Grenville, and if he had a fault it was Addison's, " Too fond to rule alone." But it is one which almost always accompanies the consciousness of great powers, and when indulged to excess is only the price we have to pay for securing those great powers to the public service. This particular quality Mr. Pitt displayed on several well-known occasions. He displayed it in his attitude towards Shelburne in 1783, he displayed it in his communications with the Prince of Wales in 1788, and also on various subsequent occasions to which we have referred Pitt was determined to be master. And so was Walpole, so was Chatham, and so was Sir Robert Peel.

It was certainly not to Pitt's credit that he allowed himself to be plundered by his servants and tradespeople on such a monstrous scale, that after the enjoyment for seventeen years of £10,000 a year he owed nearly £50,000. When some of his friends undertook to go through his accounts, they found incredible amounts charged for the ordinary necessaries of life. Nine hundredweight of butcher's meat in a week, is one item mentioned by Lord Carrington ; poultry and fish were in proportion ; and the only excuse for Pitt is, that he was plunged in public affairs at so early an age that he had no time to learn the value of money, or the necessity of economy, until he became hopelessly entangled. To a young man with no patrimony, who becomes Prime Minister of England at twenty-four years of age, much may be forgiven in the way of pecuniary mismanagement.

Of Pitt at his ease—Pitt in his hour of recreation and social pleasure, we have pictures both in his youth and middle age which show that, whatever he may have

been in public, in private life he must have been one of
the most delightful of companions. We learn a good deal
of him as a young man from the *Diary* of Mr. Wilberforce, with whom he made a prolonged stay in the summer
of 1783. Wilberforce's house at Wimbledon was noted
for its kitchen-garden, its peas and its strawberries.
Here Pitt and the future philanthropist, with two or
three friends of the same age, Edward Eliot, Henry
Banks, and Pepper Arden, enjoyed themselves like school-
boys, spending the hot days upon the river, dining at
5 o'clock, and strolling about the fields till supper-time.
Wilberforce records with triumph that he succeeded on
Sunday in getting Pitt and Pepper Arden to church.
Those who only knew Pitt in public life had no idea of
what he was in company of this kind—the gayest and
most frolicsome of the party, full of practical jokes, and
at the same time showing himself as well qualified as
Johnson to fight his way by his literature and his wit.
Pitt was only twenty-four, in the bloom of youth and
youthful spirits, yet already looked up to as one of the
first statesmen of the age; had led the House of Commons
with marked success against an overwhelming array of
talent and experience, had already been Chancellor of the
Exchequer, and might at that moment have been Prime
Minister. Life can have few better things to offer than
that combination of youthful buoyancy and merriment
with the dignity and fame of riper age which was the
happy lot of William Pitt.

In September the whole party went to Corfe Castle, in
Dorsetshire, to shoot partridges, Pitt's favourite amusement, where the fortunes of England were nearly changed
by the alleged shortsightedness of Wilberforce, who, in
firing at a bird, narrowly missed his future chief. After

a week in the stubbles, Pitt started on a trip to France, which lasted about six. He noticed the condition of the people as he travelled through the country, and found it better than he had expected. He was presented to the King and Queen, who made much of him; and he went stag-hunting at Fontainebleau, looking a very clumsy figure, says Wilberforce, in his big jack-boots. He got home again on the 24th of October, and never again quitted the shores of England.

Pitt was particularly fond of partridge-shooting, and we find frequent allusions to it in his correspondence. When he was out of office he took a farm near Walmer for the express purpose of enjoying himself after his own fashion. Lady Hester, who was then living with him, used to carry his luncheon to the farm-house, and tells us of the high spirits which he used to enjoy on these occasions, and the great hunches of bread and cheese which he would eat. When he returned to Walmer in the evening he would, perhaps, find Dundas, or some other intimate friend, arrived from town either to talk over public affairs with him, or discuss the comparative merits of *Virgil* and *Lucan*. I have often wondered if they ever adjourned to the rampart outside the dining-room, and drank their port by the cannon which are, or were, situated on it, looking across the channel the while and straining their eyes for the first glimpse of the Boulogne flotilla.

Hollwood, however, near Bromley, was Pitt's favourite residence. It was at no great distance from Hayes, his birthplace, and when a boy he used to go bird's-nesting in the Hollwood plantations. He had always wished to be the owner of it; and his wish was gratified shortly after he became Prime Minister. Here he was as partial

to his axe and pruning-knife as Mr. Gladstone himself;
and Wilberforce has described the day they spent cutting
paths under the trees and through the underwood. The
necessity of selling Hollwood in 1801 was a greater blow
to him than the necessity of quitting office. All Pitt's
tastes were innocent, for I decline to call his love of
port wine by any other name. At an early age he renounced the gaming-table, but was able, to the last, to
take pleasure in a round game, especially "speculation."
To women, as a rule, he was cold. "Pretty girlibus in-
differentissimus," said the Rolliad. But he had heart
enough to fall in love with one, Miss Eleanor Eden,
the daughter of Lord Auckland, who is said to have returned the affection, of which she was in every way
worthy. But his debts and uncertain pecuniary prospects
prevented him from making her an offer, though he fully
explained himself to her father. Lord Auckland's place
was at Westerham, near Hollwood, and it was among
these beautiful sunny woods that their attachment sprang
up. When Pitt was on his death-bed he found that
what the Whigs had laughed at so loudly was one of
those things which bring a man peace at the last. He
had so long neglected prayer, he said, that he feared it
was of no use then. But he looked back with satisfaction on " the innocence of his life."

So lived and died William Pitt, the greatest Parliamentary statesman whom England has produced, if
greatness is to be measured not merely by the genius
of the individual but by the quality of the circumstances
among which his lot is cast, and the magnitude of the difficulties which he is called on to confront and overcome.
Chatham is a splendid figure in our annals; but he never
for one moment attained the moral grandeur of his son.

He never was, for he never had the chance of being, the one man upon whom, through long years of danger both from foreign and domestic enemies, a nation reposed with confidence, whose removal from power was the signal for general despair, whose restoration revived the public spirit as sunrise renews the daylight, and whose death was lamented by the tears not only of personal friends and Parliamentary supporters, but by thousands who had never seen him, yet felt themselves reduced to sudden helplessness by the loss of their tried protector. Such a position as this no other man in English history has ever occupied; and this, which is wholly independent of particular measures or combinations, is Pitt's title to immortality.

CHAPTER II.

LORD LIVERPOOL.

LIVERPOOL.—PORTLAND.—PERCEVAL.—CASTLEREAGH.—WELLESLEY.—THE
PENINSULAR WAR.—THE PEACE.—DISTRESS IN THE COUNTRY.—THE
SIX ACTS.—ROMAN CATHOLIC CLAIMS.—FINANCE.

OF that constellation of statesmen who illumined the last
years of the Georgian era none sank to his rest amid so
little public observation, or lingered for so brief a period
on the lips of men, as he who had been first among them.
Castlereagh, Canning, Wellesley, Peel, Wellington, Lyndhurst, each and all, though doubtless in very different degrees, have been objects of interest and curiosity ever since
the grave closed over them, and have bequeathed to posterity numerous still unsettled questions in the spheres of
both ethics and politics.   Round every one of them quite a
small literature has sprung up ; and over the policy of
some and the character of others controversy still rages
with few symptoms of abatement.   Lord Liverpool alone,
who for nearly fifteen years was the chief of this brilliant
group, who gave his name to a Government second only
in duration to the Ministries of Pitt and Walpole, and
richer even than these in the harvest of glory which it
reaped, passed suddenly into the darkness without seeming
to be missed, and leaving behind him scarce a trace of his
living greatness in the pages of political literature.

Lord Liverpool, however, is much more entitled to the gratitude and admiration of posterity than some statesmen who have enjoyed much more of it. He was one of that class of Ministers whom we should be very glad to see more numerous : patient, prudent, and patriotic ; careless of his own fame, so that those measures were pursued which he considered for the public good ; shunning rather than courting popular applause; and by his clear common sense, his unselfishness, and his equanimity, solving problems and surmounting difficulties which more brilliant men are wont either to create or to exasperate. Both in 1806 and in 1809 he might have been Prime Minister had he chosen. But he recoiled from the first place, nor did he finally accept it till he saw that without him the Tory Party must be broken up, and the Whigs admitted in a body. Thus, he was not a man either to originate a great policy, to make personal enemies, or to be mixed up in political intrigues and back-stairs conspiracies. His career, accordingly, was deficient in all those elements which excite wonder and curiosity. No " revelations," no scandals, no racy anecdotes were to be expected from his private papers. There were no aspersions on his character which his family might have been eager to refute; no passages in his career which might seem to require vindication. Thus, many of the ordinary motives to which the publication of political biographies and the private papers of deceased statesmen may reasonably be attributed, were in his case wanting. And the literary warfare which usually follows such productions, and keeps alive the memory of men not above mediocrity, has not yet been kindled by the quiet virtues of Lord Liverpool.

Mr. Pitt died, as we have seen, in January 1806, and Mr. Fox survived him only six months. With the dis-

appearance of these two great men who had trodden the
stage of politics, the one for a quarter of a century, the
other for a whole generation, taller by a head than their
contemporaries, and both marked out by a certain elevation
of tone and vigour of character as natural leaders of mankind, English politics take a new point of departure. We
find ourselves, undoubtedly, on a lower level. Great men
remain; but they are not in their proper places. Others
are to come; but they are, as yet, in *statu pupillari*. During
the twenty years that elapsed between the death of Mr.
Fox and the accession to power of Mr. Canning, neither
the Whigs nor the Tories were under the influence of
commanding minds, capable of guiding and leading public
opinion; of making Government august and faction contemptible. At the same time, I think it will hereafter be
allowed that the Tory leaders of that stormy age have
been judged with a severity very much in excess of their
deserts; and that if the dangers through which they
steered us in safety, and the novelty of the problems which
confronted them as soon as they arrived in port, are fairly
weighed and counted, they are rather entitled to our
gratitude and respect for what they did than to our satire
for what they left undone.

At the death of Mr. Pitt in January 1806 Lord Hawkesbury was thirty-five years of age. Though the son of a
peer, he was not within the charmed circle of the great
families, some connection with which was necessary even
to a Tory who had neither glittering talents nor professional distinction to bring him into public notice. The
Jenkinsons were a wealthy county family, long seated at
Walcot near Charlbury, in Oxfordshire. The first who
raised the family to consequence is said to have been that
Antony Jenkinson who, in the reign of Queen Elizabeth,

was distinguished as a traveller and diplomatist. His descendant in 1620 purchased the manor of Hawkesbury in Gloucestershire. And in 1661 the Jenkinson of that day was made a baronet by Charles II. They represented Oxfordshire in Parliament for many generations, but about the middle of the last century they were compelled to part with the Walcot property, and henceforth their connection with the county of Oxford seems to have been lost. His father, the first Lord Liverpool, was private secretary to Lord Bute, and afterwards became the leader of the King's friends. He was Secretary at War under Lord North, and a member of the Board of Trade under Mr. Pitt, a post for which his knowledge of finance and commerce particularly qualified him. In 1786 he was created Baron Hawkesbury, and, in 1806, Earl of Liverpool. His eldest son, Robert Banks, was born on the 7th of June 1770, just two months after the birth of Mr. Canning. He was educated at Charterhouse and Christchurch, where he was Canning's friend and contemporary, and was bred to politics by his father, who early directed his attention to those commercial studies of which he was so fond himself. In 1791 he was returned to Parliament for Rye. He at once began to take an active part in the debates and distinguished himself on several occasions during Pitt's first Administration. On the breaking out of the war, he paid a visit to the Continent, and stayed some time at Coblentz while the Austrian and Prussian armies were quartered in that fortress. He speaks highly of the discipline and personal appearance of the Prussian soldiers, but thinks that Austria, owing to the greater magnitude of her empire, and her more plentiful supplies of men, must prove in the long run the stouter belligerent of the two : a calculation that was verified by events. And he quotes a curious saying of the Duke of Brunswick, that no country need be alarmed at the prospect of a Prussian invasion, because the Prussian soldiers were insensible to female beauty. "Ils sont grands bêtes," the Duke continued, "mais pourtant ils savent bien leur affaire." On his return home he was appointed to a seat at the India Board : and three years afterwards he was made Master of the Mint, a post that he occupied down to the retirement of Mr. Pitt.

In the Addington Administration, Lord Hawkesbury was Secretary of State for Foreign Affairs, in which capacity it fell to his lot to negotiate the Treaty of Amiens, a task which he seems to have performed with adequate ability, notwithstanding Mr. Fox's denunciations of him when he was first appointed to the office. In his correspondence with the French Government, we are informed for the first time of a curious scheme that was devised in Paris for bribing the family of Napoleon to dissuade him from his demands on England. Joseph, Lucien, and Josephine are the three Bonapartes named. Talleyrand thought it might be done, and meant to get something by the job. Lord Whitworth, however, was less sanguine, and the result justified his foresight. This notable device broke down on more than one point. It was not repudiated by the English Ministry ; but Addington and Hawkesbury did not see how it was possible to go higher than a hundred thousand pounds. If a much larger sum were expended, how would it be possible to account for it to the House of Commons ? Whitworth thought nothing could be done under at least a million ; and that the bargain would be cheap at two. But while the Secretary and the Ambassador were disputing about the price, Joseph and Lucien and Madame, who were all quite willing to earn it, seem to have discovered that the task was beyond their powers ; and though it was never formally abandoned, the English ambassador soon became convinced of its futility, and, demanding his passports, quitted Paris on the 12th of May. On the 18th of that month, war was declared against France.*

No objections of any moment were raised to the principle of the war, however severely the conduct of Ministers was criticised. But it led to the downfall of Addington. Though incapable of anything like factious opposition, Mr. Pitt was compelled to acknowledge that in that financial ability which was necessary to provide for a war expenditure Addington was totally deficient, and, the public taking the same view, in the spring of 1804, Mr. Pitt was recalled to the Treasury. But the change made no substantial difference to the subject of the present memoir. He exchanged the Foreign Office for the Home, partly because Mr. Pitt had hoped to strengthen his Administration by the accession of Lord Moira, who must in that case have taken the Foreign Office, a plan that was subsequently abandoned : partly because it was thought desirable that Lord Hawkesbury, who had been called up to the Lords in 1803, should continue to lead the Upper House, which he could not have done had he remained Foreign Secretary while another Peer was at the Home Office, the senior department of the two : and partly in deference to the King, who liked Lord Hawkesbury personally, and wished him to occupy that place in the Ministry which brought the holder of it most frequently into the royal presence. Though by this arrangement the services of Lord Hawkesbury were lost to that department for which we are inclined to think he was best qualified, he himself was rather a gainer than a loser by it. As the recognized leader of the Tory Party in the House of Lords,

* For the origin of the war *see* page 59.

in a Ministry of which Pitt was chief, he assumed a position second only to that of Pitt himself, and acquired a title to the loyalty of that statesman's friends which his tenure of office under Addington would never have secured him. Seeing that Grenville would not, and that Canning could not, be their leader, it must already have occurred to many of Mr. Pitt's supporters that the future successor of that statesman was to be found in the new Home Secretary.

During the last brief administration of Pitt, Lord Hawkesbury conducted himself with his usual good sense and good temper. Canning, who was now Treasurer of the Navy, thought proper to attack him very violently, and to insinuate that the seals of the Foreign Office had been taken from him because Pitt was dissatisfied with his conduct of it. The injured statesman at once sent in his resignation, but was easily mollified by the entreaties and apologies of Pitt, and induced to remain in office on condition that a public disavowal of the calumny should be made as soon as possible. To this Pitt readily consented, and Canning, at the same time expressing his regret very handsomely, a reconciliation was soon effected, and, what is more remarkable, was permanent. It is to this placable and easy-going disposition, to which the burden of a sustained resentment is more grievous than the original affront, that many men are indebted for success apparently beyond their merits. Among the various causes which account for the rise of Lord Liverpool, this happy gift of nature was by no means among the least important.

Another proof of that practical sagacity and liberal temperament for which he was remarkable is to be found in the advice which about this time he tendered to the Roman Catholics. He reminded them of the absolute impossibility of a Relief Bill being carried at that season, and pointed out the bad effect which their perseverance in demanding it was calculated to produce upon the minds of men at present not wholly indisposed to them. To have carried a Roman Catholic Relief Bill, in spite of the King's resistance and the powerful political party which he had in reserve, was manifestly impossible ; and if the Whigs did not know it to be impossible, it says but little for their sagacity. At all events, they discovered it two years afterwards, when Fox and Grenville failed, equally with Pitt and Canning, to effect this great change. It is remarkable how soon the consequences ensued which Lord Hawkesbury had foreseen. He had always been a favourite with George the Third, and, though a loyal follower of Pitt, had always rather inclined to the other division of the Tory Party which the King especially affected. To both the King and Lord Hawkesbury the continued estrangement between Pitt and Addington, who, with a *clientèle* of some forty members, stood sullenly aloof from the Treasury Benches, must have been extremely painful. And now the very blunder of the Romanists which Lord Hawkesbury had so accurately appreciated was found to pave the way for a reconciliation between them. Lord Fingall, who at this time was the head of the Roman Catholic interest, was supposed to be secretly encouraged by the Grenville party to urge its wrongs upon Parliament both in season and out of season. This conduct had exactly the effect upon Mr. Pitt which Hawkesbury had foreseen. It sickened him with the whole party, and drew him nearer to the ex-Minister who represented the anti-Catholic party.

Lord Hawkesbury saw the opportunity, and knew right well how agreeable he should make himself to his royal

master by taking prompt advantage of it. He sounded
Addington, who, though he was by no means adverse to
the *redintegratio amoris* now proposed to him, thought
proper to affect much indifference. He spoke of the overtures made to him as a flirtation not likely to come to
much, and professed the utmost reluctance to being thrust
into the House of Lords. Pitt's reasons, however, for
raising him to this dignity seem to have been founded in
a real regard for his friend's interests. No man, he said,
in a letter to Lord Hawkesbury, which Mr. Yonge,* we
think, has been the first to bring to light, "no man can be
of any consequence in the second situation in such a body
as the House of Commons who is not an able debater, and
has not, above all, the talents of quick reply." "Good
sense," he added, "good manners, dignity, and a reasonable
speaking will carry a man through in the first situation
when he has all the advantage of authority." This is a
curious and valuable fragment which has thus been rescued
from oblivion, applicable to all times ; and one is struck
at once with the conspicuous illustrations which it drew
from the after career of him to whom it was addressed,
Lord Liverpool himself.

Ultimately, as we know, Addington closed with the terms
offered him and became Lord Sidmouth, with the presidency
of the Council and the lead of the House of Lords. And
this was Hawkesbury's first appearance in a part which he
afterwards may be said to have made his own—the part of
political mediator. As, however, might be expected from
the characters of the two men, Pitt was the more sincere
of the two in the accommodation which Lord Hawkesbury
had effected. Sidmouth was dissatisfied not only with his

---

* *Life of Lord Liverpool*, by C. D. Yonge, Regius Professor of History and
English Literature in Queen's College, Belfast. 3 vols. 1868.

share of patronage but also with his position in the Cabinet, and retired from it in less than twelve months. But the junction, short-lived as it was, had borne good fruit. Many of Addington's supporters remained attached to Mr. Pitt, and nothing but his death prevented the schism in the party from being completely healed. His second administration, however, owing partly to Addington and partly to Grenville, had been much weaker than his first; and at the moment of his death the Tory body had not yet regained its former cohesion and unanimity.

Accordingly, when on Pitt's death Lord Hawkesbury was sent for by the King and desired to form an Administration, he and all the late colleagues of Mr. Pitt unanimously declined the task; and the result was the Ministry of "All the Talents," opposition to which was led by Lord Hawkesbury in the House of Lords and Mr. Perceval in the House of Commons. As the House of Commons consisted of the same men after Mr. Pitt's death as it did before, as the Tory Party commanded an undoubted majority, and as in the very next year they returned to power in spite of an unfavourable election, it is difficult to understand what possessed them in the interim, or why a Portland or Perceval Administration could not have been formed in 1806 as well as in 1807. It could not have been the mere fact that Fox, who was dead in 1807, was alive in 1806; for even Addington had stood up against Fox, and either Canning or Castlereagh was more formidable in debate than Addington. I suppose the history of it lies in the difficulty created by Lord Sidmouth. If he claimed a right to be Mr. Pitt's successor, it is probable enough that Hawkesbury, Melville, Canning, Castlereagh, and others would deride the claim, while all the rank and file of the old Pittite Tories would have followed him with extreme reluctance even had he been allowed to make it good. At the same time he commanded sufficient votes in the House of Commons to make a Tory Administration under any chief except Pitt impossible unless it pleased him to support it. Thus either a Ministry with Addington at the head of it or a Ministry with Addington opposed to it would have been equally weak; and Lord Hawkesbury and the rest of the Tories chose the only alternative open to them and retired from the field altogether. It was the wisest step they could have taken. He joined the Whig Cabinet as Lord Privy Seal, and his popularity with the English people was destroyed for ever. He still retained some political and parliamentary influence, and his experience of office, combined with his Protestant zeal, still made him a useful colleague. But he sank into the second rank and never again was spoken of as even a possible Prime Minister.

After the death of Fox, in July 1806, Lord Grenville determined to dissolve Parliament in the autumn; and perhaps one of the few mistakes that Lord Hawkesbury ever made in his life was a letter which he wrote to the King recommending him to forbid the dissolution. The existing House of Commons had sat for only four sessions; and there was no special reason for dismissing it before its time. The Ministry had endured no defeat. The Sovereign had no constitutional reason for supposing that his servants were distasteful to the representatives of the people; in which case, of course, he is always entitled to ask them if they really are so. Yet Lord Grenville did not hesitate to dissolve upon the mere general ground that the House of Commons was less favourable to Government than it was capable of being made. Nevertheless, I quite agree with Mr. Yonge that George the Third was right in rejecting Lord Hawkes-

bury's advice and allowing the dissolution to proceed.
Lord Hawkesbury seems to have been strangely blind to
the compensating inference to be drawn from it, that what
was sauce for the Tories was sauce also for the Whigs. A
General Election, he says, would determine in favour of
Ministers " the opinion of many persons who are undecided at present; and in the event of your Majesty's feeling
it expedient to change your Administration, it would de-
prive their successors of the advantage of that measure
which would be essential to the establishment of their
power." Events showed him his mistake. In October
1806, Lord Grenville dissolved Parliament and obtained a
ministerial majority. In the following March, George the
Third dismissed Lord Grenville, and replaced the Tories in
power, under the nominal authority of the Duke of Portland, but in reality under the lead of Lord Hawkesbury.
By this time his Lordship had come to see the question
differently. Parliament was dissolved again, without any
better reason than Grenville had been able to show for it;
and the Tory majority was brought back which the last
dissolution had dispersed.

At the present day, when some little controversy has
arisen touching the true grounds of an appeal to the
people before the House of Commons has completed its
term of seven years, it may be as well that the public
should know what the leaders of both the great parties
in the State, Lord Grenville, Lord Howick, and Lord
Erskine on the one side, and Lord Hawkesbury and Lord
Eldon on the other, did not hesitate to do, sixty years
ago. It is quite clear that in the opinion of George the
Third, who was not likely to be favourable to ministerial
encroachments, the Prime Minister of the day did in fact
" carry a dissolution in his pocket."

The Whigs were " out for their lives." But they had been in long enough, however, to work irreparable mischief. Bent at once on reversing the whole policy of their predecessors, they lost the golden opportunity for destroying the power of Napoleon, which presented itself after the battle of Eylau, when, if the 50,000 British troops held in readiness by Lord Castlereagh, to be thrown in a body on any point in the enemy's position where their action seemed most likely to be decisive, had been landed in the north of Germany, to operate on the French communications, his ruin was apparently inevitable. The Liberal Party rushed at once into the opposite extreme. They frittered away our force in unsuccessful expeditions to the Dardanelles, to Egypt, and to South America; they refused to send a man or a guinea to help the Emperor Alexander in his life and death struggle with the French ; and they effectually prevented their successors from affording him any immediate relief by totally dismantling the transport service. The result was the alienation of Russia from Great Britain, the battle of Friedland which compelled her to become the ally of France, and the Treaty of Tilsit, which for a brief period seemed to place Europe at Napoleon's feet. The Liberal policy at this juncture of our affairs is computed to have cost this country something like four hundred millions.

The new Prime Minister was the Duke of Portland, the same, curiously enough, who, having presided as a Whig over the coalition between Fox and North, survived to head the Tories against the coalition between Fox and Grenville. But the Duke was in bad health ; and during the two years and a half that his Government lasted, he was rarely seen in his place and did not make a single speech. It was under this nominal chief, however, that the most high-handed measures of the whole war were adopted, namely, the seizure of the Danish Fleet in September 1807, a measure directly forced upon us by the policy of the preceding Government, and the issue of the "Orders in Council" in answer to the "Berlin Decree," November 21st, 1806, which had, however, been provoked by a still earlier "Order" of the English Government. By the "Orders in Council" are usually understood those which were issued on the 7th of January and the 11th of November 1807. But these were only parts of a series of decrees issued alternately by England and France between May 1806 and October 1810, the first having been the work of Lord Grenville's Government in which Fox was Foreign Secretary. The policy which they represented was not, therefore, peculiar to the Tories, and was actually inaugurated by the Whigs, who declared the whole of the coast between the Elbe and Brest to be in a state of blockade, though only a small extent of it was effectively blockaded. Napoleon retaliated by the "Berlin Decree" : which was followed by the "Orders" of January 1807, provoking fresh severities from Napoleon, and further ones in turn from England. Then came the "Milan Decree" of December 1807; and the English "Orders" of April 1809, the series being finally completed by the "French Decrees of St. Cloud and Fontainebleau" in 1810, ordering all British property found in every place occupied by French troops to be seized and burned. The policy of retaliation, however, was found not to answer, and one of the first acts of Lord Liverpool's Administration was to abandon it.

The quarrel between Lord Castlereagh and Mr. Canning, of which we shall have more to say hereafter, broke up the Government in the summer of 1809 ; and Lord Liver-

pool* still declining the Treasury, Mr. Perceval became
the next Prime Minister. That he was a good Protestant
and a bad belligerent are the two worst things that have
been said of him. He was honest, adroit, courageous,
and distinguished for his skill in debate. Lord Eldon
speaks highly in his letters of "little P." as he calls him,
and he seems to have been highly popular with all that
section of the Tories. But though decidedly a very able
man, he had neither the information nor the genius
essential to an English Minister at that momentous
epoch. In his view of the Peninsular War he resembled
those foolish speculators who never can be made to see
that the surest road to ruin is to starve the speculations they engage in. His favourite phrase was their
favourite phrase; the folly, that is, of throwing good
money after bad, forgetful that if people always acted on
this maxim, few undertakings which the world has ever
seen could have succeeded. Or to put it in another way:
Perceval always took the money consideration first, and
the moral consideration second. There are some circumstances in which if a man is placed, such a balance
of advantages is madness. It is better to lose one's whole
fortune than to lose all which makes fortune worth having.
And such was really the alternative presented to us between
the Peace of Tilsit and the French invasion of Russia.
Now, to this conception of the crisis the intellect of Mr.
Perceval was incapable of rising. But, unluckily, like
many other men of narrow views, he was gifted with that
strength of will and decision of manner by which weaker
natures are subdued in spite, it may be, both of higher
culture and more enlightened opinions. Though far less
capable of appreciating the character of the struggle than

* He had become Lord Liverpool by the death of his father, Dec. 17, 1808.

several among them, Mr. Perceval's will became a law to his colleagues, and completely overruled the better judgment and more special experience of Lord Liverpool.

Lord Liverpool, who had resumed the Home Department under the Duke of Portland, became Secretary for War and the Colonies under Mr. Perceval, in 1809 ; and it was during the three years in which he held this office that his conduct is most open to criticism. Before, however, we determine how far Lord Liverpool was to blame for the treatment of the Duke of Wellington's army in the earlier stages of the Peninsular War, we must determine how far he was to blame under whom Lord Liverpool was acting. In his History of the Peninsular War Sir William Napier charged Perceval by name with having withheld the necessary supplies from the army in Spain, and then seeking to " throw on the General the responsibility of failure." In 1811 the Duke of Wellington himself complained to Wellesley Pole of the " little dirty feelings " in Ministers which had hitherto impeded the contest ; and adds that he doubts if they had either " the inclination or the nerve to do what they ought." Lord Wellesley says practically the same thing. He had been brought into the Cabinet for the express purpose of inspiring new energy into the prosecution of the war, but always found himself thwarted by the narrower conceptions and equally indomitable will of Mr. Perceval. " Lord Liverpool, however," so Lord Wellesley states himself, " usually agreed with Lord Wellesley in the necessity and policy of extending our efforts, if practicable, but submitted entirely to Mr. Perceval's statement of the impracticability." He tells a story of his colleague which illustrates his accommodating temper, and readiness to " submit " to others in a remarkable degree. " General Walker," says he, " had

persuaded Lord Liverpool to send him with 3,000 men
to Santona, but Lord Wellesley dissuaded Lord Liverpool
from it. He admitted Santona was an important point,
' but, for God's sake,' said he, ' let's have no more expeditions of our own, but keep our force collected and make
a steady exertion upon one point. Send the men to Lord
Wellington ; if he thinks they would be most useful at
Santona, no doubt he will send them there.' Lord Liverpool gave up the point very good-humouredly." I should
fancy that this is what he always did, that he was just as
agreeable to General Walker as he was to Lord Wellesley,
and gave his consent to the one and saw it overruled
by the other with equal good humour.

Mr. Perceval, however, has found a powerful advocate
in Mr. Walpole, his biographer, who quotes a letter written
in 1835 by the Duke of Wellington himself to Mr. Dudley
Perceval, the son of the Prime Minister, in answer to an
inquiry whether there was any justification for the charges
brought against his father. The Duke, wonderful to relate,
declared that he had no recollection of having made any
complaints at all, and that he had no doubt that he was
supported by the Government of the day, to the best of
their ability.* This is one of those contradictions which,
now that everyone is dead who could have thrown any
light upon the subject, must for ever remain inexplicable.
If we acquit Mr. Perceval, we must also acquit Lord
Liverpool; and if the Duke's language in 1811 meant
nothing, we may suppose that it meant nothing in 1812
and 1813, when Lord Liverpool sat in Perceval's seat.
It should be added, indeed, that many of Lord Wellington's
complaints during the later stages of the war, referred

---

* Cf. *Greville Journals*, June 1835, vol. iii. p. 271. The Duke here says
that Napier had not treated Perceval fairly

only to stores and clothing, with which Lord Liverpool had nothing to do; and that, in the *Life of Mr. Herries,** who was then Commissary-General, published four years ago by his son, Mr. Edward Herries, the whole question is discussed at great length, and it is shown that Lord Wellington himself was not always correctly informed of the source of the delays from which he suffered.

On the whole, however, I am afraid the weight of evidence is against the Ministry. It is difficult to read the memoirs and biographies which relate to this period, without coming to the conclusion that the Tory Government of 1809–1812 was, as a body, afraid of the Opposition; and that whenever any proposal for increasing our strength in the Peninsula was under consideration the Cabinet was haunted by the reflection of what Mr. Whitbread would say, or what Mr. Brougham would say, or of the punishment Lord Grey would inflict upon them. Hence all those suggestions communicated in Lord Liverpool's despatches, which, whatever he might say of them afterwards, must have mortified Lord Wellington to the core. To withdraw the British troops from Spain; to withdraw them from the Peninsula altogether; to reflect on the power of Napoleon; to consider the wrath of the Opposition; to ask himself, in God's name, where the money was to come from; these were the unworthy suggestions constantly forced upon the great Captain, he who, like Asia in "Hyperion," was already

Prophesying of his glory,

and beheld in imagination the British flag flying over the plain of Vittoria, and the scarlet uniforms threading the

---

* *Memoirs of the Public Life of the Right Hon. John Charles Herries*, by his son, Edward Herries, C.B., with an Introduction by Sir Charles Herries, K.C.B., January 1880.

distant Pyrenees. Even with these drawbacks, however,
great things were accomplished. The Tories, after all,
stood their ground; Wellington was supported; and the
battle of Salamanca put a new complexion on the war.

Lord Wellesley, however, was not satisfied, and still complained that he was reduced to a cypher. But there were
faults on both sides. If Perceval was narrow-minded and
dogmatic, and, like most inferior men, fond of asserting an
authority which he was afraid other people might forget,
Wellesley, on the other hand, was proud, exacting, and
reserved. It was said of him that he " Sultanised" his
department, and he seems to have required of his colleagues a degree of homage and assiduity which they
naturally declined to render. He, too, often mistook
London for Calcutta, and affected a kind of Oriental
seclusion, surrounded by a little circle of admirers who
brought him the news of the day, and to whom he de-
claimed in turn on the imbecility of the rest of the
Government. He gradually discontinued his attendance
at the Cabinets, and was not often seen in his place in
the House of Lords. His followers had the courage to
point out to him that if he would only exert in Parliament
or in Downing Street half the eloquence which he wasted
in his own dining-room, he would be sure to carry all
before him. He used to say that he had tried it, and in
vain ; and in this frame of mind, of course, he determined to
resign. The truth is, he could not brook contradiction.
When he had delivered his opinion at the Council Table,
it was to be so. Further argument was an insult. At the
same time, we must all to some extent sympathise with
Wellesley. He was greatly the intellectual superior of all
his colleagues. He was rich in knowledge and accomplish-
ments, of which they new nothing. He had enjoyed pecu-

liar opportunities of becoming acquainted with the affairs of the Peninsula, and with the plans and resources of his brother, Lord Wellington. What would have been bad enough to a man of Wellesley's temperament, under any conditions, under these became absolutely intolerable.

To a right understanding, however, of the relative positions of the two men, it is necessary to remember what we have already pointed out, that Wellesley in default of Canning, and Perceval in default of Sidmouth, were the heads of two rival parties, and that Wellesley came into the Cabinet as the representative of Canning's ideas, and was associated in the minds of his colleagues with all that made Canning so obnoxious to them. It is abundantly clear, from the first, that there was no love lost between them, and the Marquis, soon finding out how the land lay, commenced, greatly to his discredit, the formation of an anti-Perceval party, which was to place him in the Minister's seat. He relied on the support, it seems, of certain members of the House of Commons, who were ashamed of being led by a lawyer, and one so technical as Perceval is said to have been, as, for instance, when he spent nearly an hour in explaining to the House of Commons the different ways in which drunkenness could be detected. Whether it was this peculiarity or any other which gave umbrage to the Irish members, we cannot tell. But they were reported to be ready in a body to desert to Wellesley. Any gentlemen disposed to take part in this intrigue, were to be brought home to dinner from the House in twos and threes till they gradually came to know one another, and to be able to act in concert. Whether Perceval knew of this remarkable device or not, is uncertain. But it must have tended very greatly to sweeten the intercourse between himself and his colleague if he did. It is said, too, that Wellesley looked forward to the defeat of the Government on the motion of Lord Porchester for censuring the Walcheren expedition, in the expectation that in that event he would be called upon to form an Administration, and that he was greatly disappointed when, after a defence by Perceval, Castlereagh, and, be it remembered to his honour, by Mr. Canning too, his colleagues were victorious by a majority of forty-two.

Notwithstanding, however, the marked disaffection of Lord Wellesley, his presence in the Cabinet was supposed to be of so much importance to it, that any hint of his intention to resign produced a general consternation. Several times he was dissuaded from taking this extreme step, but at last it became evident that he could be restrained no longer, and Perceval, dreading the effect of its announcement on his own Government, besought him to keep it a secret for a month, for a fortnight, for a week even. Wellesley consented, but by some means or other the secret oozed out, and Perceval at once rushed off to the Prince Regent, and begged that Wellesley might be dismissed that moment, and Castlereagh appointed in his place. As Wellesley must be lost in any case, it was better that his departure should be their act than his. If the Government dismissed him, it might seem they could afford to do without him; but if he left them of his own accord, it might suggest to the world that he was leaving a falling house. The Prince, however, very properly refused to listen to Perceval's suggestion. Wellesley was allowed to resign in due form and at his own time; but before the effect of his retirement on the fortunes of the Government could be seen, it was brought to a tragic end. Lord Wellesley resigned on the 18th of

February. Some little time was necessarily consumed in the Ministerial arrangements which followed, and on the 11th of May, before their stability could be tested, Mr. Perceval was shot dead in the Lobby of the House of Commons by the madman Bellingham.

To understand what followed, it is necessary to go back to the preceding year, 1811, when the King's illness returned upon him, and it became necessary a second time to make provision for a Regency. Lord Grenville then paid the penalty of his junction with the Whigs, and contributed very largely, by his conduct on that occasion, to defer their return to power for nearly twenty years, and his own for ever. The Government proposed to re-enact the obnoxious restrictions of 1788, which the Whigs had so vigorously denounced ; and when the Prince was called upon to draw up an answer to the address of the two Houses, inviting him to accept the Regency, he entrusted the task to Lord Grenville and Lord Grey. They composed an answer in which these restrictions were not even glanced at. Sheridan at once represented to the Prince that there was a want of deference in the language of the two Whig lords, to which he ought not to submit. He himself was empowered to frame a new reply. His composition was preferred ; and the Whig statesmen, after a grave and dignified remonstrance, withdrew from the royal confidence. But—and herein lies the whole moral of the incident—the reason why the restrictions were *not* glanced at was, that Lord Grenville had in 1788 himself been a party to them, and now refused to tarnish his reputation for consistency by consenting to any relaxation of them. There can be no doubt that this little specimen of what he had to expect from " the friends of his youth " materially modified the Prince's eagerness in the following year to bring the two Lords into the Cabinet.

On the resignation of Lord Wellesley, which, as we have seen, finally took place on the 18th of February 1812, the Prince had commanded Mr. Perceval to invite Lords Grey and Grenville to join the Administration. This time they had contented themselves with answering that the differences between themselves and His Royal Highness's Ministers were too great to permit of such a union. Accordingly, on Mr. Perceval's death, he empowered Lord Wellesley to construct a new Government.* It was agreed that Lord Wellesley should apply to the Whigs, and Mr. Canning to the Tories. But both applications failed. Lord Liverpool saw an insuperable obstacle in the Roman Catholic question; and the Whigs in the one fact that the Regent had named his own Prime Minister. Wellesley—or the Prince—endeavoured to bribe them by giving them a majority of one in the Cabinet. But the Whigs only replied that they could not join a Cabinet constructed on "a system of counteraction inconsistent with the prosecution of any uniform or beneficial policy." On this particular point we think the Whigs were in the right; for in times of war, or other great public dangers demanding vigorous and united action, a Cabinet in which the advocates and the opponents of energetic measures are evenly balanced seems a practical absurdity. Canning himself, however, told Mr. Stapleton, his secretary, that the first was the real ground on which the negotiations failed; the Whigs insisting now, as twenty years before, on the inalienable right of the Party, and not the

---

* Lord Wellesley had two commissions: first of all to lay before the Prince the plan of an Administration; and secondly, to form one, himself as Prime Minister. The difference is not unimportant. See Chapter IV.

Sovereign, to name the Prime Minister. On Lord Wellesley's failure Lord Moira undertook the task, but with the
same success. There was no other resource, therefore,
but to fall back on the existing Ministry, and on the
8th of June 1812, Lord Liverpool announced to the
House of Lords that he had accepted the office of the
First Lord of the Treasury. His Government was looked
upon at first as only a midsummer dream, just as Pitt's
had been called only a mince-pie administration. But
Pitt's lasted eighteen, and Lord Liverpool's fifteen years.

Lord Liverpool, it is said, might have been Prime
Minister on three previous occasions, namely, in 1806,
1807, and 1809, had he chosen to pluck the fruit which
hung within his grasp. It is true that on each of these
occasions he was "sent for"; but whether that honour
necessarily implies that the person so summoned is the
one whom the Sovereign intends to be Prime Minister, is
still, I think, a moot point in the relations between the
Crown and its servants. A very interesting correspondence
on this point took place between the Duke of Wellington
and Mr. Canning in 1827, the Duke maintaining the
negative and Mr. Canning the affirmative of this proposition. Circumstances have occurred quite recently, and
may very soon occur again to invest this same question
with new interest and to illustrate its practical importance.
It certainly seems to me that except under peculiar
circumstances, or the existence of some private understanding to the contrary, the Minister or Ministers summoned to the councils of their Sovereign would have a
right to expect that he was prepared to avail himself
of their services, either jointly or severally, in the construction of a new Administration. In 1807 Lord Liverpool and Lord Eldon, and in 1809 Lord Liverpool and

Mr. Perceval, were sent for together; the presumption being that the King knew them to be ready to co-operate, and designed one of them for the Treasury.*

Toryism, in one form or another, had now been predominant for exactly forty-two years. Within that period the English Tories had lost America, but they had saved Europe. Had they not been thwarted by a backstairs intrigue, they would probably have composed Ireland. They had stood forward as the advocates and representatives of Parliamentary Reform, Roman Catholic Emancipation, and Free Trade. The first had been postponed in consequence of the French Revolution; the second in deference to the Royal will, in accordance as it was with the public opinion of the day. The third had been to some extent carried out, and would have been carried still further, but for the opposition of the Liberal Party in the House of Commons. They had placed the Royal prerogative on a rational and constitutional basis, restoring to the Crown such powers as could usefully be exercised under a Parliamentary Monarchy, but rejecting the system which aimed at the dissolution of Party. Though the section which had been in power since Mr. Pitt's death had failed to appreciate the war policy of Wellesley and Canning, they had equally refused to listen to the despairing declamations of the Whigs; they had stood firm according to their lights, and were now about to reap their reward in a series of brilliant triumphs on which Lord Liverpool reposed for life.

It is easy to see that the very same qualities which rendered Lord Liverpool an indifferent War Minister, contributed largely to his success at the head of a divided

* See Chapter IV.

Cabinet, and that the obliging disposition and tolerance
of contradiction which made his weakness in the one
position constituted his strength in the other. When
Lord Liverpool took office in 1812, his Government included neither Mr. Canning nor Lord Wellesley, who,
with a little following of their own, occupied a position of
neutrality, nor the Grenvilles, who were openly hostile ;
so that, with the preponderance of debating power greatly
on the side of the Whigs, he had to maintain his position
with little more than half the numerical strength which, at
one time, supported Mr. Pitt. The triumphant conclusion
of the war, and the glories of Vittoria and Waterloo, sustained him for a time. But with the return of peace he
could hardly have held his own, if his happy disposition
had not enabled him to re-combine, under his own wing,
all the scattered sections of the old Tory Party, till,
finally, in 1822, it was stronger than it had been at any
time since the end of Pitt's first administration. Canning
was the first to come back, in 1816 ; then followed the
Grenvilles, in 1817, disgusted with the Whig opposition
to the defensive measures of the Government. An enlightened commercial policy began to revive with the
accession of Mr. Huskisson ; and all these men of such
various temperaments and opinions, whom neither the
brilliant genius and hereditary claims of Mr. Canning,
nor the immense fame, high character, and vigorous intellect of the Duke of Wellington could hold together,
worked harmoniously for years under the gentle sway of
Lord Liverpool. It must be universally admitted that the
Tory policy down to 1815 had been a brilliant success ;
and that the statesmen who, in the teeth of a violent opposition, had carried on the Peninsular War perseveringly and
triumphantly ; who had sustained the spirits of Europe by

their stubborn defiance of the whole power of France; who had organized confederation after confederation against the common foe till he finally fell before them; and took their seats amidst the pacificators of Europe garlanded with the glories of Waterloo; occupy a position in modern history of almost unexampled splendour.

But the foreign policy of this country during his long administration was so much under the control first of Lord Castlereagh, and afterwards of Mr. Canning, and Lord Liverpool seems to have left this department so much in the hands of his lieutenants, that I shall postpone considering it at any length till I come to Mr. Canning's administration. We know, briefly, that there was hardly any settlement of Europe after the fall of Napoleon which Lord Liverpool would not have preferred to the resumption of hostilities. The war had been undertaken by England to save herself and the continent from a European dictator. That end accomplished, she asked for nothing more. She claimed no share of the territories which the great Powers, having rescued them from the original spoiler, now proceeded to redistribute among themselves. On one or two points Lord Liverpool felt rather strongly. The dismemberment of Saxony was one of these. The union of Holland and Belgium, always a favourite idea with English statesmen, was another. But it is clear that he did not think either of these objects of sufficient importance to justify our running any risk of rekindling the general conflagration. England having already made such vast sacrifices in the interests of collective Europe, was surely entitled to consider that she had done enough.

This was probably the sincere conviction of Lord Liverpool, whose object all along was to keep us as free from continental entanglements as he could. Lord Wellesley complained of his dislike of such connections even while the war was in progress; and here we at once recognize the influence of Mr. Pitt's teaching before circumstances had made them a necessity. The Holy Alliance, as many Radicals still seem in need of being told, was a perfectly harmless piece of folly, and wholly unconnected with the compact entered into by the Military Powers some years later for the maintenance of legitimate monarchy and the repression of popular agitation. The announcement of the first was 'acknowledged by the English Government with a polite smile and a civil expression of regret that the forms of the English Constitution did not permit the King of England to become a member of it. The second was repudiated by the Tory Party immediately and decisively. The Tory Party had done its work in Europe when Napoleon was finally overthrown. They would have nothing to do with the new-fangled doctrine of intervention, intended by the absolute sovereigns to stamp out the embers which the French Revolution had still left smouldering in their dominions.

Let this be borne in mind. Of the attitude of the English Tories towards the Continental Powers from 1815 to 1830, the most cursory glance into the memoirs and State papers of the period is sufficient to inform us. Yet not one man in a hundred who inveighs against Liverpool and Castlereagh, as the supporters of the absolute monarchies in their league against popular liberty, takes the trouble to examine the evidence. There was little or no difference in principle between the policy of Lord Castlereagh and Mr. Canning.* When the Duke of Wellington was setting out to join the Congress of Verona, his instructions, drawn up by the former, were passed on to

* But cf. infra, Chapter III.

him by the latter without the alteration of a word. It was Lord Castlereagh who told Spain that the recognition of her revolted colonies was only a question of time. The language of the English Government on French intervention in Spain in 1823, and on Spanish intervention in Portugal three years later, is quite sufficient by itself to clear the memory of the Tory Party from the charge of complicity with despotism.

The truth is that Lord Liverpool and Lord Castlereagh were guided in all they did by the traditional policy of Great Britain, the cultivation, namely, of German alliances as a barrier against French ambition. This had been equally the policy of both parties in the State. I have already pointed out how grossly it was abused by the Whigs in the reigns of George the First and George the Second. But it was the abuse of it, and not the use to which the Tories had objected; and when a second emergency arose similar to that which had originally called it into being, Mr. Pitt and his successors recurred to it as a matter of course. All that it was necessary to do for the preservation of this system was done by Lord Liverpool and Lord Castlereagh, but no more. If Mr. Bright himself had been Foreign Minister, England could not have protested more warmly than she did against the "mutual insurance system" which had been established by the Great Powers. Lord Liverpool's objection to go to war for the Constitutionalists was founded on no kind of sympathy with the autocrats, but exclusively on practical grounds, such as stayed our intervention, once, between Russia and Hungary, and again, between Germany and Denmark. In fact, some of Lord Liverpool's reasoning seems to have been literally reproduced in the despatches and speeches of Earl Russell. The only difference is this, that whereas to the Spanish

Liberals we had never promised any help, the Danes rose in arms mainly on the strength of such a promise.

If further evidence is wanting in proof of Lord Liverpool's disposition, the following passage from one of his letters to Mr. Canning, October 1826, *apropos* of French intervention in Portugal, might surely be conclusive :—

Secondly, I would call upon allied Powers to use their strenous efforts in order to compel Spain to give the necessary satisfaction; founding it upon the principle that, as both Spain and Portugal were independent kingdoms, neither had a right to interfere in the internal concerns of the other.

Thirdly, I would announce to the allies, that if they declined the proposed intervention, or should fail in compelling Spain to retrace her steps, we should *be forced to play the whole game of Liberal institutions in Spain as well as in Portugal*; that we should send the Spanish patriots now in England or on the Continent to Gibraltar and to Portugal, and should spare no exertion to raise the standard of the constitution again in Spain.

Thus the military Powers were warned that the moment they violated the Treaty of Vienna by interfering with the independence of other countries, we should meet their aggression by proclaiming constitutional principles in the states which they invaded. What more could be done ?

I have already stated that after the resignation of Mr. Pitt in 1801, Toryism began to run in two distinct channels, the one representing the original and more liberal Toryism of Pitt himself, the other the narrower creed, which was favoured by the King, and was probably much more in harmony with the general feeling of the country. The distinction between the two hardly made itself felt down to the beginning of the Regency. When both Pitt and Fox had entirely abandoned the Roman Catholic Question for the time being, the Tory ranks were closed up ; and when Lord Grenville was unwise enough to bring it forward again after Fox's death, it destroyed his Government. It seems to me that, quite independently of the King's wishes, it would not have been sound policy to attempt to settle this question as long as the war lasted. I have not forgotten Sydney Smith's argument on the subject; but that does not come across my own. The English people were making unheard-of exertions, and bearing the most grievous burdens in defence, not only of their independence, but of the political Constitution which was openly menaced by their enemies. They did so in the full confidence that their rulers would maintain that Constitution, and they adored the King for his devotion to it. What might have been the effect on public feeling, and on the fortitude and loyalty of the nation, had Roman Catholic Emancipation been forced on them in 1806 ? But after the restoration of peace, and when the King's recovery had become hopeless, the case was altered; and then it was that the line of demarcation between the two sections of the Tory party again became perceptible, and an operative force in public life. Thenceforward Lord Liverpool must share with Mr. Peel, the Duke of Wellington, Lord Sidmouth, Lord Eldon, and many more, the responsibility of maintaining restrictions which Mr. Canning, Lord Wellesley, Lord Castlereagh, and the politicians who more particularly represented " Mr. Pitt's friends," were anxious to remove.

He had never, however, belonged to the "no surrender" party; and it is clear that to the last he looked upon the question as one to be decided by expediency. He continued to believe that to remove the restrictions complained of would be inexpedient. He seems to have had little faith in the efficacy of "securities," and none at all in the professions of the Romish clergy. He foresaw clearly enough that the admission of Roman Catholics to political power would endanger the Established Church, and would not pacify the people. And in both of these predictions he has been abundantly justified by events. The assertion of abstract right he met with a direct negative. All His Majesty's subjects were entitled to the enjoyment of equal rights; granted: but it must be upon the same conditions. The Roman Catholic and Protestant populations of these islands did not live on the same conditions, inasmuch as one gave only a divided allegiance to the sovereign of the country. This distinction, he maintained, was at once fatal to the argument from abstract right. He was likewise one of those who thought that, owing to the peculiar nature of the Roman Catholic religion, it was idle to expect that religious peace would be the fruits of concession. Discord, bitter and lasting, would be prolonged between the two parties, when one felt itself aggrieved, and the other felt encouraged by success to press forward to still further encroachments.

That the majority of the inhabitants of any country, told by the head, have a right to choose their own religion, was a doctrine not then in fashion. And how Lord Liverpool would have dealt with it can only be a matter of conjecture. He would probably have said that such doctrine, if true in theory, is impossible in practice. He would have pointed out that if the majority may choose their religion, the minority may preserve to itself the right of endowing it or not; that religion and religious endowments are two distinct things; and that freedom to choose the one is not to be confounded with liberty to seize the other. The fallacy involved in this assertion of the rights of the majority, and in this equivocal usage of the word "religion," can only be evaded by acceptance of the broad principle that the majority has a right to lay hands upon every kind of property in the country. This question, not less in 1825 than in 1868, was mixed up with considerations which had really nothing to do with it. Probably there was never in the world a man less bigoted than Lord

Liverpool; though, of course, his opposition in this case was denounced as bigotry. Bigotry is simply the belief that your own creed is absolutely true and that every other one is absolutely false; that salvation is the privilege of the one, and damnation the meed of all the rest. But the Roman Catholics were not excluded from power because they were the children of Satan, but because they were subjects of the Pope. The propriety of tolerating an *imperium in imperio* of this description is a purely civil question, on which political philosophers might easily take opposite sides. This was the spirit in which men like Wellington, Liverpool, and Peel discussed the subject. And it is probable that the Prime Minister, had he lived, would have yielded, like the Duke of Wellington, and conceded to political considerations what had never in his own mind been a matter of religious principle.

It is, however, in connection with a totally different class of questions that Lord Liverpool is principally remembered. It has already been stated that his attention had early been directed to commercial and financial studies, and that on questions of this nature he agreed with the friends of Mr. Pitt. He was not naturally, therefore, inclined to restrictions upon trade, and was so far the representative of the earlier Tory creed. But England, as has been truly said, at the conclusion of the war in 1815, was in the position of a great county family which has spent half as much as it is worth in a contested election. The English people were thoroughly proud of the war; but ere the Waterloo corn had disappeared from its trampled ridges it became apparent to Ministers that they would have to deal with an amount of public misery which glory could neither cure nor silence. What was to be done? In assuming that the landed interest had the first claim on his consideration, Lord Liverpool was but reflecting the sentiment of both Whigs and Tories. But the measures which he took for relieving it, though from his own point of view they could not be called unjust, were certainly not far-sighted. The collapse of agriculture which occurred at the return of peace was due in great part to the unnatural inflation of agriculture which had been fostered by the war. The true remedy was a return to the conditions which existed before the war broke out. If all the land unsuitable to the growth of wheat which had been ploughed up between 1793 and 1813 had been reconverted into pasture as soon as war prices disappeared, though the agricultural interest would have been pinched sharply at the moment, corn culture in this country would have found its natural level sixty years ago, and immense future disappointments and widespread ruin have been averted.*

Instead of that, Lord Liverpool was unfortunately prevailed upon to prohibit the importation of foreign wheat whenever the average price was under eighty shillings a quarter. The pressure put upon him was very great, no doubt. Lord Redesdale, writing to Mr. Abbot in 1815, computes that rates, tithes, and other charges amounted in his part of the country to a hundred per cent. on the farmer's rental. "The ruin of the farmers," he adds, "has been more immediately effected by the failure of so many country banks and their inability to sell their produce at any price. The speculators had accumulated vast quantities of produce, particularly corn.

---

* A good deal of such land had been so treated immediately after the Repeal of the Orders in Council, and the retreat of Napoleon from Moscow. But partly owing to the Corn Law, partly to a recovery of prices brought about by other causes, in 1818 it was again replaced under tillage. But had English agriculture only been left to the operation of natural laws in 1815, we should have escaped the agricultural distresses of the present day.

The consumer generally buys of the speculator, who is now the seller and not the buyer. According to the best information I can obtain, the landlords will fall short of their Michaelmas receipts from their agricultural tenants upon an average of one half, and on the Lady Day receipts a larger proportion. Of course the money lent by the country banks which have failed is calling in; and the Chipping Norton Bank alone had lent above £40,000 to the farmers in their neighbourhood, one half of whom will probably be ruined by being compelled to pay at this moment. For the banks which stand are also calling in their outstanding debts, and will advance nothing."*

The majorities by which the Corn Law of 1815 was carried were not mere party majorities. The divisions in the House of Commons at various stages of the Bill were as follows : 209 to 66, 241 to 38, 158 to 35, 207 to 77, 184 to 78, 245 to 77, and 213 to 72. Even Sir Francis Burdett said " he saw no objection to the Bill," and it must be remembered at the same time that some kind of protective duties had always been recognized as necessary by both parties in the State. Many persons are still to be found who imagine that the " Corn Laws " were the invention of the Tory Cabinet of Lord Liverpool. They were nothing of the kind. The State had always, from the earliest times, considered itself bound to afford artificial encouragement to agriculture ; sometimes by bounties upon exports, sometimes by duties upon imports. But that it was possible to leave it altogether alone had occurred only to a very few political economists at the beginning of the present century. Statesmen, moreover, have to consider not only what is politic in the abstract, but what is capable of being

* *Lord Colchester's Diary*, vol. ii. p. 560.

done under the circumstances of any given moment. And I do not see how it was possible for Lord Liverpool to have done more than leave the Corn Laws as he found them, importation being prohibited even then when wheat was under 63s. Sir G. C. Lewis reproaches the Government with not having adopted " the liberal and enlightened commercial policy recommended by Lord Grenville and other members of the Opposition." But if we are to accept the protest drawn up by Lord Grenville, which Mr. MacCulloch seems to take as an adequate exposition of this "liberal and enlightened policy," I confess I fail to discern its great practical value. It is an abstract condemnation of the protective system in which I believe Lord Liverpool would have agreed with him; but it indicates no loop-hole of escape from the difficulties with which Government was surrounded, nor points out any means by which the sudden abolition of a system under which the whole nation had grown up, to which all classes were accustomed, and on which the most important class of all was at the time dependent for existence, could, at a moment of immense social suffering and financial confusion, have been safely and successfully undertaken. Pitt might have been equal to the task, but I think no living statesman of that day would have been found so. The Corn Law of 1815 was not, then, in any strict sense of the term a party measure ; was it, then, a class measure, a purely selfish measure ? I think not.

It must be remembered that one cardinal principle of the Tory Party from the Revolution downwards, a principle endorsed by Lord Shelburne, a man of liberal commercial views, endorsed by Mr. Pitt, and accepted by all his successors, including the Duke of Wellington, Mr. Canning, and Lord Beaconsfield, was this, that not only

8 *

did the landed interest produce a better governing class than any other interest in the country, but was in itself the surest foundation and mainstay of our national greatness and prosperity. Whatever, therefore, was injurious to the landed interest was injurious to the whole community. I believe that this doctrine was accepted as an axiom, not only by the Tory Party proper, but by the vast majority of the middle classes who were of no party at all. The worst consequence of the Reform Bill of 1832, in the eyes of the Duke of Wellington, was that we should gradually cease to be governed by "the gentlemen of the country." Mr. Disraeli, addressing his constituents at Shrewsbury in 1843, said :

> I never will commit myself upon this great question to petty economical details ; I will not pledge myself to miserable questions of sixpence in seven shillings and sixpence or eight shillings of duties about corn ; I do not care whether your corn sells for this sum or that, or whether it is under a sliding scale or a fixed duty ; but what I want, and what I wish to secure, and what, as far as my energies go, I will secure, is the preponderance of the landed interest. . . . I take the only broad and only safe line, namely, that what we ought to uphold is, the preponderance of the landed interest ; that the preponderance of the landed interest has made England ; that it is an immense element of political power and stability ; that we should never have been able to undertake the great war in which we embarked in the memory of many present ; that we could never have been able to conquer the greatest military genius the world ever saw, with the greatest means at his disposal, and to hurl him from his throne, if we had not had a territorial aristocracy to give stability to our Constitution.

Now, let us compare with these passages what Mr. Gladstone said of the same class, "the gentlemen of the country," only fourteen years ago in introducing the Irish Land Act. He alluded first in general terms to the " immense mass of public duties bearing upon every subject of political, moral, and social interest, discharged without fee or reward, which has honourably distinguished for so many generations the landlords of England. This fixed and

happy usage I take to be a just relic and true descendant of
the feudal system which never took a real or genuine root
in Ireland." And then he went on to describe more particularly the position of the English landed gentry, to which he
hoped in time it might be possible to assimilate the Irish :

A position marked by residence, by personal familiarity, and by sympathy
with the people among whom they live, by long traditional connection handed
on from generation to generation, and marked by a constant discharge of
duty in every form that can be suggested—be it as to the administration of
justice, be it as to the defence of the country, be it as to the supply of social
or spiritual or moral or educational wants, be it for any purpose whatever
that is recognized as good and beneficial in a civilized society.

Well, this is pretty well. Now, I say that measures devised for securing the prosperity and permanence of such a
class as this, are something more than measures for the
gratification of selfishness and cupidity. In framing laws
for the benefit of agriculture, the Tory Government was
acting on a theory—on a political theory as well as on
a social fact. If the landed interest was supposed to
benefit by the imposition of protective duties, the whole
community was supposed to benefit by the services of the
landed interest. The theory may be right or wrong ; Mr.
Gladstone says it is right. That point must be discussed
by writers on political philosophy. I am concerned only
with the history of statesmen and parties, and I say that
this belief in the governing qualities of the aristocracy and
their value to the entire nation has, by a large and independent party in this country, numbering in its ranks
some of the most eminent public men whom England has
produced, the present Prime Minister among the number,
been honestly entertained as a great political principle,
independent of its material consequences, ever since the
division of parties which took place in 1688.

As far as Lord Liverpool himself was concerned he

avowedly introduced the Bill of 1815 merely as an experiment, saying that if it was found not to answer, it could easily be repealed ; and, after an abortive effort to improve it in 1822, he had determined in 1826 to retrace his steps, and revert to a more liberal system.   He and Mr. Huskisson were engaged in the execution of this design when he was seized with his last illness, in the winter of 1826–7, and his complete incapacitation for business, followed by the death of Mr. Canning only six months afterwards, threw the whole scheme into abeyance.   More agitating questions speedily arose, and for nearly another ten years the Corn Laws were forgotten.   Had either Liverpool or Canning lived, Free Trade would probably have been established by the last surviving inheritors of the principles of Mr. Pitt.

War is one of those evils which affects different nations in very different degrees, according to the nature of the part which they are called upon to take in it.   In Continental States, with a purely agricultural population, where invaders and invaded know it only by its horrors and its burdens, it is, of course, an unmitigated curse to all but the very few who participate in its honours and rewards, or who benefit by the demand for military supplies and equipage.   But in an insular country, which is at the same time a great naval and commercial country, such is far from being the case.   If she is practically secure against invasion, she can carry on her own industries unmolested, while the industries of all neighbouring countries are languishing or extinguished.   If she is mistress of the sea, the whole carrying trade of the world naturally flows into her hands.   The demand for her goods enriches the manufacturer, who in turn has more to spend on the luxuries and conveniences of life.   As the foreign supply of corn is impeded the home supply rises in price, and the farmer shares in the general prosperity. The poor do not share in it to an equal extent, for their wages do not rise in proportion to the price of commodities. But still they are in constant employment, and never feel the pangs of want. The large class of persons who live on fixed incomes, and feel all the weight of taxation without any of the compensating advantages to which we have referred, are, of course, great sufferers. But there will also be nearly as large a class who are not only not sufferers, but are actual gainers by war. It is easy to see, however, that in exact proportion to the profits created by this artificial stimulus will be the loss inflicted by its withdrawal: and this is precisely what happened in England in 1816. With the restoration of peace she lost all her lucrative monopolies. She at once began to suffer from all the consequences of over-production. She could not find a market for her commodities, except at greatly reduced prices. There was less money to spend either in production or consumption; labourers and artizans were thrown out of work; and the peace which was to have brought happiness to everyone brought bankruptcy and misery to millions.

The financial policy of Lord Liverpool's Government, in the face of this national distress, has always been stigmatized as one of the two great blots upon Toryism, as the severity with which the popular disturbances of the period were suppressed is alleged to be the other. Too little allowance, however, seems to have been made for the fact that, if the original proposals of the Government had been accepted, the burden of taxation on the community at large need not have been so heavy. At the end of the war the Property Tax of 10 per cent. levied on all incomes above £200 a year yielded an annual revenue of

£15,000,000. This, no doubt, was a war tax, originally imposed on the understanding that it should cease with the return of peace ; but when our expenditure had been reduced to as low a point as was consistent with the necessities of the public service,* it still remained impossible to abandon the whole of this large contingent. Government proposed, therefore, to reduce it by one half, which would have left them with £7,500,000 from this source. But the House of Commons would not listen to the proposal. The whole tax was taken off at once, and the deficit had to be made up by other means. Two hundred a year seventy years ago meant a good deal more than it means now, and the Property Tax, therefore, did not touch the very poor at all. The Tory plan was to retain as much of it as would enable Government to dispense with the necessity of levying fresh taxes on the people. This was surely a wise and popular policy, and the kind of breach of faith with the public involved in it is not one of which modern financiers, at all events, have much reason to complain. It would have been the lesser evil of the two.

Driven from this resource, however, the Government, it may readily be owned, did not adopt the wiser of the two alternatives before them. The expenditure for the year 1816 was calculated at £66,581,295. The revenue without the Property Tax was only £58,470,000, leaving a deficit of rather more than eight millions. The half of the Property Tax, therefore, which the Ministry had proposed to retain would just have made up the required sum. To obtain this sum the Ministers had only to divert to the revenue of the year a portion of the amount annually set aside for the Sinking Fund, and their difficulties would have vanished at once. Instead of this they

* Walpole.

resolved to keep up the Sinking Fund and borrow the amount required. The Sinking Fund was intended to pay off the National Debt; but to pay off old debts by the creation of new ones, though it may sometimes be necessary, is not economy. We make no progress towards solvency, even if we do not retrograde, by such a system; and this truth, indeed, is so obvious that we cannot suppose the Government to have been altogether blind to it. The pertinacity with which they adhered to the Sinking Fund arose probably from a conviction that it was worth some pecuniary sacrifice to keep the obligation before the eyes of the country. As long as the Sinking Fund remained in existence, there was a standing memento of what it was our duty to perform. But the required sacrifice was too great. To govern the country as economically as possible, and to devote scrupulously every penny of the surplus to the reduction of the debt, was all that could be done consistently with financial common sense.* At the same time, we are bound to remember what was the original proposal of the Tory Government: the retention, namely, of half the Property Tax, which would have rendered further loans unnecessary, and would have been a direct boon to the working classes.

With governing economically the Tories of that age have always been accredited by all who have ever glanced at the subject. There is no history of our expenditure from 1816 to 1830 to be found which does not bear evidence to this truth.† The Finance Committee appointed by the Govern-

---

* This was done by the Duke of Wellington's Government in 1829.

† See among others, *History of Commerce*, by Professor Leoni Levi; *History of England from 1815 to 1860*, by Mr. Spencer Walpole; *History of Taxation*, by Stephen Dowell, Esq., Assistant-Solicitor of Inland Revenue *Practical Results of Reform Act of 1832*, by Sir John Walsh; *Gladstone's Gleanings*, vol. i. p. 137; *Memoirs of the Right Hon. T. C. Herries*, 1880.

ment in 1817 was the commencement of a system of economy which lasted to the end of the Tory period. Between 1820 and 1825* the military and naval estimates were reduced from £16,008,700 to £13,894,877, and between 1820 and 1830 the total expenditure was reduced from £58,073,314 to £47,812,000. Yet, notwithstanding these reductions, the Tories were accused of every kind of extravagance and profusion. One of the loudest cries at the General Election of 1830 was the demand for retrenchment, a number of seats being won for the Whig Party solely by the pledges to which they did not scruple to commit themselves on this very question. Yet when Lord Althorpe brought in his first Budget in 1831 he was obliged to confess that he could not bring the public expenditure one penny below the point at which it then stood! If it is true that history never reproduces itself, its echoes are at times astonishingly loud and clear.

Mr. Vansittart was certainly not a brilliant Chancellor of the Exchequer, but he was not worse than Sir Charles Wood ; and for half the period now under consideration he was not Chancellor of the Exchequer at all. Our financial policy from the Peace to the Reform Bill must be judged as a whole. During nine years out of the sixteen, at all events, it was economical and successful. That Ministers should have floundered a little at first when suddenly plunged into the ocean of difficulties which the Peace provided for them is not very wonderful. That they righted themselves in a very few years, and continued to hold a steady course through all the embarrassments and temptations which beset the remainder of their passage, are facts which would long ago have effaced all memory of their earlier errors had they been called by any other name.

* These figures are Mr. Walpole's. Professor Levi makes the reduction less.

The Bank Acts, to which I shall refer more particularly in my chapter on Sir Robert Peel, are universally allowed to have been wise. The conduct of the Government during the commercial crisis of 1825 is extolled by all the best authorities. The panic began in the middle of the autumn and reached its height by Christmas. Sixty-three country banks stopped payment. The bullion in the Bank of England was reduced to half a million, and the Government was urgently pressed again to suspend cash payments. " To their infinite credit," says Tooke,* they refused to do so, and thus saved the country from a remedy worse than the disease. With the Tories in, 1802 and 1819, began the Factory Legislation which has been one of the greatest boons conferred on the working classes in the nineteenth century. They passed the first Act which recognized the right of the people to combine for the augmentation of wages ; they reformed the Criminal Code ; and they gave us for the first time an admirable system of police.

It is childish to argue that such measures were not Tory measures, because they were originally suggested by men who were not Tories. In the first place, only one of them had been suggested by a man who was not a Tory ; and, in the second place, if we apply this test to all the great measures which have been passed during the present century, we shall find that neither party in the State is entitled to the credit of any one of them. It has been said, so often that I am almost ashamed to repeat it, that, under a system of Party Government, the Ministers of the Crown are very unlikely to be the initiators of great social and political changes. They must wait till they see a public opinion in

* *History of Prices*, ii. 169.

favour of them strong enough to overcome the opposition which they are certain to excite; and this public opinion can only be created by the efforts of independent individuals. Philosophers and philanthropists are the usual pioneers of social changes. Many beneficial laws we owe to more polluted sources. But whatever the source, the demand almost always arises from without; and the Minister who is the first to understand when it must be taken up, and enrolled among the wants which it is the duty of Government to supply, is the man to whom the credit of practical legislation on the subject is, by the custom of Parliamentary Government, universally allowed. In other words, there are two parties to every great change of this description, the thinkers and the actors. To the first belong men like Adam Smith, Price, Romilly, Mackintosh, Cobbett, Cobden, and Mill; to the second, such men as Pitt, Peel, Stanley, the late Lord Derby, and Lord Russell. Mr. Gladstone and Lord Beaconsfield may be said to belong to both. But, as a general rule, when we attribute to a political party the merit of such and such a measure, we mean the merit which belongs to the active and constructive element in the result.

The policy to which I here appeal is summed up by a highly-competent authority, though a very unwilling witness, in the following terms:—

The financial history of the three years was very remarkable. For the first time since the conclusion of the Great War, the finances of the country had been conducted on an intelligible system. The old Sinking Fund had been abolished, and a new Sinking Fund, which the country had proved able to maintain, had been substituted for it. The funded debt had been reduced from £796,000,000 to £778,000,000; the unfunded debt from £38,000,000 to £31,000,000. In 1823, the window-tax had been reduced by one half; in 1825, the poorer householders had been relieved from the pressure both of house-tax and window-tax. The manufacturing classes had been encouraged by the reduction of the duties on silk, wool, and iron. The consuming classes had been benefited by the reduction of duties on spirits, wines, coffee, and sugar. The useless bounties on the whale and herring fisheries had been abolished; the bounties on the linen manufacture had been repealed; and the selfish policy which vainly endeavoured to concentrate the carrying trade of the world in British bottoms had been abandoned. During the same period the Labour Laws had been repealed; and the working classes had, for the first time, been legally permitted to combine for the purpose of raising the rate of wages. Such great alterations in the commercial and industrial legislation of the kingdom had never previously been attempted by any Minister. Changes of such importance were not again suggested for another twenty years.*

It is a total mistake to suppose that the disorders and distress which clouded the last years of George the Third's reign, were due to any species of ignorance or severity peculiar to the Tory Party. Nothing of the kind. We have but to look into Hansard to see at once that between the Opposition and the Government there was, on most of the points under consideration, no difference of principle whatever. The well-known "six Acts" seem to have been forced upon the Government by the little knot of revolutionaries, who took advantage of the popular suffering to fan into sedition what would otherwise have evaporated in harmless remonstrance. When men like Thistlewood and his associates were at work among the lower orders it was impossible for the Government to remain quiet. And members of the Whig Party are known to have declared that they would have been obliged to do the same thing had they been in office themselves. The amount of solemn nonsense which has been written on this subject is really almost appalling. To begin with, the "six Acts" were not measures of severity forced on a reluctant Parliament by an overbearing Ministry. The Opposition was divided into two parties, and both, we are

* Walpole, vol. ii. p 119.

told, looked with favour on the Government proposals.*
"Moderate men," who had previously doubted the necessity for the Government measures, were at once convinced
by the discovery of the Cato Street conspiracy.† And
now what *were* these measures ?

The first of the six Acts was to prevent bodies of men from assembling
for the purpose of military drill. By the second, Justices of the Peace were
authorized to issue warrants in certain counties of England and Scotland, to
search for arms or other weapons dangerous to the public peace, on a sworn
information. By the third, the court was authorized, in the event of the
accused allowing judgment to go by default, to order the seizure of all copies
of a seditious or blasphemous libel, to be restored if the person accused were
afterwards acquitted ; and for the second offence, transportation might be
inflicted. By the fourth, no more than fifty persons were to be allowed to as-
semble, except in borough or county meetings called by a magistrate ; and the
carrying of arms and flags at such meetings was prohibited, and extensive
powers given to Justices of Peace or county magistrates, for dispersing
them. In addition to these Acts a Bill was introduced by the Lord
Chancellor into the House of Lords, to prevent traversing or postponing the
trial to the next assizes in cases of misdemeanour. And another was introduced into the House of Commons by Lord Castlereagh subjecting news-
papers to certain stamps, and to prevent the abuses arising from the
publication of blasphemous and seditious libels. The first and third of these
Acts, prohibiting military training and authorizing the seizure of seditious
publications, alone were proposed to be permanent ; the second and fourth
were temporary only, and have long since expired.

I scarcely think that, on the whole, I could find a better
representative of the "regulation" Liberalism by which so
much of our modern English history has, so to speak, been
made to order, than the gentleman of whose work I have
already availed myself so largely, Mr. Spencer Walpole.
Without saying anything either for or against his authority

* " ' The Radicals,' wrote Brougham, ' have made themselves so odious,
that a number even of our own way of thinking would be well enough pleased
to see them and their vile press put down at all hazards.' The more Liberal
element among the Opposition were far from unanimous in their desire to
resist the Ministry. But the less Liberal element among them were even
more anxious than Lord Sidmouth and Lord Eldon for repressive measures "
Walpole, vol. i. p. 515.

† *Ibid.*, p. 529.

as a scientific historian, I think we may accept his opinions as fairly representing the class of Liberals to which he belongs. Now he, be it remembered, true to his political instincts, condemns the six Acts *en bloc*, and in the most unsparing manner. Yet, as soon as we come to details, what do we find? "Two out of the 'Six Acts' do not deserve to be remembered with any feelings of asperity. The Traversing Bill, in its ultimate shape, was a beneficial reform; the Military Training Bill has remained the law of the land to the present day." The Seizure of Arms Bill "was almost forced on the Government by the follies of the Radicals themselves. Watson, who had been concerned in the Spa Fields riots, had the folly to boast at a Smithfield meeting that there were 800,000 Radicals in arms." Of the Seditious Meetings Bill, after launching much invective at it, he tells us in the end that "the passing of the Seditious Meetings Bill disconcerted Thistlewood's* views." There remain, therefore, only the two Bills relating to "seditious and blasphemous libels," and the imposition of a stamp duty on pamphlets, to the latter of which Mr. Walpole owns that there was "no objection," to sustain the whole weight of the declamation which this gentleman has aimed at the Government. If two out of the six Acts were beneficial; if a third was forced upon the Government by the action of the Radicals; if a fourth had the effect of "disconcerting" the views of the ringleaders of a dangerous conspiracy; and if to another there was "no objection," I think we may leave the defence of the Six Acts in Mr. Walpole's hands. "The measures of the Ministry," he concludes, "however reprehensible they may seem in other respects, had one justification; they were successful. The firmness of the

---

* The leader of the conspirators.

authorities checked the disorders which were everywhere
menacing the country, and convinced the leaders of the
Radicals, or those of them who were still at large, that it
was impossible to pursue their designs against the Government." Englishmen of the present day will be inclined to
believe that this by itself was no small service to the public.

Mr. Walpole is fond of repeating that the conspiracy
was "contemptible"; that the conspirators were "obscure persons," and so forth, and seems to derive great
support from this reflection. All I can say is that, if a
conspiracy is contemptible, of which the members have the
villainy to plan, and the daring to attempt, the assassination of an entire Cabinet, the conspiracy which wrought
the murder of Lord Frederick Cavendish and Mr. Bourke
has been very harshly spoken of; and that, if all obscure
persons are to be at liberty to conspire against the lives
and properties of their neighbours, simply because they
are obscure, there is not a country in Europe that would
not shortly be knee-deep in blood.

Of all the tasks, great and various as they were, which
awaited the statesmen of the Regency, two stand out in
bold relief and overshadow all the others. These two were
the readjustment of our financial system and the direction
of our foreign policy amid the many new and conflicting
obligations and interests with which it was now entangled.
Lord Liverpool addressed himself to the first of these tasks;
Lord Castlereagh, and afterwards Mr. Canning, to the
second. When the religious difficulty of the day is added
to these, we shall see that a statesman's hands must have
been tolerably full, without adding to his burden by extending the field of legislation. The currency, the corn-
laws, and the Catholics found ample employment for Lord
Liverpool, though he always continued to keep an eye on

his Foreign Minister, to know all that was done in his department, and to offer many excellent suggestions. If a Hercules of legislation could have done all this, and taken up the other questions we have mentioned at the same time, we can only say again that Lord Liverpool was not this Hercules. Not that his name is altogether unconnected with social reform. He took a lively interest in Mr. Peel's Factory Act; he was the author of some beneficial changes in the Game Laws; and, as we see from the lately published Report of the Agricultural Commission, his Government had the honour of passing the first Allotment Act.

Lord Liverpool was an essentially fair-minded man, of great common-sense and great business capacity. He had not the genius which discerns from afar the signs of the times and treats present evils by the light of them; but he did what more brilliant men might have failed to do. He held together, for ten or twelve years, a Cabinet composed of very discordant materials, and was thus enabled to secure for his Government the support of both the old Conservative Tories and the younger advocates of Reform, who began to grow impatient of abuses. Without some such combination it is doubtful how far the country could have been governed at all during the critical period which followed the conclusion of the war. His high character, tact, moderation, and perfect disinterestedness secured for us a strong Government at the time when it was most wanted, and this, at all events, is a claim upon our gratitude which is never likely to be disputed.

CHAPTER III.

MR. CANNING.

IT is a singular feature in the career of Mr. Canning that the shortest and least important stage of it was that in which he played the first part. As Foreign Minister he has been considered the founder of a school; and though it is perfectly true that in many points he was anticipated by Lord Castlereagh, between whom and himself there was little real difference of principle, yet it was reserved for Mr. Canning to bring the new system to maturity and complete the process of disentangling England from those more intimate relations with the military Powers, which, indispensable as they were during the ascendency of Napoleon, could not have been maintained afterwards without contracting liabilities and espousing doctrines which the country would never have endured. But as Prime Minister he left his mark on nothing. He entered on his "inheritance," as he himself termed it, in April, and he died in August—the last of the followers of Mr. Pitt who took any active part in public life. His death, like that of his great master, marks an epoch in our political history. For, though another race of great Tory statesmen, far superior in abilities to either Lord Liverpool, the Duke of Portland, or Mr. Perceval, were ready to take his place, the principles of the Tory Party underwent a greater change after 1827 than they did in 1806. Mr. Canning was the only living statesman who could have kept the old *régime* together, and with it those ideas of government which are the growth of an age of aristocracy. In addition to his eminent abilities and the benefits of his early training, he had the breadth of view and the elevation of sentiment which were necessary to win the confidence of the people, and retain that hold over their passions, which the statesmen on whom the conduct of the Tory Party devolved at his death were less qualified to exercise. The halo which surrounded the Duke of Wellington, derived exclusively from his military glory, began to wane like the sun beneath the ocean as he dipped into politics, and only shone again with unclouded brightness when he emerged from the waters.

Mr. Canning was born in London on the 11th of April 1770, of an old Warwickshire family, a branch of which settled in Ireland, and in 1818 obtained the peerage of Garvagh. The head of this branch was the father of three sons, of whom the eldest was the statesman's father, disinherited—so runs the story—in consequence of his marriage; the second the father of the first Lord Garvagh; and the youngest, of Lord Stratford de Redcliffe. It was this uncle, then engaged in business in London, who, on the death of his elder brother in 1771, took charge of his infant son, and brought him up like his own. His mother, who had been a Miss Costello and was a very pretty woman, adopted the stage as a profession, where she attained a certain measure of success. She did not live to see her son Prime Minister, though she very narrowly missed it; as she died on the 27th of March 1827, exactly fifteen days before the seals were delivered to him.

9 *

Canning was educated first at a private school near Winchester, and afterwards at Eton, where, together with Hookham Frere and the two Smiths, he founded the *Microcosm*, for the copyright of which Knight the publisher thought it worth his while to give fifty guineas, before the young proprietors had left school. Canning was captain of Eton in 1787, and in October of that year he went up to Christ Church. In the following year he gained the Chancellor's prize for Latin verse, the subject being the Pilgrimage to Mecca, and, having taken his bachelor's degree, repaired to London and enrolled himself at Lincoln's Inn. His uncle was a Whig, and frequently entertained the Whig leader at his table; and here the young student met Fox, Fitzpatrick, and Sheridan, who introduced him to Devonshire House, and to all the most beautiful and fashionable women of the Whig party. Young Canning was well qualified to shine in such circles, and speedily attracted marked attention. But he early recognized in Pitt the political hero of the age; nor did Pitt himself, to whom he had been presented while still an undergraduate, by Lord Hawkesbury, fail to discern in him, even at that early age, the promise of a valuable ally.

Soon after he was settled in London, the Minister sent for him, and he at once consented to the proposal that he should enter Parliament for the Ministerial borough of Newport, for which place he took his seat in the session of 1793. He delivered a very effective maiden speech on the 31st of January, 1794, and his own account of it, contained in a letter to his friend, Lord Boringdon, will be found very interesting. The subject was the subsidy proposed to be granted to the King of Sardinia :—

I intended to have told you at full length what were my feelings at getting up and being pointed at by the Speaker, and hearing my name called from all sides of the House; how I trembled lest I should hesitate, or misplace a word, in the two or three first sentences, while all was dead silence around me, and my own voice sounded to my ears quite like some other gentleman's; how, in about ten minutes or less, I got warmed in collision with Fox's arguments, and did not even care twopence for anybody or anything; how I was roused in about half an hour from this pleasing state of self-sufficiency by accidentally casting my eyes on the Opposition bench for the purpose of paying compliments to Fox, and assuring him of my respect and admiration, and there seeing certain members of the Opposition laughing (as I thought) and quizzing me; how this accident abashed me, and, together with my being out of breath, rendered me incapable of uttering; how those who sat below me on the Treasury bench, seeing what it was that distressed me, cheered loudly, and the House joined them; and how, in less than a minute, straining every nerve in my body, and plucking up every bit of resolution in my heart, I went on more boldly than ever, and getting into a part of my subject that I liked, and having the House with me, got happily and triumphantly to the end.

To all this I had some intention of adding (if I could so far subdue my natural modesty) some account of the reception which it met from those with whom it was most my interest and ambition that it should be well received, but I find it impossible to do so, and I must, therefore, defer all that I have to tell you on such subjects till I see you in England.

The speech is said to have been marred to some extent by a too palpable imitation of Burke, whose style did not sit well on so young and vivacious an orator. Canning had the good sense to recognise his mistake, and dropped the attempt forthwith. In 1796 he was made Under-Secretary for Foreign Affairs, Lord Grenville being his chief; and in November 1797 he started the *Anti-Jacobin*. The journal was a brilliant success, numbering among its contributors his old Eton friends of the *Microcosm*, together with George Ellis, Lord Carlisle, Lord Wellesley, and, according to rumour, even Pitt himself. The *Anti-Jacobin* quite eclipsed the *Rolliad*, and thoroughly succeeded in turning the laugh against the Liberals; and when the Opposition leaders and revolutionary principles had once been made to look ridiculous, the Tory victory was complete. Why the publication was stopped in the following July I have never been able to ascertain. In 1801 Canning retired from office with Mr. Pitt, having married, the year before, Miss Scott, the daughter of General Scott and sister of the Duchess of Portland, with a portion of a hundred thousand pounds. The pension of five hundred a year, to which he became entitled on resigning his appointment, he desired to have settled on his mother and sisters, to whom through life he ever showed the most affectionate solicitude.

It is well known that during the administration of Mr. Addington, Pitt absented himself a good deal both from the House of Commons and from London, residing principally at Walmer Castle, and amusing himself with a farm which he had purchased. But his political friends were not so well satisfied with his retirement as he was himself, and Canning in particular urged him to return to the field with solicitations which in time became irksome. He also took upon himself to fight Pitt's battles in his absence, and to speak on his behalf and in his name with rather more confidence and presumption than were agreeable to his august patron. But Pitt was a remarkably good-natured man, and seems, moreover, to have treated his *protégé* with a kind of fatherly indulgence, not always, perhaps, to Canning's own advantage. Canning's threat of resignation when Addington was re-admitted to the Cabinet in 1804, and the manner in which it appears to have been received by Pitt, is an instance in point. Canning made a confidant of Lady Hester, and between the uncle and niece his ruffled plumes were smoothed, and he continued a member of the Government.

The Peace of Amiens was signed in March 1802, and so unsatisfactory did its terms appear to many of Pitt's old friends, that Lord Grenville, Lord Spencer, the Marquis of Buckingham, and Mr. Windham at once went into violent opposition. Pitt, of course, withheld Canning from attacking it, but he could not prevent him from saying everywhere that Pitt ought to return to office, and was the only man at such a crisis fit to be trusted with the Government of the country ; or from pursuing the unfortunate Minister with squibs and epigrams, which neither he nor his friends forgave to the last hour of their lives. It was about this time that he wrote the well-known song, *The Pilot that weathered the Storm*, which can hardly have failed to lead public opinion in the direction which he wished it to take. He continued, however, to support the Government with great ability ; and on the 8th of December 1802, on the question of the national defences, made one of the finest speeches which ever fell from his lips, reminding us more than once of the first Philippic of Demosthenes. But as time went on, and it became more and more evident that Napoleon had no intention of abiding by the terms of peace, and that a fresh war was every day becoming more imminent, the Pittite party in the House of Commons began to show less and less forbearance to the Government, and Pitt himself at length re-appeared upon the scene, to the infinite delight of his impetuous subaltern, though he was unwilling at first to push matters to extremities. The point on which Napoleon laid so much stress was our failure to evacuate Malta within the time specified by the Treaty, overlooking the fact that this step had been made conditional on the fulfilment by himself of other pledges which he had systematically violated. It is unnecessary to defend the conduct of the British Government at this juncture, as Mr. Fox himself always admitted that the second French war was inevitable, whatever the first might have been. But it soon became evident that Addington was not equal to the conduct of it. Independently of the inadequacy of his measures, he did not possess the confidence of the foreign Powers in alliance with Great Britain. " Si ce Ministère dure," said Count Woronzow, the Russian Ambassador in England, " la Grande Bretagne ne durera pas."

War was declared on the 18th of March 1803, and in the following June Canning supported a vote of censure on the Government, moved by Colonel Patten, member for Newton in Lancashire. But the House of Commons was in no mood to support any motion of the kind. The Opposition were unwilling as yet to turn out Addington in order to bring in Pitt; and Pitt's own supporters in the Tory Party were too few to do it by themselves, even had Pitt himself desired that result, which he did not. He himself moved the Orders of the Day, being unwilling either to condemn or to acquit his former friend ; but the House declined the compromise by an immense majority, and afterwards rejected the main question by nearly as large a one. Pitt's idea was that it was useless to rake up the past : though he could not conscientiously say that the Ministry had been blameless. But with regard to the future he was determined to "oppose most decidedly, and with all his power, any weak or pernicious half measures, unequal to the pressure of the moment."

The time soon came when he was obliged to be as good as his word. He had not been Chancellor of the Exchequer seventeen years for nothing. He, and perhaps he alone, fully comprehended our resources ; and though he wished that the renewal of the war could have been deferred for two or three years, by which time we should have been still better prepared to sustain it, he saw at once that misplaced economy at such a moment as that when Napoleon was only watching his opportunity to swoop down upon us with two hundred thousand men was nothing less than a crime. Neither the army nor the navy were on a thoroughly efficient footing; the latter, especially, had been reduced to such a pass by Lord St. Vincent, who would persist in believing that war was impossible, that we were for some time in a much more critical condition than is commonly understood. "Let us be masters of the Channel for six hours," said Napoleon, "and we are masters of the world!" In August 1804* it seemed quite possible that the French might be masters of the Channel for six hours. Fortunately for ourselves, the French admiral, with whom Napoleon had concocted all the details of his grand design, died just at the moment when it ought to have been put in execution, and before a fit successor could be found the opportunity was lost. But in the month of August 1804 it undoubtedly existed, and its existence was the fault of the Ministry.

In a letter to George Rose, of November 11th, 1803, Pitt complains of "the unaccountable negligence and inactivity of the Government," and in the following month he brought forward a motion on the state of the Navy in a speech which might be studied with great advantage at the present moment. It will be seen, then—and this is the point I wish to make clear—that Canning's attacks on the Ministry were abundantly justified by their conduct, and that, however much Mr. Addington and his own personal friends might think themselves aggrieved by them, the country was really indebted to him. We see, too, plainly, that with the development of Napoleon's ambition, Pitt's conception of the war, and the sacrifices necessary to be made by this country, had enlarged also, and that,

* This must not be confounded with the affair of 1805.

however much he might feel himself restrained by his original undertaking to support the Government, his views were identical with Canning's.

Canning, who protested under Addington, protested again under the Duke of Portland, and was sacrificed to the powerful influences arrayed upon the other side. He protested again, as an independent member, during the Ministry of Mr. Perceval, and though, no doubt, it was in a great measure owing to him, and the Pittite Tories who supported him, that the Peninsular War was not abandoned, yet he was taunted by the other section of the Party with being actuated by unworthy motives, and his memory has come down to us, even to this day, still bearing the marks of their resentment. This unhappy misunderstanding, which had its origin during the first years of this century, poisoned the minds of a later generation against the pupil of Mr. Pitt, and caused even the great soldier, who was far more indebted to him than he ever understood, to stand aloof from him in his hour of need, and drive him into the arms of a party whom he himself had always regarded with distrust. As there can be no doubt that the conduct of Sir Robert Peel and the Duke of Wellington, in refusing to act cordially with Mr. Canning in 1827, exercised the most disastrous influence on the fortunes of the Tory Party, and on the fortunes of the English Constitution,* the various events and transactions which, by contributing to fasten on Mr. Canning the character of an intriguer, lay at the root of this unlucky schism, become invested with a deep and an abiding interest for us, and in any history of the Tory Party must occupy a prominent place.

To trace the mischief to its source we must go to the

* See Chap. IV.

Diary of the first Lord Malmesbury, who says that Canning was Mr. Pitt's spoiled child, and implies that his head had been turned by his rapid rise in public life. It is easy to understand that older men than himself, and men of higher birth and rank, would be offended by the forwardness of the great man's *protégé*, and regard his satire as impertinence, whether levelled at themselves or others. With this previous impression on their minds, they would be prepared, of course, to place the most unfavourable construction on his conduct whenever it was called in question, and, to whatever dispute he was a party, to find him in the wrong. Canning had himself and his patron to thank for the existence of this prejudice in the political circles of the day. But in the particular controversies in which it operated to his disadvantage I believe he was always in the right, and that, had there been no *arrière pensée* in the way, nobody would have thought otherwise.

After the formation of Lord Grenville's Government Canning was more than once offered high office by his former chief, but declined to join him by himself, as he felt he should be surrounded by Whigs, and that his relations with Mr. Fox would necessarily be extremely uncomfortable. But the offer is worth mentioning for the sake of the reply which on one occasion it drew from Mr. Canning, showing how true he still remained to the central article of the Tory faith. "If Lord Grenville means to make his Government all that it ought to be, the King must be admitted into it (be consulted), then he will retrieve the first false step, which is a cause of the great part of the present aversion to him." Lord Malmesbury's comment on his refusal was : "He may be safely trusted, for, I repeat, he is honourable and honest."

As has been very truly said, Canning's position after the death of Mr. Pitt was like Becky Sharpe's at Gaunt House when left alone with the ladies after dinner. He was made to feel the full weight of all the petty jealousies and animosities which he had kindled during his patron's lifetime ; and unfortunately, perhaps, for himself, among his political friends was a statesman of consummate ability who was not calculated to set him the best possible example of conciliation or modesty. This was Lord Wellesley, who had lately returned from India, and understood as well as Canning the mistake that had been committed by the Government in withdrawing the British forces from the Peninsula. On the dismissal of Lord Grenville the two sections of the Tory party, the Pittites, represented by Canning, and the followers of Addington, now Lord Sidmouth, represented by Mr. Perceval, finding it impossible to agree, a neutral Prime Minister was appointed in the person of the Duke of Portland, already with one foot in the grave, and totally unequal to his duties. In this administration Canning was Secretary of State for Foreign Affairs, and Lord Castlereagh Secretary for War.* It cannot be said that there was any want of spirit or energy in the earlier operations of the Government. The seizure of the Danish Fleet by Lord Cathcart in September 1807, planned by Canning, was not only " an act of vigour," but a very successful act of vigour, which effectually checkmated the combination formed against us by Napoleon in the North of Europe. The Orders in Council,† though the full effects of them were not foreseen at the moment, showed, at all events, the lengths to which England was prepared to go against her formidable enemy.

* War and the Colonies.
† See Chap. II.

Canning, however, had been seriously annoyed by a resolution adopted, in his absence, at a meeting of the Cabinet, approving of the Convention of Cintra. The Minister by whose advice this step was taken was Lord Castlereagh—a circumstance which did not contribute to smooth the relations between himself and the Secretary for War, already slightly strained by the opinions which Canning was known to have expressed on the Corunna campaign: "The advance into Spain under Sir John Moore, who had an army in Portugal of about 12,000 men, did not take place till some weeks after the Convention at Cintra (Aug. 30, 1808) had been signed. The delay was occasioned by the tardy departure from England of the reinforcements to join him. Had they arrived in Spain in the middle of August, they would have found the Spanish armies undefeated. But when the British army was in a position to advance, Napoleon had, with his wonted celerity, defeated and dispersed the Spanish forces, and opened for himself the road to Madrid."* The policy of "too late" is unhappily no novelty in the military history of England.

Canning took advantage of the disaster to force on the Government the necessity of our being more efficiently represented in Spain, and Lord Wellesley accepted the embassy on the express condition that Sir Arthur should be sent back to Portugal with an efficient force at his command. The General was sent, but not the army; which, by Lord Castlereagh's orders, was despatched to Flushing, and perished of disease in the island of Walcheren. Had these troops formed part of Sir Arthur Wellesley's army, the fruits of the battle of Talavera would not have been lost, and the effect of the diversion

* Stapleton's *Canning*, p. 159.

in Spain upon Napoleon's fortunes have been felt much sooner.

Canning's cup was now full. Justly irritated by the conduct of the Cabinet in the matter of the Convention of Cintra; disgusted with the mismanagement of Moore's expedition ; on discovering that the undertaking with Lord Wellesley had been violated, he could refrain no longer, and announced to the Duke of Portland, that either Lord Castlereagh must retire from the War Department or he himself from the Ministry. The Duke of Portland agreed with Mr. Canning, and communicated what had passed to Lord Eldon, Lord Camden, and Lord Bathurst, the intimate friends of Lord Castlereagh, who joined with the Duke of Portland in pressing on Mr. Canning to allow the intended change to be concealed from Lord Castlereagh till the end of the Session. Whether Mr. Canning consented to this proposal or not seems uncertain. According to the version of the affair given by Lord Colchester, he did ; according to the correspondence published in the *Annual Register*, and the excellent narrative founded on it in Twiss's *Life of Lord Eldon*, he did not; but remained under the impression that the communication had been made by Lord Camden. At all events he learned the truth on the 21st of June, the day Parliament was prorogued ; but as Lord Castlereagh was then in the middle of his preparations for the expedition, Perceval, to whom the scheme was then first communicated, is said to have persuaded his colleagues to postpone the execution of it till the issue of the expedition should be known.

It seems certain, however, that Canning was led to believe that no further delay would take place in informing Lord Castlereagh of the facts. A further delay,

nevertheless, was begged of him till the expedition should
have sailed, and then another, till the issue of the expedition should be known. These repeated solicitations
came from Lord Castlereagh's own friends, who represented to Canning that, if they had time given them,
they could break the matter to him more gently, and
gradually reconcile him to the change without any wound
to his feelings. That Canning yielded to these requests is
rather to his honour than otherwise, though those who
have had the public ear have succeeded in keeping afloat
a different version of the story. But when, towards the
end of August, the fate of the expedition became known,
and Canning found that nothing had been done or was
likely to be done, on the 6th of September he resigned.
Castlereagh, taking notice of his absence from a Cabinet,
became inquisitive, and going home to dinner with Lord
Camden, extorted from him the whole history of the
transaction. The next day he sent a challenge to Mr.
Canning, and the two statesmen met on Putney Heath,
when Canning was slightly wounded and Castlereagh lost
a button off his coat : the *Morning Chronicle* thanking
Mr. Canning for the service he had intended to his
country.

It is clear to me that Castlereagh had no ground of
quarrel with Canning, who, in a very difficult situation,
had acted for the best, and had been deceived by the moral
cowardice of others. To determine whether a man has
acted rightly in any given emergency, it is often a good
plan to consider what would have happened had he acted
differently. In this case there were the conventional
three courses open to Mr. Canning. He might have remained in the Cabinet, a silent spectator of the mismanagement which he believed to be disastrous to the

country, and for which he would then have been responsible. He might have insisted peremptorily on a change
being made at once, and have resigned if it was refused. Or he might have done what he did—have yielded
to the united solicitations of the King, the Prime Minister,
and Lord Castlereagh's own friends, who represented to
him that his resignation would break up the Government,
and that more harm would be done to the public service
by such a catastrophe than by allowing Lord Castlereagh
to remain in office three months longer.

Of these three courses, no man with any keen sense of
public duty could have adopted the first. Had he adopted
the second, it seems equally certain that, whether his
own resignation or Lord Castlereagh's had been the
consequence, the Government must have come to the
ground — a calamity much greater in times of public
danger than is commonly supposed—and the breach between the two sections of the Tory Party have been
bitterly exasperated. With these alternatives before him,
and the counsel of Lord Castlereagh's own friends to
guide him, is Mr. Canning to be blamed for one moment
for the course which he adopted? He was surely right
in concluding that the honour of Lord Castlereagh was
safe in the keeping of his friends, and that they would
not advise him to do anything which was either discredit-
able to himself or unfair to his colleague. Lord Castlereagh,
however, had the Addington party on his side ; and they
were too glad to get a fresh opportunity of declaiming
against Canning to stop to inquire whether his Lordship
was not extremely wrong-headed in taking up the matter
as he did. So it became an article of faith with that
section of the Tories that Mr. Canning had behaved badly
to Lord Castlereagh. He was already declared to have

behaved badly to Mr. Addington ; and with these two previous convictions recorded against him, he was immediately to be put upon his trial on a third charge—that, namely, of behaving badly to Mr. Perceval.

When it became evident that a successor to the Duke of Portland would shortly have to be found, Canning told Mr. Perceval that he thought the choice lay between themselves, adding that, though he could not consent to act under him in the House of Commons, his retirement, should it be necessary, would make no difference in their friendship. This was an intimation to Perceval that he considered his own claim to the Treasury the stronger of the two, and was prepared to submit it to the King ; but that if considerations of convenience dictated the choice of Perceval, he should recognize their weight and acquiesce in the arrangement amicably, though unable himself to form a part of it. That he should have been ready with suggestions for facilitating his own promotion to the Treasury was, of course, to be expected. He proposed that Perceval should either be Chancellor of the Duchy of Lancaster for life with a Peerage, or succeed Lord Eldon on the woolsack. Lord Eldon had not then established his great reputation, and Perceval, who had been both Solicitor-General and Attorney-General, had the usual qualifications for the post. It was all very well for Perceval's friends, after he had been actually Prime Minister, to describe such proposals as insulting. But at the present time I should say there is hardly a politician to be found who would not agree with me that they were fully equal to his merits.

Canning, moreover, impressed upon the King the necessity of having the next Prime Minister in the House of Commons, and as in that case if it was not Canning it must

10

be Perceval, he had a right to credit himself with having helped in Perceval's elevation. If a man goes to the dispenser of Office, and says to him, "Now, I want this place for myself, but if you cannot give it to me then give it to my friend," is he doing his friend a good turn or not? That Perceval honestly recognized the superiority of Mr. Canning, is, we think, evident. Canning said to him, "When you are First Lord as well as Chancellor of the Exchequer, you will be double yourself in strength in the House of Commons, and you may go on without me." To which Perceval rejoined, with as much good sense as point, "It may be very true that any man who holds both these offices is of twice the importance and weight in public opinion; but Canning single, is of more Parliamentary weight than Perceval double." There is no reason to doubt, we say, that this was his sincere opinion. But Perceval was surrounded by friends who regarded himself and Mr. Canning as the two representative men of the two rival Tory sections—the faithful few who were called "the friends of Mr. Pitt," and the grosser multitude who had followed the lead of Mr. Addington. It is perfectly natural that they should have endeavoured to persuade both himself and themselves and the world at large that he was a much greater man than he was. It is impossible to understand the history of the twenty years which followed the death of Mr. Pitt, unless we always bear in mind that throughout the whole of that period the Tories, as of old, had a King *de facto* and a King *de jure* too. "He has a knack of versifying," said Curl, of Pope, "but in prose I think myself a match for him." This was the sort of distinction which his friends desired to have it thought existed between Perceval and Canning. The latter had a knack of writing squibs, but in all affairs of solid business, little P, they said, was quite his equal. Perceval himself, we may believe, did not swallow all this flattery. But he swallowed more of it than was good for him, and we can only smile when he talks of being extinguished by a coronet.*

An attempt has been made to exalt the character of Castlereagh at the expense of both Pitt and Canning, who, it is said, did nòt understand his larger conceptions of the war and the scale on which our military operations ought to be conducted. It is forgotten that all Castlereagh's measures at the time referred to had the full concurrence of Pitt, and therefore also of Canning. They were both privy to his scheme for landing 40,000 men in the north of Europe. It was not to the magnitude of his plans, but to the misdirection of them, that Canning took objection.

I must pass very briefly over the next thirteen years, the period which intervened between Mr. Canning's retirement from the Foreign Office in 1809 and his return to it in 1822. Mr. Canning continued his support in Parliament to the Peninsular War, and helped greatly to fortify the resolution of the Government in persevering with the contest. Both in 1810 and 1811 he made some very fine speeches on this subject, one of which is distinguished by a very happy reference to the *Merchant of Venice*. An Opposition speaker had recommended that we should leave Spain to her fate, in order that on the destruction of her Empire we might seize on her American Colonies. Mr. Canning said that considering all that England had affected to feel for the condition of the Spaniards,—her sympathy, condolence, and admiration—a speech which implied that we were really thinking all the time of her

---

* Scott saw nothing strange in the offer of a Peerage to Perceval.—Lockhart, vol. ii., p. 263.

Colonies, reminded him of Shylock's lament over Jessica, whom he would not have minded seeing dead at his feet had she only brought him back his ducats.

In 1811 Mr. Canning made his two famous speeches on the Report of the Bullion Committee, of which Mr. Horner was Chairman and Mr. Huskisson a leading member. Mr. Canning himself was a decided bullionist, and strongly in favour of an ultimate return to cash payments; but not of an immediate return. He thought it must be made dependent on the restoration of peace, when the gold we had exported during the war would come back to us from abroad. Notwithstanding that financial questions had never much occupied his attention, the mastery of the subject which he displayed, when called upon to take part in the debates, excited the admiration of both parties. " He played with the most knotty subtleties of the question," said Mr. Horner, " as if he had long been perfectly familiar with it." Those who wish for a fuller account of this controversy, and a justification of Mr. Canning's financial theories, will find what they want in the *Political Life of Mr. Canning*.*

After the assassination of Mr. Perceval, Canning was again offered the Foreign Office by Lord Liverpool; but he declined to serve under Lord Castlereagh, who was to retain the lead of the House of Commons, and continued without office till, in 1814, he went as Ambassador Extraordinary to Portugal, with a salary of £14,000 a year; and his speech in defence of himself in Parliament, where the appointment was stigmatised as a job, is among the best he ever made. In 1816 he re-entered the Government as President of the Board of Control, only to

* Vol. iii. chap. xiii.

quit it again after the trial of Queen Caroline, in consequence of the offence which he had given to George the Fourth by his opposition to the Divorce Clause. Again, after a time, Lord Liverpool invited him into the Cabinet, but the King would not listen to the proposal ; and Canning had accepted the office of Governor-General of India, and was on the point of sailing, when the death of Lord Londonderry brought the Foreign Office to his feet. Lord Liverpool told the King roundly that Canning must be Secretary; the Duke of Wellington, to his honour, came to the support of the Prime Minister ; and he bowed to the necessity at once.

The key to Canning's foreign policy is to be found in his correspondence with Sir Henry Wellesley, then our ambassador at Vienna. At this period it is well known that the great military Powers of the Continent had combined for the purpose of trampling out the embers of the French Revolution which still continued to smoulder in Europe, and crushing all insurrectionary movements against the legitimate dynasties. It may be convenient, perhaps, before proceeding any further, to recount very briefly the progress of European diplomacy from Napoleon's abdication in 1814 to the Congress of Vienna in 1822. The first Peace of Paris, following what the Allies conceived to be the final downfall of Napoleon, was signed on the 30th of May 1814, and settled the relations between the other great Powers and France. The Congress of Vienna followed in November of the same year to settle the affairs of Europe, and the rearrangements of territory rendered necessary by the long war. The Congress sat through the winter, and had practically concluded its labours, when the news arrived of Napoleon's escape from Elba, and the Treaty of Vienna was signed by the Allies on the 25th of

March 1815, for the purpose of resisting and redeposing him. After the Waterloo campaign came the second Peace of Paris, imposing harder terms on France than the first had done, and providing for the army of occupation. This was signed on the 20th of November 1815. The pacification and reconstruction of the Continental kingdoms were finally completed by the Treaty of Aix-la-Chapelle in 1818, which embodied in itself the provisions of the Treaty of Paris and the *recez* of the Congress of Vienna.

As the Protocols attached to this Treaty and signed by all the Plenipotentiaries were frequently referred to afterwards, it may be as well to quote the most important of them to see clearly what it was to which the Tory Government had committed us.

The Convention of the 9th of October, which definitely regulated the execution of the engagements agreed to in the treaty of peace, November 20th, 1815, is considered by the Sovereigns who concurred therein as the accomplishment of the work of peace, and as the completion of the political system destined to ensure its solidity.

The intimate union established among the Monarchs who are joint parties to this system, by their own principles, no less than by the interests of their people, appears to Europe the most sacred pledge of its future tranquillity.

The object of this union is as simple as it is great and salutary. It does not tend to any new political combination—to any change in the relations sanctioned by existing treaties. Calm and consistent in its proceedings, it has no other object than the maintenance of peace, and the guarantee of those transactions on which peace was founded and consolidated.

The Sovereigns, in forming this august union, have regarded as its fundamental basis their invariable resolution never to depart, either among themselves or in their relations with other States, from the strictest observation of the principles of the rights of nations; principles which, in their application to a state of permanent peace, can alone effectually guarantee the independence of each Government and the stability of the general association.

The Treaty of Aix-la-Chapelle was signed, as we have seen, in 1818. Two years afterwards the revolution broke out in Spain, Italy, and Naples, which, together with the Eastern Question, gave ample employment to European statesmen for the rest of Mr. Canning's life. The Congress of Troppau was convened in October 1820, to consider how these popular movements should be dealt with. It was adjourned to Laybach, from which the Continental Powers issued a circular in December, explaining their views of the crisis and the obligations attaching to all the signatories of the Treaty of Aix-la-Chapelle. The circular was answered by Lord Castlereagh in a famous State Paper, of which we shall shortly hear more, sent round to all the British representatives in January 1821. In September 1822 a great effort was made to find some common basis of action by the Congress of Verona. But all in vain. The great Powers had determined on their course of action, and even the Duke of Wellington failed to make any impression on his former friends. He told the Emperor of Russia that there was "no sympathy, and would be none, between England and Revolutionists and Jacobins anywhere. The system of English government was founded on respect for property. Jacobinism, or Revolution, in the sense which His Imperial Majesty applied to the term, was the confiscation of property. All for which England ever pleaded was the right of nations to set up over themselves whatever form of government they thought best, and to be left to manage their own affairs so long as they left other nations to manage theirs. Neither he nor the Government he represented was blind to the many defects which disfigured the Spanish Constitution.* But they were satisfied that the best remedy for them would be provided by time, and to that greatest of all practical reformers he advised that Spain and her Constitution should be left."† It was just at this time that Mr. Canning became

---

* Spanish Constitution, *i.e.* of 1812.
† Gleig's *Life of Wellington*, vol. iii. pp. 157, 158.

Foreign Minister, and we shall find in his correspondence almost identically the same language.

Austria, however, had already marched an army into Naples, and France was preparing to march another into Spain. These movements, which, if not a direct violation of the spirit of the aforesaid compact, certainly bore a strong resemblance to it, England was unable to prevent. The military Powers succeeded in their objects, and absolutism was restored in Italy and in Spain, not to be finally deposed again till long after the death of Mr. Canning. In Portugal the course of affairs was much more complicated. There were three parties in that country: the Revolutionary Party, the Constitutional Party, and the Despotic Party. Mr. Canning sided with the second, and endeavoured to maintain John VI., who, with his Minister Palmella, was at the head of it, against both the Democrats and the Autocrats, the latter led by the King's second son, Don Miguel. Here Canning was successful. In 1823 he sent a squadron to the Tagus, which effectually disconcerted a *coup d'état* attempted by Don Miguel; and, after the King's death, a British force was sent to maintain the authority of the Regent Isabella against a threatened invasion by Spain in favour of the Miguelites. At Canning's death, in August 1827, Portugal was tranquil and the Constitutional Party in peaceable possession of the government. In Portugal the case had arisen which Canning put hypothetically to Sir Henry Wellesley in 1823.* Our interests and our obligations both pointed the same way. It was decidedly our interest to prevent the western coast of the Peninsula from falling into the power of Spain, then under the tutelage of France, and we were under

* *See* page 157.

treaty obligations to assist Portugal even had our interests been different.

The contention of our Allies throughout had been that, by the general understanding founded on the Congress of Vienna, and embodied in the Treaty of 1818, England had become a consenting party to the policy of repression, not necessarily to any active participation in it, but to a moral approval—benevolent neutrality, at least—and they were offended by the very different tone adopted by the English Press and by the Opposition in the House of Commons. Lord Castlereagh, no less than Canning, at once protested against this construction of our duties. *Non hæc in fædera veni* was the burden of his song from the beginning. In the answer to the Laybach circular, which we have already mentioned, he defined what he conceived to be the extent of our engagements. England did stand pledged to uphold the territorial arrangements established at the Congress of Vienna. The invasion of a weaker State by a stronger one for the purposes of conquest would demand our immediate interference. But with the internal affairs of each separate State we had nothing to do. We could neither share in nor approve of, though we might not feel called on to resist, the intervention of one ally to put down internal disturbances in the dominions of another. We had never committed ourselves to any such principle as that, and must, as a general rule, protest against it, though exceptional circumstances might, in some cases, be thought to justify it ; the exception being where the security of the intervening State was threatened by rebellion on its frontier.

This exception was certainly a loop-hole by which the allied Powers might justify a good deal which the English people would have condemned. But the point is that in

1825, more than two years after Castlereagh's death, and after the recognition of the Spanish colonies, when George the Fourth addressed a memorandum to his Cabinet requesting to know whether his Government was still to be carried on according to the Treaties of 1814, 1815, and 1818, he was unanimously referred to the above Circular, which had been issued with his own approval and the approval of the Government, and was now declared by the Cabinet in which Canning was Foreign Minister to represent their policy.* Canning, therefore, was content that his foreign policy should be identified with Castlereagh's Circular. This is point number one to be remembered. Canning repeats to Sir Henry Wellesley over and over again

---

* *Vide* Cabinet Memorandum, January 29, 1825. All the Ministers, including, of course, the Duke of Wellington, being present, except Lord Bexley.

"Upon communicating freely with each other their respective individual opinions, Your Majesty's servants have found so entire an agreement to subsist between them, as to the substance of the answer to be returned to Your Majesty's question, that they humbly request Your Majesty's permission to give that answer generally and collectively.

"Your Majesty's servants think it their duty to remind Your Majesty that a divergence of opinion between Your Majesty and your Allies, as to the nature of their engagements for the maintenance of the peace of Europe, began to appear even in the negotiations of 1815, and Your Majesty's Plenipotentiary, upon that occasion, declared to Your Majesty's Allies the extent to which alone Your Majesty would be a party to such engagements.

"This divergence became still more apparent in the Conferences at Aix-la-Chapelle in 1818; and after several intermediate explanations, the allied Governments still persisting in their own interpretation of the principles of those treaties, and even in representing Your Majesty as concurring in such interpretation, Your Majesty found it necessary to proclaim to the world, by the Circular Note of the late Lord Londonderry of the 19th January 1821 Your Majesty's dissent from that interpretation.

"Your Majesty's servants feel it to be their duty, therefore, to state that they fully recognize the principles of policy laid down in 1814, 1815, and 1818, in the sense given to them repeatedly by Your Majesty's Plenipotentiary, and specially in the Circular so issued by Your Majesty's command in 1821, and in no other."—*Life of Canning*, p. 419.

that the Allies have no right to call upon us to interfere
"internally" with other countries, but that we have a
right to call upon them not to interfere "externally."
All our guarantees, he says, were territorial, not political.
We desired that the internal tranquillity of every State
should be maintained, but we were not prepared to say
that Monarchy was the only condition by which that end
could be secured. There was one glory of the moon and
another of the sun, said Canning, and though he would
support absolute monarchy, where it was the old-established
form of Government, seemed the natural growth of the
soil, and suited to the habits of the people, he could be no
party to forcing it on a reluctant population. Each
country must settle these questions for itself. England
might have her preferences, and was at liberty to avow
them. But all she could be required to do by force of
arms was to defend the balance of power and the general
territorial settlement effected in 1816. How, then, did
the writer of the despatches of 1823 differ from the
writer of the Circular of 1821? and what was the real
difference between the policy of Canning and the policy of
Castlereagh and Wellington?

The difference was one, I think, rather in degree than
in kind. Canning, if unable to prevent, would show his
displeasure at, the interference of one State in the domestic
quarrels of another in a more marked manner than
Castlereagh. If we turn to the Parliamentary debates,
and especially to Lord Castlereagh's speech, on the
"conduct of the Allies," in March 1821, just after his
answer to the Circular, we shall discover, perhaps, the
point at which he and Canning would have parted company. While condemning, in formal terms, and as a
general principle, as strongly as Canning could have done,

the doctrine of development which the great Powers were applying to the settlement of Vienna, it is clear that the elder Minister viewed it more indulgently than the younger one, was more disposed to make allowance for it, and less inclined to visit it with any practical marks of disapproval. The Duke of Wellington agreed with him; and hence, although Castlereagh himself had admitted that the recognition of the Spanish-American Colonies was only a question of time, the Duke resisted it when proposed by Canning as a measure of retaliation consequent on the prolonged occupation of Spain by a French army invited thither by Ferdinand the Seventh to support absolutism. Canning said that this was a violation of the spirit, not only of the Treaty of Aix-la-Chapelle, but also of the Treaty of Utrecht, and was determined that, if French influence was finally to predominate in Spain, it should not predominate in the "Indies."

So, again, in 1826, when it was in his power to prevent the invasion of Portugal by Spain, he sent a British force to the Tagus.* Canning believed that the Treaty of Vienna gave us a right to prevent such intervention, but whether, or in what way, we should exercise that right was a question to be determined in each case by considerations of prudence, and by the direction in which English interests inclined the balance.† Canning, in fact, was the first statesman

* The force disembarked on January 1st, 1827. A squadron had been sent for the protection of John the Sixth in 1823.

† "If we have been neutral between France and Spain, it is not because we admitted the war to be the natural fruit of the Alliance, but because it is a war of two nations with both of which we are in amity, and to neither of which we are bound by any obligation to take any part at all. But it *would* be our *interest* to prevent the aggrandizement of France at the expense of Spain; and to that object we acknowledge ourselves to be pledged, and contend that Austria and Russia and Prussia are pledged equally with us by the Alliance. So much for our obligations and our interests. The Allies, we

who distinctly laid down the doctrine of English interests, afterwards acted on by Lord Palmerston * and Lord Beaconsfield, as the guiding star of English policy. In Nov. 1822 he wrote to Sir Charles Bagot, our Ambassador at St. Petersburg, as follows :—" Ten years have made a world of difference, and prepared a very different sort of world to bustle in than that which I should have found in 1812. For fame, it is a squeezed orange; but for public good there is something to do, and I will try—but it must be cautiously—to do it. You know my politics well enough to know what I mean when I say that for *Europe* I shall be desirous *now* and *then* to read *England.*" And about a year afterwards, in a great speech at Plymouth, he said :— " The language of modern philosophy is widely and diffusely benevolent ; it professes the perfection of our species, and the amelioration of the lot of all mankind. Gentlemen, I hope that my heart beats as high for the general interests of humanity, I hope I have as friendly a disposition towards other nations of the earth as anyone who vaunts his philanthropy most highly ; but I am contented to confess that, in the conduct of political affairs, the grand object of my contemplation is the interest of England. Not, gentlemen, that the interest of England

say, have no right, under the Alliance, to call upon us to aid or abet a forcible interference in the internal affairs of any country, for the purpose or under the pretext of putting down extravagant theories of liberty. But we *have* a right to call upon *them*, as they upon us, to check the aggression of State against State, and to preserve the territorial balance of Europe. We abstained from taking any part in the war between France and Spain, because we were under no obligation to take any ; and because, where no obligation exists, a Government is free without dishonour to consult the interest of the nation which it governs. But if France attempts conquest, interest and obligation point the same way ; and the obligation in that case is confessedly common to us and to our Allies."—Canning to Sir Henry Wellesley, September 16, 1823.

* *Vide supra*, p. 108.

is an interest which stands isolated and alone. The situation which she holds forbids an exclusive selfishness. Her prosperity must contribute to the prosperity of surrounding nations, and her stability to the safety of the world."*

On the other hand, it must be allowed that the motives and sentiments by which Wellington and Castlereagh were actuated are not altogether undeserving of our sympathy. During the closing years of one of the most momentous struggles recorded in modern history, Wellington, Castlereagh, and the Sovereigns of Austria, Russia, and Prussia had been, so to speak, brothers in arms. The memories of that glorious period could not be dissolved in a day. It was impossible that the two great English statesmen should see the conduct of the Allied Sovereigns in the light in which it appeared to those who were unconnected with them by similar associations. The attitude of Mr. Canning would seem to the Duke of Wellington an ungracious attitude. He did not understand, as Canning did, the growth of public opinion in England, and thought, perhaps, as Prince Metternich thought, that the Government could do what it liked, and that if there was any display of unfriendly feeling towards the Allies, either in the House of Commons or the country, Ministers were to blame for it. Canning laboured hard to convince Metternich of his error ; but if we are to judge from subsequent events, it was long before he found it out.

It was implied, if not openly asserted, by some members of the English Opposition, that the Allied Sovereigns were right in their interpretation of our treaty engagements, and that they did extend to co-operation with the legiti-

* See also the last letter which he ever wrote to Lord Liverpool, Feb. 4, 1827.—*Canning and His Times*, p. 563.

mate monarchies in crushing revolutionary movements. I cannot discover, however, any ground for the contention, except as far as France was concerned. By the Treaty of Aix-la-Chapelle, in 1818, we did· pledge ourselves to resist any fresh effort of the French Jacobins to disturb the Restoration. With Napoleon still alive, France still smarting under her defeat, the Radical Party gaining ground in the large towns, and the army of occupation withdrawn, such an agreement was perfectly justifiable. But, good or bad, wise or unwise, Mr. Canning himself was a party to it and was one of the English Plenipotentiaries who attended at the Congress.

It has been alleged that the language of Lord Castlereagh's despatches does not always coincide with what he actually addressed to his correspondents : and that he misled the great Powers by professions of friendship which were not suffered to appear in the papers laid before Parliament.* I have been unable to discover any serious discrepancy, and, so far as the Laybach Circular is concerned, Mr. Canning's own words appear conclusive. Mr. Walpole says that the English people doubted the sincerity of Lord Castlereagh's answer. But in the letter already mentioned Mr. Canning, referring to this very document, says :—

It was not only the language, which was held by the Government, therefore, but it was in the firm belief that in that language they were sincere ; it was not those speeches of Lord Liverpool and myself (which give Prince Metternich so much uneasiness), but it was the confidence in our real feeling of all that we expressed that satisfied the country; that induced them to consider our neutral position in the Spanish question as one chosen by our-

* *Vide* Greville, vol. i. p. 105, who directly charges Lord Castlereagh with having written one thing for the Austrian Minister and another for the English Parliament. But till better proof of it is forthcoming, I shall decline to believe anything dishonourable of Lord Castlereagh. Canning, at all events, suspected nothing of the kind,

selves, from a just regard for British interests, and not from a compliance with foreign dictation, or in enmity to national freedom. Prince Metternich must not suppose, therefore (and I entreat you not to encourage him in supposing), that our language belied our sentiments; or that we had, either of us, any reserve or qualification, in our own minds, of the opinions which we declared to Parliament; or that, if Parliament and the nation had been absolutely without an opinion upon the subject, we should have held either a different language or a different conduct with respect to Spain. Prince Metternich must take us such as we are, for better for worse; and we are such as we *seem*, such as we profess ourselves to Parliament and to the world.—*Life of Canning*, p. 379.

By the language of the Government, which the people believed to be sincere, Canning here means the language of Lord Castlereagh's Reply; and by the speeches of Lord Liverpool and himself, he seems to refer more particularly to speeches delivered in the spring of 1821, severely censuring the Laybach Circular, and defending Lord Castlereagh's answer to it. It is easy to suppose that both Lord Castlereagh and Wellington may have been anxious to soften down unpalatable truths as far as they could, and that in so doing they may have occasionally created wrong impressions.* If there is any truth in what I have said on a previous page, posterity, I think, will not be inclined to judge them harshly. But in the main, the whole Tory party meant the same thing. They—Castlereagh as well as Canning—occupied a midway position between the Absolutists on the one hand and the Revolutionary party on the other; and this position they were anxious to maintain without turning to the right or to the left. Of course they pleased nobody. They gave great offence to the Allied Powers by condemning the Laybach Circular and repudiating the obligations which they tried to fasten on this country. They gave great offence to the Whig Party at home by refusing to do more. They would interfere neither

* For the "wrong impressions" created by the Whigs on the Radical Party at Madrid, see Canning's Speech, April 28th, 1823.

against revolution nor on behalf of revolution. The obligations which they had contracted at Vienna and Aix-la-Chapelle were limited, in their judgment, to the maintenance of the balance of power as established at the Peace, and to the protection of the territorial arrangements then concluded against all disturbance from without. As long as no external encroachment on this system was attempted, thrones might be set up and pulled down, constitutions granted and withdrawn, rebellions flourish or decline, and England had no part to play but that of a disinterested spectator, who might, indeed, advise or mediate, if required, but was under no obligation to intervene in any other form. She might, by antecedent treaties, have incurred different liabilities in the case of particular nations —as she had done in the case of Portugal. But this was all that she was forced to do by the three treaties of 1814, 1815, and 1818, to which George the Fourth referred.

This was the Tory principle. Individual Ministers would very likely differ with regard to the various applications of it: and in the interpretations of those " rights of nations " which, by the Protocol I have quoted, the Powers pledged themselves to respect. One might be more disposed to sympathize with the monarchical, and another with the popular party ; all would not think exactly alike. But they all agreed in three things : first, that the Austrian occupation of Naples was not a territorial aggression, and did not come within the class of wrongs, if wrong it was, which England was bound to resist ; secondly, that for England to go to war, except in the case of such aggression, would be downright madness ; and, thirdly, that to persist in protests and remonstrances of a violent or menacing description, unless we were prepared to fight, was useless and undignified, and a wanton waste of British influence. Canning himself was decided on this point. When England had remonstrated once, and remonstrated in vain, she had done enough; and if we wish to see a full exemplification of the mischief that may be done by these perpetual complaints, which those to whom they are addressed soon learn to regard as the gods of Epicurus regarded the complaints of mankind—

Like a tale of little meaning, though the words are strong—

we need only refer to the debates on foreign affairs and the speeches of Lord Derby and Mr. Disraeli between 1860 and 1865.

Canning was extremely reluctant to do anything which might kindle another European war, because, as he was fond of saying, it would be " a war of opinion." Wars carried on for dynastic and commercial objects admitted of compromise. Religious and political contests were necessarily impatient of it; and a war between the two antagonistic principles of monarchy and democracy might last another thirty years. He undoubtedly advocated a system of neutrality more absolute than is prudent, perhaps, at the present day. Before the discovery of steam, and while the Russian and Anglo-Indian Empires were so far apart that no man ever dreamed of a collision, England stood in little need of European allies. She had already proved what she could do against a world in arms; and sixty years ago could have done it again. But the conditions of the question are widely different at the present day, and were another Canning to arise in our own generation his language would probably be different.

It is, further, to be remembered that the cases of Spain, Portugal, and Naples were very different from each other. We have seen what the Duke of Wellington said about the French occupation of Spain. But he approved of the occu-

pation of Naples, and thought it would have been better
had the period fixed for the duration of it been five, or even
seven years, instead of three. The distinction was that in
Spain Ferdinand, on his restoration, found the Constitution
of 1812 established. Under it the Spaniards had helped
to achieve their independence, and when the King annulled
it he had promised that the Cortes should be speedily called
together, and a more carefully considered representative
system established in its place. This promise he never
kept, and then the Revolution broke out. But nothing of
the kind had ever happened in Naples. The Neapolitan
people had never possessed a constitution. The King had
neither overthrown any popular government which he found
in existence, nor broken any pledge to introduce one. The
revolutionary party in Spain had some right to call itself
the constitutional, or the popular party. In Naples it was
a mere faction.

Mr. Canning's opinions on the Eastern Question, which
was fast rising in importance during the last years of his
life, are embodied in the Treaty of London (1827), and
seem covered by the general principles enunciated in the
Castlereagh Circular. The proposal of Ibrahim Pasha to
carry off the whole population of the Morea, and repeople
the country with Egyptians—a bold conception, but, unhappily for those who traffic in the crimes of "the un-
speakable," a pure fabrication—would, we presume, have
been resisted by Mr. Canning on grounds lying wholly
outside the region of diplomacy. But though willing to
mediate between Greece and Turkey, if invited to do so,
he was not in favour of any other kind of intervention,
except for the purpose of protecting British interests.
Piracy had grown to such a height in the Greek waters
that British merchant-ships could not navigate them in

safety, and a British naval force was sent out to put a stop
to it. This did, no doubt, interfere to some extent with
the operations of the belligerents; but as intervention by
the terms of the Circular was permissible where the security of a neighbouring Power was threatened by insurgents, by parity of reasoning it would be lawful where his
trade or commerce was endangered. Further than this
Mr. Canning, I imagine, was not prepared to go; and I
am much disposed to believe that he would have concurred
with the Duke of Wellington in calling the battle of
Navarino " an untoward event."

It is not sufficiently understood that the moving spring
of Canning's policy in Eastern Europe was the dread of
Muscovite aggression. What made him so anxious to
terminate hostilities between Greece and Turkey was the
hourly dread of an alliance between Greece and Russia.
Had the latter Power appeared as the ally of a Christian
people struggling for its freedom against a Mahometan
oppressor, public opinion in England would not have permitted us to take up arms for Turkey; and it was to be
feared that in that case Russia would, in Canning's own
words, swallow Greece at one mouthful and Turkey at
another. It was this consideration which induced him
very reluctantly to sanction a slight departure from the
language to which, down to 1826, he had always steadfastly
adhered. In the autumn of 1825 he told the Greek
Deputies in London that—

They forgot that there existed between England and Turkey treaties of
very ancient date, and of uninterrupted obligation, which the Turks faithfully observed, and to the protection of which British interests of a vast
amount were confided within the dominions of the Sultan, and that all these
interests must at once be put in jeopardy, and the obligation of the treaties
which secured them be at once advisedly broken by the first blow which
Great Britain should strike, *as the ally of Greece*, in hostility to Turkey. Mr.
Canning then suggested the idea of compromise with the Porte, but the

Deputies declared that the Greeks must be either "entirely independent or perish."

Mr. Canning then, having thus explained to the Deputies all that the Greeks had to expect from the British Government, endeavoured to impress upon their minds that the efforts to induce Great Britain to take part in their favour " had not only no favourable result, but were always attended by consequences prejudicial to their cause."

Every step taken by the Greeks to identify Great Britain with their undertaking, obliged her to put forth to the world some new declaration of her persevering in the system of neutrality which she had established.

In a country like England the real intentions and acts of its Government, though pretty well known, and in the result accurately judged of, were nevertheless liable to temporary misapprehensions, and the case was still more serious when the conduct of England was considered abroad.*

On the 20th of December of the same year, Sir Stratford Canning (Lord Stratford de Redcliffe) was instructed in his communications with Russia to make the disavowal of any intention to use force a *sine quâ non* in entering into any negotiations on the Greek question. The Protocol, signed by the Duke of Wellington at St. Petersburg in April 1826, after stating the terms on which England and Russia were willing to mediate between the two belligerents laid down :—

3. That in case the mediation offered by His Britannic Majesty to the Porte should not have been accepted by that Power, and whatever should be in other respects the state of relations of His Imperial Majesty with the Turkish Government, Great Britain and Russia should always consider the terms of the arrangement mentioned in the first Article of the present Protocol, as the basis of the reconciliation to be brought about by their interference, whether jointly or separately, between the Porte and the Greeks ; and they will seize all favourable occasions to give weight to their influence with the two Parties, for the purpose of effecting the same reconciliation on the same base.

4. That Great Britain and Russia reserve the right of adopting, in the end, the measures necessary to settle the details of the arrangement in question, as well as the limits of the territory, and the names of the Islands of the Archipelago to which it shall be applicable, and which it shall be proposed to the Porte to comprehend under the denomination of Greece.

5. Moreover, that His Britannic Majesty and His Imperial Majesty would

* *Political Life of Canning*, vol. ii. p. 444.

not seek, either one or the other, any augmentation of territory, any exclusive influence, or any commercial advantages for their subjects, except those which every other nation should be equally able to obtain.

And on the 4th of September 1826, Mr. Canning informed Prince Lieven that the British Government did not consider the refusal of Turkey to listen to proposals for an accommodation with Greece as affording any justifiable grounds for having recourse to war. On the 20th of November he repeated this statement.

Thus we see that within six months of the Treaty of London Canning was still firm against coercion. In the same despatch we find him suggesting what measures should be taken if Turkey remained obstinate to the last. These consist in establishing commercial relations with Greece, and other steps preparatory to a recognition of her independence, provided she showed herself capable of maintaining an independent existence, of carrying on a government of her own, and of controlling her own military and naval forces; and this recognition was to take effect only in such parts of Greece as had freed themselves from Turkish domination. This is certainly not the language of a statesman who was contemplating an immediate armed intervention in favour of the insurgents. So much for what occurred immediately before the Treaty of London. This document, to which the Duke of Wellington was no party, set out by asserting that the continuation of hostilities in the Archipelago "produces daily fresh impediments to the commerce of the European States, and gives occasion to piracies which not only expose the subjects of the high contracting Powers to considerable losses, but besides render necessary burdensome measures of protection and repression." The contracting Powers are " penetrated with the necessity of putting an end to this sanguinary contest," and for that purpose such and such terms of peace were to be recommended to the acceptance of both parties. A demand for an immediate armistice was to be made at the same time.

And now comes the "additional and secret article" on which so much stress has been laid. It provides that if Turkey does not accept the proposed mediation within one month she is to be informed that "the inconveniences pointed out in the public treaty" impose upon the contracting Powers "the necessity of taking immediate measures for an approximation with the Greeks." This approximation is to be brought about by establishing commercial relations with them as Canning had suggested, and by appointing and receiving consuls "so long as there shall exist among them authorities capable of maintaining such relations." If the Porte does not adopt the armistice within one month, or if the Greeks refuse to execute it, the Powers will "exert all the means which circumstances may suggest to their prudence to obtain the immediate effect of it," and will prevent as far as possible all collisions between the contending parties, "without, however, taking any part in the hostilities between the two." And the Powers undertook to send instructions to their naval officers in the Levant in conformity with these provisions. If all these efforts are fruitless, "the high contracting Powers will nevertheless continue to prosecute the work of pacification on the bases agreed upon between them,* and they authorize their representatives in London to discuss and determine the ulterior measures to which it may become necessary to resort." By these "ulterior mea-

* *I.e.* in the Protocol of 1826.

sures" Canning must be taken to have meant the
"arrangements" contemplated by the 4th Article of the
Protocol. But the Duke of Wellington foresaw that they
might bear another interpretation, and the event justified
his sagacity.

We have seen that the consequence of Turkey refusing
the proposed mediation was to be the establishment of commercial relations with the Greeks, where they had authorities capable of maintaining them; and that Canning's
proposal was a recognition of independence wherever
they had freed their own territory from Turkish domination, on condition that they possessed the materials
for a regular government. We have seen also that, while
resolved on the prevention of collisions between the two
belligerents in the waters of the Levant, the Powers
pledged themselves to abstain from taking any part in
the actual hostilities between them. How collisions were
to be prevented without practically taking part in the
hostilities between the two parties it is difficult to understand. But it is clear enough that our operations were to
be limited to keeping the peace of the sea, and that the
measures adopted for enforcing the armistice had no reference to any direct coercion of the Turkish Government
into accepting the proposals recommended to it. It was
evidently contemplated that the war by land might continue; and that the Turks might obtain such successes as
should make the Greeks incapable of maintaining those
authorities which were necessary to the continuance of
commercial relations with them. Otherwise what was the
meaning of making those relations with them dependent
on their being capable of maintaining such authorities?
But at the same time it must be allowed that the words
of the Treaty are, to some slight extent, a deflection from

the words of the Protocol, though it seems impossible to believe that any forcible intervention by land was ever seriously contemplated by Canning.

Be this as it may, however, Canning's motive was the same, the necessity, that is, of putting an end to the hostilities between Greece and Turkey, before war should break out between Turkey and Russia, and the latter be enabled to make a cat's-paw of the insurgents for overthrowing the balance of power in the east of Europe altogether. Buonapartism was now extinct; nothing was to be apprehended from France; and English statesmen were waking up to what Canning had all along perceived, that the next enemy which European independence would have to fear was Russia.

Of Canning's opinions on Reform and Emancipation a better opportunity for discussion will be found in the following chapters,* as they are inextricably woven up with the conduct and opinions of the next two statesmen on my list, the Duke and Sir Robert Peel. But with the formation of Mr. Canning's ministry, and the intrigues of which he was accused in connection with it, we may deal at once. The best account of the transaction is to be found in Sir George Cornwall Lewis's *Administrations of Great Britain*, though this great authority partly contradicts himself on one point material to the reputation of Mr. Canning.

Early in the year 1827 it became known that Lord Liverpool could never return to public life, and the King at once sent for Mr. Canning, with whom, through the mediation of Sir William Knighton, he had now become thoroughly reconciled.† In Lord Liverpool's Government

---

* See pages 203–207.
† *Canning and his Times* (Stapleton), p. 43.

Catholic Emancipation had been an open question, and it was still thought better to keep it on the same footing. Canning had consented to serve under Lord Liverpool, who on this point represented the Protestant section of the Cabinet, because as long as Lord Liverpool was Prime Minister his own claim to the highest place was, of course, in abeyance.   With Lord Liverpool's retirement, however, Canning's claim revived; and, this being universally admitted, his exclusion must have rested entirely on his support of Emancipation.   But no Cabinet in which its legitimate chief was refused his proper rank exclusively on the ground of his opinions on this single question could be said to be constituted on a footing of neutrality.   To make one man Premier, who confessedly had only the second claim, because he was a Protestant, and to exclude another, who confessedly had the first claim, because he was a Catholic, was not to hold the balance equally between the two parties.   For Canning, excluded as a Catholic, to have taken office under a Minister appointed because he was a Protestant, would have destroyed the very semblance of neutrality.   As Canning had been the leader of the Emancipationist party among the Tories, he could not have acted in this manner without a clear breach of faith towards his followers.

But it is urged that he was guilty of something much worse than this, and deliberately laid a trap both for the King and his colleagues. He offered to resign and give the King the chance of forming a Ministry out of the Protestant party exclusively.   This, it is said, he did, knowing all the time that such a scheme was practically impossible, and that the attempt could only end in forcing the King back upon himself. But was it impossible ?   Sir G. C. Lewis says in one passage that it was; and on almost the next page we find the following remarkable statement :—

It appears to us that if Mr. Peel believed in his own arguments on the Catholic question; if he really thought that the existing system ought to be maintained as an integral part of the British Constitution; then he ought to have urged upon the King the formation of an administration upon the principle of resistance to the Catholic claims, and to have himself offered to take a leading part in it.

Exactly what Canning himself said. Sir George continues :—

If, however, he had a lurking consciousness that his arguments were unsound and his policy mischievous, and a case of necessity for conceding the Catholic claims might speedily arise, then he ought to have openly renounced his advocacy of a cause which he felt to be untenable. If he was sincerely persuaded of the goodness of his cause, he ought to have formed an anti-Catholic Government. If not, he ought not to have refused to join Mr. Canning's Ministry.

Clearly, then, on the hypothesis that Peel and Wellington were sincere, the attempt could not have been so hopeless as to make it disingenuous to suggest it, or it would have been equally absurd for Sir G. C. Lewis to recommend it; and Canning was bound to suppose that Peel and his party were sincere. If it is thought that Sir G. C. Lewis, himself a Liberal, may have taken too unfavourable a view of Peel's conduct, we may turn to an unimpeachable witness in the person of Sir Walter Scott, an old Tory if there ever was one. "They," said he, meaning the Protestant section, "should either have made a stand without Canning, or a stand with him," and he goes on to point out the evil effects of doing what they actually did. The utter impossibility of an exclusively Protestant administration with two-thirds of the English people and the King himself in its favour, seems a wholly unwarrantable assumption, and we have no right whatever to suppose that it was present to Canning's mind for a moment.* Besides, such an administration absolutely was formed six months after Canning's death; and was not materially weakened by the secession of Mr. Canning's friends. The Wellington Government, from that moment, became an absolutely anti-Catholic Government, and might have lasted, as such, for some years longer had the Duke chosen to face the consequences.

The part played by Peel and Wellington in this transaction will come under consideration further on. I shall only add here that it was by no means only the Duke of Wellington who thought he had reason to complain of Mr. Canning. Mr. Canning's correspondence between 1823 and 1826 contains several allusions to what he thought unfair dealing on the Duke's part; consulting with the King, for instance, about letters to be written to Canning and never telling Canning that he had done so. Canning also complains rather bitterly that the chief patronage ministers in the Government, and especially Lord Eldon, gave him so small a share of it as considerably to heighten his difficulties " in conducting the King's business in the House of Commons."

When Canning resolved to form a Government independent of the Peelite Tories, he had not only the section of the aristocracy to reckon with which formed a part of that connection ; he had also given mortal offence to many of the Whig grandees, and, as Croker pointed out to him, was pitting himself against the great boroughmongers on both sides of the House. Canning's answer, with which we should compare his reply to Lord Grenville in 1806, was remarkable, and forms a fitting conclusion to this chapter. " Am I to suppose," says he, " that you

---

* It was very odd, Lord Eldon said, if, out of a thousand members of the Legislature, a Protestant Government could not be constructed.

consider the King as completely in the hands of the Tory aristocracy as his father, or rather as George the Second, was in the hands of the Whigs? *If so, then George the Third reigned, and Mr. Pitt (both father and son) administered the Government in vain.* I have a better opinion of the real vigour of the Crown when it chooses to put forth its own strength, and I am not without some reliance on the body of the people." Such may be called the dying words of the illustrious statesman who inherited the principles of Mr. Pitt; and herein speaks the genuine Toryism of which Mr. Pitt was the founder, and which, relying on popular support, he conducted to victory against overwhelming odds entrenched in a position which seemed impregnable. Had Canning lived, could he have perpetuated the system? Under new conditions, and different guarantees for its stability, is it ever destined to be revived? It is clear from the above letter that, in Mr. Canning's opinion, George the Third and Mr. Pitt had *not* failed in their efforts to emancipate the Crown, and this is important evidence against the contrary opinion of Lord Beaconsfield, who thought that they had. I read this letter in the *Croker Papers* with very great interest, as it shows how truly Canning was the διάδοχος of Pitt, and how closely he had cherished through life that great principle which, so far, I have endeavoured to represent as the differential element of Toryism. As long as a man held firm to this, no matter what his opinion on Reform, or religion, or finance, so long was he a Tory. And such a man was Mr. Canning.

There is no doubt that in his conduct on this occasion Mr. Canning conceived himself to be acting over again the part of Pitt in 1783. The two situations were not analogous throughout, because George the Fourth, had he been left entirely to himself, would probably have preferred someone else. But after Wellington and Peel had themselves destroyed their own chances and determined the King in Canning's favour, they did correspond very closely. When the Duke of Rutland forced his way into the Royal presence and presented his sovereign with a memorial, signed by eight Dukes, against the appointment of Mr. Canning, on pain of their support being at once withdrawn from His Majesty's Government, we see that half a century of power had worked much the same effect upon the Tories as, according to Macaulay, it had once produced upon the Whigs. Neither the Duke of Newcastle, nor the Duke of Bedford, nor Mr. Fox, nor Lord Grey could have done more.

The feelings which Mr. Canning was known to entertain against combinations or cabals of this description, and which he had inherited from his great master, caused the Duke of Wellington with some want of insight to suspect him of being "hostile to the aristocracy." Nothing could be more untrue. Never was there a stauncher supporter of the old borough system, which was the stronghold of the aristocracy. But he wished them to keep their own place in the economy of the Constitution, and not to swamp the monarchy.

Of Mr. Canning's eloquence, some of its greatest admirers have doubted the sincerity. But the doubt seems to have no better foundation than the common prejudice against brilliancy, suggesting that, as all is not gold that glitters, therefore nothing that glitters can be gold. Mr. Canning's whole career gives the lie to this unworthy imputation. It would be difficult to point out what he gained, except the satisfaction of his conscience, either by his fidelity to the Roman Catholic claims, or his support of the Peninsular War.

Mr. Canning was one of the very few orators on record who could be plain, nervous, and concise, or rich, glowing, and figurative, at will. Two finer similies are not, perhaps, to be found in any orator than the comparison between the state of Europe in 1813 and the appearance of a country in which a great deluge has just begun to subside, and "the spires and turrets of ancient establishments to reappear above the waters," and that between England in time of peace and a man-of-war lying quietly at anchor, to be found in the Plymouth speech of 1823.* With the power of exposition for which Mr. Gladstone in his best days was remarkable, he united the rhetorical art of Lord Beaconsfield, to which his great rival was a stranger. He never quite reached either the grandeur of Mr. Pitt or the passion of Mr. Fox. But in logic and wit, in beauty of imagery and splendour of diction united, he exhibited a combination not perhaps to be found in either.

He died on the 8th of August 1827, from the consequences of a cold caught during the Duke of York's funeral, having been Prime Minister only four months. Did it ever cross the minds of either Sir Robert Peel or the Duke of Wellington that they had acted ungenerously for nothing, and that they might have had all they coveted without the burden of a reminiscence which must occasionally have been painful to both?

* See also Speech on Army Estimates, Dec. 8th, 1802; the Bullion Speeches, 1811; on thanks to Lord Wellington, July 7th, 1813; on Embassy to Lisbon, March 6th, 1817; on Spain, April 28th, 1822; and on sending British troops to Portugal, Dec. 1826.

CHAPTER IV.

THE DUKE OF WELLINGTON.

WE have now reached a point in the history of Toryism at which its good genius deserted it, and it becomes for a considerable period of time a history of failure. Aware as I am of the presumption of differing from Lord Beaconsfield, I cannot bring myself to adopt, without large reser vations, his estimate of the English Government from 1815 to 1828. At the close of the war the English Ministers found themselves confronted with enormous difficulties both at home and abroad. The distress of the agricultural and manufacturing interests was universal and acute. The financial embarrassments of the Government were overwhelming. Taking advantage of both, and making a cat's-paw of the working classes, the remnant of the Jacobins, in concert with Continental conspirators, had revived the revolutionary schemes which Mr. Pitt had trampled under foot, and were plotting the overthrow of the Constitution. Abroad we were engaged in the task of reconstructing the map of Europe which the French Revolution had destroyed, in mediating between the Great Powers, and in resisting their attempts to drag this country into a coalition against popular liberty. With these vast and varied questions to occupy their attention, I cannot think that the Government are so much to be blamed for not having dealt more promptly with Emancipation and Reform.

That they made mistakes is only to say that they were human. The Corn Law and the Sinking Fund were unsuccessful experiments; but the fallacies on which they were founded were not peculiar to the Tories, who were preparing to abandon the one when Lord Liverpool died, and abandoned the other within a very short time of his retirement. Their policy on the currency question, and their behaviour on more than one great commercial crisis when public credit was trembling in the balance, is allowed by all our greatest economic authorities to have been marked by both wisdom and courage. Of the preventive measures which they found it necessary to adopt, we are, perhaps, better able to judge at the present moment than we were forty years ago, when we had not yet realised the consequences which may flow from the neglect of such precautions. Lord Liverpool and his colleagues were charged with the government of the country, with the maintenance of law and order, with the security of life and property; and when they knew that desperate men were concocting schemes of plunder and massacre, they are not to be severely taken to task because they might not always draw the line with perfect accuracy between distress and disaffection? I do not think that many impartial readers at the present day will say much against the Six Acts. The Moderate Liberal party of that day had nothing to say against them. It is the evil of all periods of turbulence and treason that they compel the innocent to bear the burden of restraint intended only to press upon the guilty.

The Cato Street conspiracy was not the only evidence of such designs which the Ministers possessed; and to have taken no measures to defeat them would have been only less criminal on the part of the Government than to have secretly connived at them. These measures, moreover, as a Liberal historian allows, had at least the merit of being successful;* and measures can hardly be called successful if the dangers which they are intended to avert have no existence. I say the Ministry would have deserved punishment themselves had they acted otherwise. While to lay any stress on a shade of more or less in legislation of this kind, to insist that the Government shall always keep its foot exactly on the narrow line between too much rigour and too little, is idle pedantry with which it is waste of common sense to argue.

To the part played by our Government in the settlement of Europe it is easy to take objections, but it is not so easy to say how they could have prevented it. The obvious work for the Congress of Vienna to have undertaken was the restitution of Europe to the *status quo ante bellum*. This would have been a logical, a generous, and a truly Conservative policy. But it never seems to have entered into the heads of any one of the Plenipotentiaries, and one would be inclined to believe that it had become a practical impossibility. On this hypothesis, what was the next best arrangement? One that, with the smallest derangement of national tradition and national sentiment, should offer the strongest barrier to any future scheme of French ambition? Supposing that France was the quarter from which danger to Europe was to be apprehended, the answer would be in the affirmative; and we must remember that the policy of the Congress was regulated

* Walpole's *History of England.*

throughout on that assumption ; that it was conducted by men in whose minds the Napoleonic system, with all its tyranny and violence, was still fresh ; while the wounds which its founder had inflicted were still bleeding ; by soldiers who had fought with him for years ; by kings on whose necks he had set his foot : and can we be surprised that they did not meet together in the philosophic and statesman-like temper which modern critics think they ought to have displayed. Neither the restoration of the kingdom of Poland, nor the maintenance of a kingdom of Italy would have strengthened the barrier against France, from whom alone at that time any danger was apprehended. The former was obviously a source of weakness to Russia, who, though not more unselfish than the other great Powers, had suffered severely in the cause of European independence, and was regarded very naturally by England as one of its bulwarks. The kingdom of Saxony paid the penalty of its adhesion to Napoleon ; but its division was a State necessity, not an act of mere vindictiveness.

Lord Castlereagh swam with the stream. He too was impressed with the idea that to strengthen the three great military monarchies was the first duty of the Congress. But he went no farther. Lord Beaconsfield judges the foreign policy of the " Mediocrities " solely by the second Peace of Paris. He should have remembered the firm stand made by the English Government from 1818 to 1828 against the new Continental system which came in after the Settlement of Vienna, and that much greater praise is due to Castlereagh and Canning for their resistance to the one than blame for their acceptance of the other. Besides, as I have also pointed out in the chapter on Lord Liverpool, had Lord Castlereagh and the Duke of

Wellington been ever so strongly disposed to resist the
new settlement of Europe, they could only have done so
by force of arms, which would at once have brought back
Napoleon, and have given all the states of Europe their
battles to fight over again.   Canning proved this in 1823,
and was no more in a position to go to arms to prevent the
French invasion of Spain than Lord Liverpool had been
to prevent the partition of Saxony.

I repeat, therefore, that from 1815 to 1828 the Tory
administration of this country was, on the whole, a successful one.   Confronted with domestic difficulties of an
entirely novel character, the English Ministry made more
than one false step, which they frankly recognized and
retraced before many years had passed.   But they governed
the country and maintained the authority of the law, when
revolution, making a tool of suffering, was again con-
spiring against the State, and ready with its usual weapons.
They persevered in their duty, against all the taunts of a
factious Opposition which could have done nothing else
itself had it suddenly been called to power ; and so clearly
was it seen to be in the right that the old Liberal section
of the Tory Party who, under Lord Grenville, had for some
time acted with the Whigs, returned to their allegiance,
convinced that the duty of all Englishmen, who were
Englishmen first and party men afterwards, was to rally
round Lord Liverpool's administration.   They saved this
country from great commercial and monetary disasters,
and disentangled her from the continental engagements
which she had contracted during the war, as soon as they
perceived the true nature of the obligations' which the
military powers were for grafting on them.   If these
services do not entitle the Ministers who governed England
from the battle of Waterloo to the death of Mr. Canning,

to a more favourable verdict than they have received at the hands of modern historians,* it can only be because such men have fallen into the common mistake of supposing that Governments are capable of doing two things at once—of undertaking great political and constitutional reforms in the face of a wide-spread revolutionary conspiracy, while engaged at the same time in the solution of the most delicate financial problems, and in extricating their country with peace and honour from the most embarrassing foreign complications.

I say it was impossible. Everybody has allowed that Mr. Gladstone's Irish difficulties alone were a sufficient excuse for the dearth of legislation which marked his last five years of office. What, then, must have been the position of a Ministry in 1816, with questions on its hands, the accumulated growth of twenty years of war, with a state of public feeling bitterly hostile to political and social changes, identified as they were with the revolutionary theories against which Englishmen had been fighting since they were children; and distracted by continental difficulties which absorbed the whole attention of the ablest members of the Cabinet? They took those questions which pressed more immediately for solution, and left the remainder to their successors.

I do not think, therefore, that down to the beginning of the year 1828 the administration of affairs by the Tory Party is open to the censures which have been so freely bestowed on it. The Ministers were not all men of equal ability; and affairs were not conducted without serious and various mistakes. But show me an administration

---

* Among these, of course, I do not include Lord Beaconsfield, whose account of the Mediocrities was written forty years ago, under very peculiar circumstances, and with little or nothing but oral tradition to guide him.

in which they ever have been ! On the whole, the Government was carried on with dignity, firmness, and good sense. Our finances were placed upon a sound basis. The country was governed cheaply ; and continued to maintain abroad the position which we had won by our exertions during the great war. The people after a time became prosperous and contented, and the demand for reform had all but completely died away. In 1827, when asked how the Whig reformers could join Mr. Canning who was a staunch opponent of reform, Lord Althorpe replied that the Whigs did not intend to raise the question any more. Everything, in fact, in January 1828, seemed to justify the hopes of the high Tory Party that the Duke was "in for his life," and that their own principles and policy were now finally re-established on a basis more solid and more permanent than they had ever occupied before. And I think it must be admitted that the Ministers who had brought us to this happy consummation could not have been the blunderers which they have been painted. In fact, the very conditions on which Lord Beaconsfield relies for the justification of his estimate of what the Duke of Wellington might have done, are fatal to the criticisms which he has levelled at the Duke's predecessors.

There never was such an opportunity of forming a strong and enlightened administration, and rendering the Tory Party famous and popular in the country, as on the junction of the friends of Mr. Canning, after his decease, with the followers of the Duke of Wellington. All personal jealousies had ceased, and men like Mr. Huskisson, Mr. Lambe (Lord Melbourne), and Lord Palmerston had, without reluctance or reserve, recognized the leadership of Mr. Peel, then only in the perfection of his manhood, and were acting with him with deference and cordiality. The times were ripe for a calm, prudent, and statesman-like settlement of two great questions: the admission of Roman Catholics into the House of Commons, and some reconstruction of that Assembly itself. Very moderate measures would have sufficed.

But what was it that made the times ripe " for the settle-

ment of these two questions"? What but the disappearance
of those threatening symptoms which had marked the
beginning of the Regency, and the general tranquillity and
satisfaction which prevailed throughout the country. Elsewhere Lord Beaconsfield has told us that these questions
might have been settled by Lord Liverpool. I have already
explained why, in my humble opinion, Lord Liverpool may
be excused for not having undertaken these reforms, while
his lordship's own subsequent assertion that they were
ripe for settlement when the Duke of Wellington took the
helm in hand may, perhaps, excuse us for continuing
to be of opinion that they were not ripe before. The very
jealousies of which he speaks in the passage we have
quoted from Lord George Bentinck were an insuperable
bar to such a settlement.

But it is quite true that when the death of Mr. Canning
had removed the only obstacle which had existed to the
cordial reunion of all the old elements of Toryism, Pittites
and Addingtonians, in a strong and united administration,
the Tories threw away the chance and showed themselves
no wiser than the Whigs had been just five and forty
years before. If the Duke and Sir Robert Peel had
possessed the very little prescience that was wanted to
have saved them from breaking with the Canningites,
they might have defied the vengeance of the Protestants.
But they had not ; and the history of the next five years
is the history of a succession of errors, by which the fair
promise of 1828 was speedily clouded over and a revolution consummated which " might have been postponed for
a generation, and never need have occurred at all in so
aggravated a form." Lord Beaconsfield was the first to
teach us that the " Venetian Constitution " was not an
unmixed blessing ; that we paid very dearly for our whistle,

in the shape of the National Debt which was created to support it ; and that the system of class legislation which was its natural consequence was not an exchange for personal Government in which the good was all on one side. But it is perfectly clear that when he wrote on these subjects in a practical, and not a speculative spirit, he fully recognized the political merits of the old *régime*, and regretted its absolute destruction.

Of the circumstances attending the formation of Mr. Canning's administration some account has already been given in the preceding chapter. On the Duke's share in them a few remarks may now be added. On the 2nd of May 1827 the Duke had declared in the House of Lords that he must be mad to think of being Minister : on the 25th of January 1828 he was gazetted First Lord of the Treasury. In the same speech he assured their Lordships that the King had never asked him to be Prime Minister : two months afterwards the King told the Duke of Buckingham that he had twice refused to be Prime Minister. On the 9th of April Mr. Peel suggested the Duke of Wellington to Canning, and soon afterwards to the King : in his letter to Mr. Canning of the 6th of May, the Duke declared that the proposal was not made " in concert with him or at his suggestion "; in other words, that he knew nothing at all about it ; for nothing less than this would have been any answer to Mr. Canning's inquiry. It should be added that, in his interview with the Duke of Buckingham, the King did not distinctly say that he had offered the Treasury to the Duke of Wellington, but only that the Duke had twice refused it ; which he is hardly likely to have done unless it had been offered him. Moreover, the Duke himself repeated to the House of Lords all the arguments which he had used to convince the King of his unfitness, which would seem to have been hardly called for had no such overture, direct or indirect, been made to him.

In order, then, to accept the Duke's version of the story, it is necessary to believe, first, that to convert him from the opinion that he would be " mad " to think of being Minister to a conviction of his own perfect fitness for the post only nine months were required, during which time nothing new had occurred to affect his own estimate of himself; secondly, that he laboured to convince the King of his own unfitness for a task which His Majesty had never proposed to him ; and, thirdly, that Mr. Peel suggested him as Prime Minister both to the King and to Mr. Canning without his own knowledge or consent.

The Duke's high character forbids us to believe for one moment that he was guilty of wilful misrepresentation. But there is a curious passage in the *Greville Memoirs* in which it is stated that he very often failed to understand what was said to him. We know that he suffered greatly from deafness, said to have been caused by the wind of a cannon-ball in the Peninsula; and it is quite possible, therefore, that he may have misunderstood both the King and Mr. Peel. His reluctance to serve under Canning seems to have been compounded of numerous ingredients, of which none, perhaps, in itself would have been sufficient to provoke his refusal, but which altogether proved invincible. He had acquiesced with a wry face in Canning's Foreign Policy. He thought that he was hostile to the aristocracy. He thought he had behaved badly to Lord Castlereagh. He believed that some communication had passed between Canning and the Whigs before the illness of Lord Liverpool. He was nettled at Mr. Canning's mode of communicating with him after he had been commissioned to form a Ministry, as neither sufficiently friendly nor sufficiently respectful. Some of his former colleagues Canning saw in person; to the Duke he only wrote. He signed himself, "Your Grace's sincere and faithful friend," instead of "Sincerely yours"; and when the Duke complained that Mr. Canning's first letter did not tell him all he wanted to know, he chose to think that Canning's answer conveyed a covert rebuke. Several of these reasons being such as could not be publicly avowed, the Duke was obliged to put others* in the foreground, of which subsequent events have certainly impaired the cogency, and of which he himself was perhaps conscious that he exaggerated the importance. This accounts for the somewhat vague and unsatisfactory character of the Duke's explanation; though I do not for a moment doubt that the objections on which he laid the greatest stress were perfectly genuine at the moment, however deepened in hue by collateral and independent circumstances.

The question which the Duke asked, in his reply to Mr. Canning's first communication, was who was to be at the head of the new Government? and Mr. Canning replied: "I believe it to be so generally understood that the King usually entrusts the formation of an Administration to the individual whom it is His Majesty's gracious intention to place at the head of it, that it did not occur to me, when I communicated to your Grace yesterday the commands which I had just received from His Majesty, to add that in the present instance His Majesty does not intend to depart from the usual course of proceedings on such occasions."

The Duke said, in answer, that his question referred to

---

* The Roman Catholic question and Foreign Policy.

a plan which Mr. Canning had recently discussed with him for placing some third person at the head of the Government, under whom they could both serve. And this we may accept as the real meaning of his inquiry. His Grace then went on to argue the point whether the person to whom the Sovereign entrusted the formation of a Government *was* always necessarily intended to be at the head of it; and he referred, in support of the negative, to the commission given to Lord Wellesley, and afterwards to Lord Moira in 1812. Canning replied that both these negotiations had been failures, but the Duke rightly said that this did not affect the argument; and on the whole, as far as this particular point was concerned, he seems to have had the best of it. It must be borne in mind, however, that the Sovereign may summon to his presence a statesman whom he wishes to consult on the formation of a Government, without its being necessarily understood that he means him to be Prime Minister. Mr. Canning himself was so consulted by George the Fourth on the 28th of March, when he gave His Majesty the advice I have already mentioned. But when the Sovereign directly authorizes any particular statesman at once to construct a new Ministry, as the King did Mr. Canning on the 10th of April, then, according to modern usage, at all events, there could be no doubt of his intentions. The negotiations of 1827 are, I think, the last occasion on which it was contemplated that the *First* Minister, the real head of the Ministry, should not be the First Lord of the Treasury.*

The Duke could never understand that he was himself misunderstood. Nobody, he said, in the House of Lords

---

* This, of course, was written before the formation of Lord Salisbury's Government.

who knew anything of his present Majesty (George IV.) would ever venture to dictate to him. Yet there is excellent reason to believe that this is just what His Majesty believed that Peel and Wellington were attempting; and there is reason to believe that it was this feeling, after all, which led to the appointment of Mr. Canning. "Your Majesty's father broke down the Whig domination," said Canning to the King. "Will Your Majesty submit to the Tory?" "No," replied the King, "I'm damned if I do!" and it was the universal belief at the time that this feeling was at the bottom of the King's determination. Whether it was language like this which induced the Duke of Wellington to believe that Canning was hostile to the aristocracy, is, of course, uncertain. Probably it was not. But this at all events was another of the counts laid against him; and it is laid with unmistakeable bitterness in a memorandum of 1827, drawn up after Canning's death. Greville knew better. Writing of the revolutionary movement in 1831, he says, "God knows how it will all end. There has been but one man for many years past able to arrest this torrent, and that was Canning; and him the Tories (i.e. the Addingtonian Tories), idiots that they were, and never discovering that he was their best friend, hunted to death with their besotted and ignorant hostility."

There is, however, this much to be said in favour of the Duke and those who thought with him, namely, that the position of the English aristocracy had been greatly altered by the French Revolution, and that language which was prudent and statesmanlike in 1784 was perhaps not quite so judicious in 1827. The birth of Radicalism had made it necessary to strengthen rather than to weaken the aristocratic element in the Constitution. Neither the home policy nor the foreign policy of the Tory party could ever be, after '93, exactly what it had been before. Perhaps even Lord Beaconsfield did not always quite remember this.*

The Administration of Lord Goderich, who succeeded Mr. Canning, did not live to meet Parliament; but the reader who desires to gain a full and impartial view of the progress of Toryism must not neglect the memoirs of Mr. Herries, who was Lord Goderich's Chancellor of the Exchequer. He, a thorough Tory, considered the Goderich Government to be a truly Tory Government, and the following statement, which he drew up in answer to the proposal that Lord Holland should be brought into the Cabinet, is worthy of all consideration. It is dated Dec. 28, 1827 :—

The present Cabinet consists in part of persons avowedly attached to the political principles which have prevailed in the Government of the country for the last forty years, and in part of individuals previously accustomed to act in opposition to those principles. . . . Of these, however, it must be added that they were distinguished from the majority of the party with which they habitually acted by the greater moderation of their principles and a greater approximation to the opinions of the persons who exercised the powers of government. The union of these moderate Whigs with the Tories was first accomplished by Mr. Canning, and in forming a Government embracing these varieties of political persuasion, it was distinctly laid down by him that the ruling character of the Government should be the same as that of Lord Liverpool. *The members of the opposite party who joined Mr. Canning accepted office under that express explanation and condition.* The Government thus constituted was therefore essentially Tory. . . . The death of Mr. Canning changed nothing in the principle on which the Government was constituted. . . . The principle so laid down and so confirmed is in fact no other than the principle of Mr. Pitt's Government transmitted through his several successors to Lord Liverpool, Mr. Canning, and Lord Goderich.

When, on the resignation of the last-named statesman, the Duke of Wellington received the King's commands to form a new Administration, the Tories who had belonged to the Government of both Lord Liverpool and Mr. Canning made no difficulty in joining him. Sir Robert Peel was Home Secretary, and Mr. Goulburn Chancellor of the Ex-

* He calls the Whigs in 1832 the leaders of the English aristocracy.

chequer. A preliminary skirmish on the question of Parliamentary Reform, which was soon to bring on a general engagement of unexpected magnitude, led the Duke into his first blunder. The borough of East Retford having been convicted of bribery, the question arose whether the franchise should be given to Birmingham or transferred to the hundred in which Retford was situated. The Government, represented in the House of Commons by Sir Robert Peel, supported the latter alternative. But Mr. Huskisson, the President of the Board of Trade, was pledged to the former, and accordingly voted in the minority. Whether the Duke would have taken any notice of the vote had he been left to himself we have no means of ascertaining. But Mr. Huskisson wrote to him the very same evening to say that he placed his office in His Grace's hands, in case he thought it desirable that he should retire from the Government. The letter, which may be seen in the Duke's correspondence, ran as follows:—

MY DEAR DUKE,

After the vote which, in regard to my own consistency and personal character, I have found myself, from the course of this evening's debate, compelled to give on the East Retford question, I owe it to you, as the head of the Administration, and to Mr. Peel, as the Leader of the House of Commons, to lose no time in affording you an opportunity of placing my office in other hands, as the only means in my power of preventing the injury to the King's service which may ensue from the appearance of disunion in His Majesty's councils, however unformed in reality, or however unimportant in itself the question which has given rise to that appearance

W. HUSKISSON

I have never been able to understand how the Duke could insist upon regarding it as equivalent to a direct resignation. Others, however, thought the same: Lord Bathurst in particular, whom the Duke consulted on the subject; and such, too, is Greville's opinion, who is not generally favourable to the Duke. The Duke, though he afterwards expressed regret for the misunderstanding, continued to father it on Mr. Huskisson, and said that the only way of undoing the effect of it was the withdrawal of the letter. He had communicated his resignation to the King, who had accepted it, and if he was now asked to remain in office, it would place the King in the position of " soliciting " a subject, which could not be thought of. Mr. Huskisson declined to adopt the Duke's suggestion, and left the Government, followed by Lord Palmerston, Lord Dudley, and Mr. Charles Grant, the more immediate friends of Mr. Canning. Perhaps the best excuse for the Duke is that the Canningite Party seemed inclined to hold their resignation over his head *in terrorem*. There had been a dispute in the Cabinet about the Corn Law Bill, when Mr. Grant resigned office because he could not have his own way. He was pacified, and came back. But when Huskisson's resignation followed, the Duke may have been excusably irritated by what seemed a repetition of the same tactics, and have been tempted into resolving that there should be no more mistakes. But when every allowance is made for these and other provocations, the fact remains that to the want of foresight displayed both by the Duke of Wellington and Mr. Peel at this particular period we owe the first step in that career which ended, whether for good or for evil, in the overthrow of the old Constitution.

Mr. Huskisson was known to share the views of Mr. Canning with regard to any essential alteration of our representative system. When, therefore, he pointed to the timely enfranchisement of a few large towns as the surest way of averting it, he might at least have been listened to. He begged for only a week's delay ;* but it was all in vain. The Tory leaders were smitten with judicial blindness. They did not see that although public opinion was not yet

* He asked to have the debate deferred for that time.

decidedly hostile to the principle of nomination, it was in daily danger of becoming so as long as it was left face to face with anomalies to which the Radicals could constantly appeal. The Duke of Wellington may have feared " the thin end of the wedge." But that was not the character of Mr. Peel. If he had only come forward at once, and, in opposing the motion for East Retford, given an undertaking at the same time that Government would bring in a general measure for correcting some of the most notorious abuses of the existing system, the question might have been settled, for that generation at least. The Tory Party, in that case, would still have included the followers of Mr. Canning. Mr. Stanley would in all probability have joined them at a later period. With an amended electorate and a new Parliament, and with all the popularity which they would have acquired by having settled the Reform question *at that time*, Ministers might have undertaken the Roman Catholic Question with perfect safety ; they need never have been committed to the principle of Protection, as they were by Sir Robert Peel himself during the Ministry of Lord Melbourne ; and I see no reason why, under Peel, Palmerston, and Lord Derby, they might not have governed England down to the death, at all events, of the last-mentioned statesman, if not, under other leaders, down even to the present moment. It was not too late even in 1830 to have anticipated the Whigs. Lord Althorpe expected them to do it. Lord Palmerston, there is reason to believe, would have rejoined them upon that condition. But the Duke seems to have had no misgivings. He was full of confidence. " You will see, we shall do very well," he said to Mrs. Arbuthnot, only just before the crash came.

Even in 1832, in my own opinion, a chance still re-

mained which was lost through the conduct of Sir Robert
Peel. But the prime opportunity was missed in 1828.
The Tory game was to have settled the Reform question
first and the Roman Catholic question afterwards. The
Government could not have lost more support among their
own party by the former than they did by the latter, while
at the same time it would have been a loss which they
were certain to repair at the first General Election that
took place. By the course which they actually pursued
they forfeited a degree of confidence which no appeal to
the people could restore, for the repeal of the Roman
Catholic disabilities, even where it was allowed to be necessary, was far from being popular ; and they brought only
a broken and dispirited party to withstand the charge of
the Whigs flushed with their unlooked-for victory, and
panting to avenge their long exclusion from power by the
complete prostration of their adversaries. The Tories,
distrustful of their leaders and quarrelling among themselves, were hardly in better plight to resist the rush of
the Whigs, than the Covenanters at Bothwell Brigg to
withstand the charge of the Life Guards. They had one
point in their favour ; they had one more chance of rallying, if they had only had the sense and courage to take
advantage of it. But they failed to do so, and the manner
of their failure it will shortly be our business to investigate.

We need not linger long at this moment over the story
of Roman Catholic Emancipation. We shall have to recur
to it hereafter in considering the career of Sir Robert Peel.
Opposition to it had never been one of the fundamental
articles of the Tory creed, and of the ten ablest men who
sprang from the loins of Toryism between 1780 and 1830
—namely, Pitt, Canning, Grenville, Castlereagh, Wellesley,
Wellington, Peel, Palmerston, Lyndhurst, and Eldon—six

were in favour of it, one really neutral, and only three against it. But after the death of Mr. Canning, the anti-Catholic section obtained so complete an ascendancy in the Government that the original tenets of the party were for the time forgotten, and Tory principles came to be identified with those statesmen who represented on this question the opinions of Mr. Addington. In proposing the Emancipation Act Peel and Wellington were supposed to be not recurring to the principles of their founder, but directly contradicting them. In the second place the Tory Leaders hardly cared to conceal that their change of front was due not to conviction but necessity. Sir Robert Peel openly avowed that his opinions had not changed, and that he made the concession as the lesser of two evils. Language of this kind did them no good with either side. A few leading men who could understand their difficulties may perhaps have been softened by it. But many of the rank and file and the majority of the outside public did not see why what had been maintained so long could not be maintained longer, if it was really for the public good.

Lord Lonsdale, who was a warm supporter of the Duke, confesses that his only doubt is whether it might not have been better to hold out and face the consequences. They certainly could not have been worse than what has occurred in Ireland since ; and it must frankly be owned that, judged merely by its efficacy in producing the particular results which were expected from it, the Emancipation Act was a total failure. The Tories who resisted it predicted the fruits which it would bear, and it *has* borne them : there is no doubt about that. So far, these gentlemen were infinitely more clear-sighted than their opponents. But the question is whether the public opinion of England, though anti-Catholic at the moment, would not very shortly have insisted on the experiment being tried ; just as it has determined that other experiments should be tried, all of which have been equally fruitless. I believe that it would ; and that the Duke of Wellington could not long have held his ground. But if he had only got rid of the Reform question first, the Roman Catholic question, whatever else it did, or failed to do, need not have broken up the party. Either way, the Government would have occupied a much stronger position after they had passed a Reform Bill than they did before. If, after the Borough system had been adjusted to the public opinion of the day, a Parliament returned by the amended constituencies had still been opposed to Emancipation, the Duke might have faced the consequences of refusing it with much less anxiety than when Parliamentary Reform was still hanging over his head.

It is to be observed that, apart from their conscientious reluctance to the principle of Emancipation, the anti-Catholic Tories in 1829, like the Protectionists in 1846, felt deeply aggrieved at the manner in which the change had been effected. In each case the intentions of the Government were kept a secret from their followers, who were allowed to go on till the last moment using the same language as of old to their own consti-tuents, only suddenly to discover, at the eleventh hour, what egregious fools they had been made. As late as December the 11th, 1828, and after matters had been arranged with the King, the Duke wrote a letter to Dr. Curtis* saying that a settlement of the question at that time was impossible ! The Duke of Wellington

---

* Roman Catholic Archbishop of Dublin. The Duke had known him at Salamanca ; and had a good deal of correspondence with him on the Roman Catholic Question.

seems to have thought in the one case as Sir Robert did in the other, that to have taken the party into his confidence would only have been to place them in a better position for resisting the proposed measure. They would have had time to organize an opposition which might have succeeded in defeating it. Practical statesmen, familiar with the conditions of Parliamentary life, and the resources of political parties, must, of course, be contradicted on questions of this nature with extreme diffidence. Yet it is impossible not to ask how, in either case, worse could have happened than did happen, however the question had been approached. The division on the second reading of the Roman Catholic Relief Bill was 353 to 173, the minority, of course, being composed of the estranged Tories. The hostility of these was quite sufficient to destroy the Government as soon as any question arose on which they could combine with the Whigs. But a much larger secession would not have been enough to enable them to reject the Bill. However much their numbers might have been increased in consequence of time being allowed them for preparation, it is absurd to suppose that they would have been sufficiently increased to prevent the passage of the measure. If we strike off fifty from one side and add them to the other, the Government would still have had a majority of eighty.

Unless, therefore, the difference between telling his party and not telling them meant the whole difference between losing the battle and winning it, it signified nothing whether a few votes more or less were gained or lost by either process. But the Duke was sure of carrying the Bill. He could only have broken up the party whatever he did, and he could not have broken it up more effectually than by the course which he pur-

sued. The same may be said of 1846. Two hundred
and fifty-two Conservative members voted against Sir
Robert Peel on the amendment of Mr. Philip Miles.
More than a hundred helped to make up the majority
which turned him out of office. What more could have
happened had he taken them into his confidence twenty
times over ? However this may be, it is beyond a doubt
that in 1829 the wound inflicted on the anti-Catholics by
the unexpected surrender of their principles was greatly
irritated by the feeling that they had been treated like
children ; and that to this, quite as much as to that, is
to be attributed their defection on the Civil List.

I must own I am at a loss to understand what gain can
ever be expected from such manœuvres. When the leader
of a party not only changes his opinions, but conceals that
change from his supporters till it is too late for them to
resist or to remonstrate, he exposes their fidelity to a
double strain : it has to bear, at one and the same time,
both the sacrifice of their principles and the betrayal of
their confidence. Surely the loyalty which is strong enough
to survive the two combined would be strong enough
to survive either by itself. The gentlemen who support
him in spite of the deceit which has been practised on
them will hardly oppose him because they have been
more openly dealt with. At all events, it seems utterly
improbable that any opposition to his plans which a knowledge of them may enable them to prepare, can be worse
or more formidable than the personal resentment which
is kindled by a sense of insult.

The motives which induced the Duke of Wellington and
Mr. Peel to make the concessions when they did are akin
to those which have influenced every concession to Ireland
that has been made since : fear of violence in one place

and fear of obstruction in another. The Duke of Wellington believed that further resistance would provoke a civil war in Ireland : Mr. Peel, that it would provoke one in the House of Commons. It is impossible to read the memorandum which he drew up on the subject, for the consideration of the King, without being deeply struck with the really unchangeable nature of the Irish difficulty. In it occurs the following passage, which, whether familiar to the Home Rulers of the present day or not, is as good a justification of their tactics as they need desire to show. If obstruction carried Emancipation, why not Separation also ?

The Parliamentary business would be impeded by the addition to the House of Commons of fifty or sixty members, whose only chance of maintaining their influence would be unremitting attendance in the House, and violent, vexatious opposition even to the details of business.— *Wellington Despatches*, vol. iv. p. 439.

The passage of the Bill was very far from preventing the apprehended evil. However, the Bill *was* passed, and, in the eyes of many honest men, the Constitution of 1688 was destroyed. This view of the event was incorrect, for the Protestant securities exacted at the Revolution settlement were directed against a change of dynasty which alone could have endangered the established religion of the country. They were no integral or essential part of the Constitution then established, but exceptional precautions against a particular exigency which ceased to be required as soon as the danger disappeared. But it was the very circumstance that their original and political value *had* totally disappeared, which led the country to invest them with an exclusively religious meaning. And to those who did so the abolition of them was a shock such as the minds of this generation, grown familiar with bloodless revolutions, can only imperfectly comprehend. Many of my readers, however, who are not beyond middle age, may remember their fathers and mothers, less than forty years ago, looking back with unabated horror to the great apostasy, and still murmuring to each other of what might have happened " had the Duke of York lived."

We are sometimes told that " there was in Church and State, before these great changes, something of the nature of a principle ; something which a statesman could appeal to without stultifying himself."* What is meant, I suppose, is that prior to the repeal of the Test and Corporation Acts in 1828 the theory of Church and State was still intact— the theory according to which citizenship and churchman-ship went together ; and no man was eligible to share in any duties of the State who was not also a member of the Church. He who stood outside one stood outside both. The Act of Indemnity which was passed every year, virtually dispensing with these conditions, did not affect the theory on which they were founded ; on the contrary, it was rather an annual recognition of it, and, no doubt, it was idle to argue, as so many people did, and still do, that it was proper to abolish the Acts in question because the operation of them was suspended. But how far the repeal of these Acts has subverted the principle of Church and State, and how far either this or any subsequent legisla-tion of the same kind could have been prevented, are different questions, which Churchmen make no attempt to answer.

It seems to me, however, that the principle of an Established Church is not necessarily dependent on the State's compelling all persons to be members of it who are desirous of filling any temporal office of trust The

* Archdeacon Denison, *Notes of My Life*.

State may adopt any given Church as its own, secure its endowments and privileges, and offer it to the nation to take or to leave. This seems to be one principle, at all events, on which establishments can be logically defended; and it is clear that this principle was not abandoned in 1828. This seems to be what Mr. Gladstone means when he speaks in his autobiography of the State "commending" any form of religion to the people; and although, no doubt, the persistent refusal of the large majority to accept that recommendation would show that the theory in that particular instance was not working, such is not the state of things which we see in England at the present day.

Like Pitt and Canning, the Duke had to "go out" for the part which he had played in politics. Lord Winchelsea, in a letter to the *Standard* of the 16th of March 1829, explaining his reasons for withdrawing his name from the subscription to King's College, which had been founded under the sanction of the Duke of Wellington, said, "That the late political events had convinced him (Lord Winchelsea) that the whole transaction (the establishment of King's College) was intended as a blind to the Protestant and High Church party; that the noble Duke, who had for some time previous to that period determined upon breaking in upon the Constitution of 1688, might the more effectually, under the cloak of some intended show of zeal for the Protestant religion, carry on his insidious design for the infringement of our liberties, and the introduction of Popery into every department of the State." This, of course, led to a duel, which was fought in Battersea fields on the 21st, of which a full and interesting account may be found in vol. iv. of the *Supplementary Despatches*, drawn up by Dr. Hume, the surgeon in attendance. Lord Winchelsea stood the Duke's shot, fired in the air, and apologised. The Duke's own defence of his conduct, in a letter to the Duke of Buckingham of the 21st April, is highly characteristic. Sir Henry Halford expressed his opinion of the duel in the following quotation :

> Querat certamen cui nil nisi vita superstes
> Subdita cui cedit Roma, cavere meum est

In the year following Emancipation, George the Fourth died, and the Revolution of July drove the elder Bourbons out of France. The effect of both these events was felt in the General Election. The revolutionary spirit woke up again, though still in a manageable form. The people began to talk about reform and retrenchment, and to exact pledges from candidates which told heavily in the day of battle ; and the Duke had to meet Parliament in the autumn with a weakened Cabinet, a diminished majority, and a disaffected party.

It was then that he made the second of the five great blunders by which his conduct was distinguished during the course of the Revolution of 1828–1832. On the 26th of October 1830 he declared, in his place in the House of Lords, not only that he would listen to no measure of Parliamentary Reform, small or great ; but that he regarded our existing system as incapable of improvement, and that, if he had to frame a new Constitution from the beginning, he should take our own as a model. The inconceivable want of judgment displayed in such a statement as this, at a moment when every friend of the aristocracy should have seen that only the most delicate and prudent management on the part of their advocates could save their power from destruction, needs no comment. The Duke himself, however, always maintained that it was not this declaration which turned him out. In a letter to General Malcom he explained at some length

what he conceived to be the reasons of his downfall.
They are what we have already stated. The vindictiveness of the anti-Catholic Tories, and the new ideas on the
subject of reform and economy which the French Revolution had set afloat. It was owing to these two causes that
when, on November 14th, Sir Henry Parnell moved that
the Civil List proposed for the new King should be referred
to a Select Committee, the Government was defeated by
a majority of twenty-nine. Though not absolutely compelled to resign by such a vote, the Duke wisely took
advantage of it to escape from a position which had now
become almost untenable. That he could do so under
cover of a defeat incurred in the service of the Crown,
instead of waiting to be beaten, as he very likely might
have been, on the question of Parliamentary Reform, which
was to be brought forward by Mr. Brougham the very next
day, was an additional reason for making the Civil List a
Cabinet question; and thus the great Minister, whose
tenure of power was expected to rival Walpole's, was
compelled to give up the helm after holding it for less
than three years.

The causes of the catastrophe have been made plain
enough in the course of these remarks. During the
thirteen years which followed the battle of Waterloo the
field had been cleared for certain great domestic questions
which the agitated state of the country, our relations with
the Continent, and the division of the Tory Party into two
camps had made it impossible to take into consideration
at an earlier period. The Duke failed to understand his
own position till it was too late. At his accession to office
the political atmosphere was tranquil. Social discontent
had for the time being subsided. The cry for reform had
dwindled to a mere echo. But the Duke might have

known that the calm would not last for ever; and that whenever the spirit of revolution was once again awakened it would not be satisfied with such measures as all moderate men would have accepted in 1828. He did not know it then; and others have not known it since. But there is still time, even now in this our day, if the English aristocracy will rouse themselves from the spell which some enemy seems to have cast over them.

It is unnecessary to repeat in any detail the history of the great constitutional change which was completed in 1832. It will be enough to note the salient points on which the issue turned, and to call attention to some aspects of the polity which was then overthrown, not, I think, generally appreciated. When the Duke of Wellington passed his celebrated encomium on the representative system which existed in 1830, he made a terrible blunder as a Parliamentary tactician. But it may be doubted whether he made an equally great one if we suppose him to have been speaking in the character of a political philosopher. In the Duke's correspondence we notice more than one allusion to the assertion of the reformers that they meant to restore the House of Commons to its original character; and he asks what character; and to what period of history they refer for the model House of Commons which they declared to have previously existed. Canning asked the same question; and there was no answer to be given to it. No such House as the reformers designed and ultimately succeeded in creating was ever before known to the English Constitution. If we look back to the days of the Plantagenets we find a House of Commons constituted on a far more popular basis than the House of Commons of a hundred years ago. But we find their functions practically limited to what are now called questions of supply. From time to time they discussed the policy of the Sovereign; but they had no power of controlling it. They were not considered to form part of the Government of the country, or competent to decide on matters of imperial interest. If, on the other hand, we look back to the House of Commons of a hundred years ago, we see a far less popular assembly than we find in the days of the Plantagenets. Now, however, it has become the chief power in the State; all the highest questions of foreign and domestic policy are ultimately referred to it; virtually it makes and unmakes Ministries; and can, in effect, insist on either peace or war. But a House of of Commons combining both these characteristics—the popular constitution of the fourteenth century with the imperial powers of the eighteenth, might have been looked for in vain in English history before 1832.

In an Assembly meant to be a democratic one, representing exclusively the middle and lower classes of society, the nomination boroughs were a glaring and monstrous anomaly. But in a House of Commons intended to be a mixed body, the constitution of which had been gradually and unconsciously adapted to its extended functions, they were no real anomaly at all. They were the means by which the Crown and the aristocracy reserved to themselves that share in the government of the country which they had always exercised hitherto, and to which the people had been so thoroughly accustomed that it was a long time before they saw anything anomalous in the machinery by which it was preserved. As the House of Commons claimed a share in the functions of the aristocracy, the aristocracy claimed a share in the constitution of the House of Commons. And it was only by means of the nomination system that the aristocratic, plutocratic, and democratic elements which were intended to be mingled in equal degrees in it, could be made to work harmoniously together.*

Elsewhere Mr. Gladstone speaks of the old system as one that was worth fighting for, founded on great principles, and defensible by strong arguments. It is, he says, a total mistake to suppose that misgovernment led to the Reform Bill. The country before 1831 was economically governed ; and it was not illiberally governed. Almost all the improvements which were carried immediately after the Reform Bill would probably have been carried just as soon had the Reform Bill never been enacted. The Corn Laws would probably have been repealed in the unreformed Parliament sooner than they were in the reformed one, and Roman Catholic Emancipation would not have been conceded by the latter so soon as it was by the former. This is a powerful testimony to the system which was supported by Mr. Canning, Sir Robert Peel, and the Duke of Wellington. Without being blind to its anomalies, they contended that no substitute for it had yet been proposed which would carry out the ends of good government with equal success, or combine in an equal degree the progress of improvement with the integrity of the Constitution, and the stability and continuity which it was above all things necessary should distinguish the counsels of the Crown.

Now without saying a word either of the abstract or the practical merits of such a form of government, I do say that it was based on a distinct idea; that it represented a political theory ; and that, in connection with this, even Gatton and Old Sarum were not the anomalies they have

---

* *Gladstone Gleanings*, vol. i. p. 77.

been supposed. It may be that in 1830 the English people had outgrown the Constitution, and that the democracy was not only ready but well qualified to take over to itself a larger share of political power. But what I do say is that the Act of 1832 was not a reform of the old Constitution but the creation of a new one. While the old one lasted, the nomination boroughs fitted into it perfectly. The system was logical, coherent, and practically useful ; and I am not prepared to admit that the Duke of Wellington's panegyric on it, though unwise to the verge of insanity, was, strictly speaking, untrue. Indeed, I am rather inclined to think that it would be no forced deduction from the statements contained in Mr. Gladstone's essay, to declare that, in all essential points, it was substantially correct.

The resignation of the Tory leaders in 1830 was to some extent influenced by the conviction that the Whigs would not be able to carry on the Government, and that they themselves must shortly be recalled to power, strengthened by the failure of their adversaries, and reconciled, perhaps, with the mutineers, whose hostility might have been satiated with the punishment they had been able to inflict. These expectations were disappointed ; and, even if he had returned to power, it is extremely doubtful how far the Duke could have relied on the unflinching support of the anti-Catholics. Many of them thought that after he had abandoned Protestantism he might be expected to abandon anything ; and that he was a more dangerous minister for the country than Lord Grey himself. The Duke of Richmond had even gone over to the Whigs in consequence. It is, indeed, to the presence of this feeling in the rank and file of the Tory Party that much of the weakness and hesitation displayed by their leaders throughout the Reform struggle is to be attributed. And thus, in more senses than one, the Emancipation Act was the parent of the Reform Act.

It seems, however, that the Whigs themselves, when they first took possession of Downing Street, were doubtful of being able to remain there without the assistance of the Tories. The talk of the party was of a junction with Sir Robert Peel, and a moderate Reform Bill; and whether any such idea was entertained by their leaders or not, we know that Lord Grey himself on more than one previous occasion had contemplated a junction with the Duke of Wellington, and that so competent a judge as Lord Hertford, even so late as February 1831, believed it to be feasible, and most desirable. It does not appear, however, that any steps were taken to bring about communications between them, the Duke's unhappy declaration of the previous October standing in the way, we suppose, of every possible compromise. If he had only been willing to do then what he was willing to do fifteen months afterwards, and practically recall that ill-timed manifesto, the revolution might still have been averted.

Nothing, however, was done, and on the 1st of March Lord John Russell introduced the Government Reform Bill. We all know that its sweeping provisions went far beyond the expectations of what would now be called the moderate men of both parties, and it is probable enough that the Ministers themselves had so framed it that they might have something to give away. But what has never been thoroughly explained is the mixture of motives which induced Sir Robert Peel to consent to take it into consideration. This decidedly was blunder number three. I quite agree with those who say that had he declined to entertain so extravagant a proposal at all, taking care at the same time to express himself in favour of a moderate

measure which should amend the details without destroying the principle of the existing system, he would have
had a majority in his favour, and would in all probability
have been at once recalled to power.* Whether Sir
Robert's mistake on the introduction of the Bill was due
to his own reluctance to resume the responsibilities of
office under circumstances of such peculiar difficulty;
whether he himself really believed that to read the Bill a
second time offered the best chance of making good terms
with the enemy, and of saving a part of the threatened
fabric from destruction ; or whether he was over-persuaded
by those canting blockheads, the pests of the political world,
who mistake words for things, and go about assuring us
that half a loaf is better than no bread, even when the
loaf is a flint—we may perhaps consider in another chapter ;
but in either case the result was the same. The principle
of the Bill was recognized : and the Radicals had got the
leverage they wanted. Nothing was hereafter to be tolerated that went behind the principle. Whereas, if this had
been rejected and a Tory Government restored on the
understanding that a different Bill should be brought in,
the chances were that Lord Grey and the more Conservative members of his party would have supported the
Tories, and the compromise would have succeeded. But
when the Bill had once been read a second time Lord
Grey was in a position to insist on a dissolution of Parliament if anything went wrong in Committee. It is
pretty certain that he would have done nothing of the kind
had the House of Commons refused even to listen to it.
This great Tory blunder placed the Whigs on firm ground;
and gave them an advantage which they maintained to
the end of the struggle.

* Croker, vol. ii. p. 110.

But even worse mistakes were to come. The first Bill was read a second time by a majority of one ; the casting vote being given by the apostate Calcraft, who, like a second Judas, shot himself five months afterwards. But an amendment moved in Committee by General Gascoigne, that it was inexpedient to increase the number of the House of Commons, was carried by a majority of eight ; and then Ministers dissolved. The Duke always thought that the King did very wrong to dissolve : that this was his capital blunder : and that public feeling would very soon have cooled down. By this time, however, it had so far been worked upon, that the country, which six months before would probably have gone against Reform, now returned a large majority in its favour, and another Bill passed through the House of Commons on the 22nd of September. It was thrown out in the Lords by a majority of forty-one on the 8th of October ; and after a winter of riots, incendiarism, and almost insurrection, a third Bill was carried through the House of Commons, and sent up to the Lords in the spring of 1832.

Both parties now became anxious for an accommodation. The Tory Party shrank from the responsibility of throwing out the Bill a second time. Lord Grey and the King shrank from the creation of Peers, which, if the Tories held out, was inevitable. There was a section of the Cabinet who would have been only too glad of an opportunity to make extensive alterations in the Bill. The Duke of Richmond, Lord Lansdowne, Lord Melbourne, Lord Palmerston, and Mr. Stanley had become convinced that they had gone too far. The more moderate among the Tories felt that now or never was the time to secure a favourable compromise. With this disposition upon both sides, considerable progress was made during the month

14

of April towards arriving at an amicable understanding. One point the Whigs had all but agreed to yield ; and that was that no £10 householder who had also a freehold in the town should vote for both the town and the county. This was always considered a very important point by the Conservatives,* and the attempt to carry it in the Bill of 1859 was one of the prominent objections raised to that measure by the Whigs. But in 1832 Lord Grey had been willing to concede it ; and so matters were progressing with every appearance of considerable amendments being accepted, when the violence and precipitation of the ultra-Tories, and the bad management of their leaders, undid all that had been done.

The second reading of the Bill had been carried in the Lords on the 14th of April by a majority of nine, with the help of the well-known "Waverers," led by Lords Harrowby and Wharncliffe, who had taken the lead in the above negotiations. It was understood by the Government that as long as there was any hope of bringing them to a satisfactory conclusion, no hostile action would be taken in Committee. When the House re-assembled after Easter, Lord Wharncliffe had an interview with Lord Grey, in which he told the Prime Minister that the Tories were bent on postponing the disfranchising clauses till after the consideration of the enfranchising ones, and that an amendment to that effect would be moved by Lord Lyndhurst. Lord Grey said it would be impossible for the Government to agree to this ; and Lord Wharncliffe, according to Greville,† said that he would try to pre-

---

* *Wellington Despatches*, vol. viii., pp. 82, 84, 272, 282, 284, 286.

† Confirmed by Lord Grey himself. Letter to Sir Herbert Taylor, May 7. I may here add that the correspondence of Lord Grey and William the Fourth, published in 1867, shows that Greville is a fairly trustworthy authority for the events of this period.

vent it from being brought forward, assuring Lord Grey at the same time that *he*, Lord Wharncliffe, would do nothing to interfere with the principle of the Bill. Lord Lyndhurst, however, assured Lord Wharncliffe afterwards that the Tory Party was determined, and that his amendment could not be abandoned without the risk of a general insurrection. Lords Harrowby and Wharncliffe then agreed to support it ; and, what was worse, allowed themselves to be dissuaded from doing what they were bound in honour, no less than by policy and courtesy, to do, namely, communicate what was coming to Lord Grey. Not a word was said to him till the afternoon of the debate, when, on Lord Lyndhurst's motion being carried by a majority of thirty-five, of which the Waverers formed part, he very naturally threw up the Bill, and resigned.

Here was blunder number four. It would have been worth any money to the Tories to have kept Lord Grey on the inclined plane of concession, and to have sown dissensions between himself and the Radicals, to say nothing of the fact that amendments of no slight value had been already agreed to. Mr. Wood, Lord Grey's son-in-law, afterwards Lord Halifax, told Greville that Government would give way " on two special points." They were ready to agree that no man voting for a town in right of a £10 house should have a vote for the county in right of any freehold in that town ; and that the representation of metropolitan districts should be confined to Marylebone. Lord Grey himself in his correspondence with Sir H. Taylor between the 7th and 15th May, repeatedly alludes to the " many things which might have been done " before the carriage of the amendment, but which he sees no possibility of carrying into effect now. " Alterations which did

14 *

not appear to us advisable," he says, "might then have been submitted to," for the purpose of carrying the Bill. On the 13th of February he was prepared to make "large concessions"; and among these, no doubt, was the exclusion of the town freeholders from the counties. He elsewhere enumerates the essential points which could not be given up, and this is not among them.* Supposing the Duke to have been acquainted with all the facts, as Lord Grey believed him to have been, his only excuse is that he relied on the possibility of forming another Administration. Besides, not only was the Amendment a mistake, as at once putting a stop to the *rapprochement* which was progressing so favourably between the moderates on both sides, but it gave the Radical Party just the opportunity which they wanted. Lord Brougham lets us into the secret. The Radicals were afraid that the Tories would be sharp enough "to avoid giving us the advantage of defeating any essential part as long as they could, and that they would throw out or alter one after the other of the lesser provisions so that we should be left in the greatest possible difficulty." What he and his friends wanted, therefore, was that their adversaries should make some move which they could allege struck at the principle of the Bill, and so bring on a crisis, upon which an appeal might be made to the country to insist upon "the Bill, the whole Bill, and nothing but the Bill," and Ministers might claim the King's consent to such a creation of peers as would bear down all opposition.†

Lord Lyndhurst's motion did just what they wanted; it did "strike at the principle of the Bill." The Whig Reform Bills of 1831–2 were no longer what they once

---

* *Grey Correspondence*, vol. ii. pp. 213, 300.
† *Life of Lord Lyndhurst*, by Sir Theodore Martin, p. 30.

might have been, measures only for conferring members
on populous and important places which were not represented, and for withdrawing from decayed boroughs
as many members as were required for that purpose.
They were Bills of which disfranchisement for its own
sake was a primary and essential part. They were
avowedly directed to the reduction of aristocratic influence in the House of Commons, as an end in itself,
quite independently of the claims of other towns to representation, which might make it necessary to transfer
to them a certain number of nomination seats. Lord
Lyndhurst's amendment said, in effect, Let us first determine what number of unrepresented towns require
representatives, and then it will be time enough to consider where they are to come from. The Government
said, Let us first determine how many small boroughs
deserve to be disfranchised, and then it will be time
enough to consider how we shall allot the seats. The
latter proposal affirmed that the representation of small
towns, the former that the non-representation of large
towns, was the great blot to be removed.

Lord Lyndhurst, from my own point of view, was right
on the question of principle, but wholly wrong on the
question of Parliamentary management. The affair had
gone too far then to make it worth while to quarrel with
the Government on an abstract question. And to the
counter plan of Reform which the Duke and others were
ready to adopt, the amendment was not essential. The
first point with them all was to exclude the freeholders
in represented towns from voting for the counties. The
second was some re-arrangement of Schedules A and B,
which should make the Bill somewhat less Radical.* The

* Those who were shocked in 1867 at the idea of a Tory Reform Bill

first point, as we have seen, the Government would probably have conceded ; the second was peculiarly fitted
for consideration in Committee. So that one fails to see
what great advantage it was expected to obtain by Lord
Lyndhurst's amendment. The Duke of Wellington, from
the tone of his letter to the Duke of Cumberland on the
27th of April, does not seem to have attached much importance to it. Is it possible that he was unaware of the
whole extent of the communications which had passed
between Lord Wharncliffe and Lord Grey; or of the very
great probability that the latter would treat the support
of Lord Lyndhurst by the Waverers as the breach of an
implied understanding which must necessarily put an end
to all further negotiations ?* The Duke never looked
with much favour on the Harrowby and Wharncliffe
tactics. And in a long letter to Lord Wharncliffe, dated
February 3rd, 1832, he gave his reasons for thinking that
no satisfactory compromise could be effected. Yet when
we read his letters of the 27th of April to the Duke of
Cumberland and Lord Bathurst, and see how nearly what
he then required approached to what the Government
were almost certainly prepared to grant,† it is, perhaps,
to be regretted that he did not think it wise to adopt a
more conciliatory attitude, and try to induce his supporters to give up the Amendment. However, if he did
not know all that Lord Wharncliffe had promised ‡ for

---

establishing Household Suffrage in the towns, will be interested in hearing
that the same franchise was suggested by Lord Aberdeen to the Duke of
Wellington in 1832, without provoking either surprise or disapproval.

　＊ See Lord Grey's letter to Sir Herbert Taylor, May 7th.

　† Sir Herbert Taylor to Lord Grey, May 27th. Conversation of Lord Grey
with the King, April 1st.—*Greville*, vol. ii. pp. 257-76. What Grey stated
as essentials were not incompatible with the Duke's or Lord Ellenborough's
suggestions.

　‡ *Greville*, vol. ii. p. 293.

himself in particular, or all that Lord Grey had been led to believe of the Opposition in general, he could not very well have interfered; while of the policy of Lyndhurst's amendment, apart from personal considerations, of course, if the Duke believed that a Tory Government could be formed, able to carry through the kind of Reform Bill which he had sketched for himself, his support cannot be called a blunder. Whether he was right or not is a moot question to the present hour. If we answer the question in the affirmative, the responsibility for what followed must rest on other shoulders.

Lord Grey, as it is known, lost not a moment in laying before the King the two alternatives of creating peers or accepting his resignation. The King chose the latter, and sent for Lord Lyndhurst, who at once referred him to the Duke, and then followed a week of "political man-œuvres," which the *Wellington Despatches*, the *Greville Memoirs*, and the *Croker Papers* have rendered more intelligible than they were forty years ago, when *Coningsby* was first published. Mr. Disraeli thought* "the future historian would be perplexed to ascertain what was the distinct object which the Duke of Wellington purposed to himself in the political manœuvres of May 1832." I think it is perfectly plain. It has now been made abundantly clear that, although William the Fourth would have insisted on some Reform Bill being passed, he would not have insisted on that particular Reform Bill; that he was, in fact, prepared to support those very alterations which the Conservative Party recommended. It is also known that the Duke of Wellington, throwing over all his former declarations, was prepared to bring in a Reform Bill, such as might easily have been accommodated to the basis on

* Cf. *Coningsby*, chap. vii.

which Lord Grey was willing to treat before the 7th of
May. We also know that there were influential members
of Lord Grey's Government who would probably have supported such a measure. And what is more important
than all is that Sir Robert Peel himself, though he refused
to join the Duke of Wellington, thought that the attempt
might be successful.

It is forgotten that the Tory Party all along had secret
sympathisers in the Ministry; that Lord Grey, but a few
years before, had been willing to join a Tory Government;
that in 1830 he had thought of making overtures to Peel;
and that the great body of the respectable classes had been
rather frightened into reform than converted to it. The
existing Parliament had six years to run; and a firm stand
taken upon moderate grounds had a reasonable prospect
of success. I do not see, therefore, that the "object"
which the Duke of Wellington proposed to himself is necessarily obscure, or that the attainment of it was necessarily
hopeless. How his efforts were nipped in the bud by the
refusal of his old colleague to support him will be told in
our chapter on Sir Robert Peel. We have heard of men
straining at gnats and swallowing camels. But Sir Robert
Peel did more : having swallowed the camel, he afterwards
strained at the gnat.

The plan of a Tory Administration in May 1832 broke
down chiefly in consequence of a declaration from Mr.
Baring, who was to have been the Tory Chancellor of the
Exchequer, that if the Whig Ministers like to come back
and carry the Bill, he for one should only be too glad to
see them do it. In these words he only spoke the sentiments of a considerable section of the Tory Party who
thought that the Whigs, having got us into the mess,
ought to see us through it, and that it was for them and

not for the Tories to carry out a revolutionary measure,
quite forgetting that in their own hands it need not have
been a revolutionary measure. On this point we shall have
a good deal more to say hereafter, but I shall lose no time
in quoting the opinion of the Duke of Wellington on this
point, which he communicated to Croker in 1846, when
Croker tried to persuade him not to remain a member of
Sir Robert Peel's Government :—

"You say," says the Duke, "that it would be better that Cobden should
be the Minister and propose the alteration of the Corn Laws. I have a good
deal of experience of the evil which can be done by a Minister of whom it is
thought that it would be preferable that he should be the person to carry a
bad measure. I recollect that in 1832 it was thought that a Government
might be formed which in completing the Reform Bill might prevent some
of its mischief. Some thought, Let the Whigs and Radicals who proposed
the measure complete it. They were successful; the formation of the new
Administration failed, and the Reform Bill was carried. All the improvements intended were rejected, and some of the very worst parts of the Bill
were carried after this failure."

After this final collapse of the Tory Party there is little
more to record. The Duke of Wellington persuaded the
Peers to let the Bill pass, and "the Venetian Constitution"
passed away. It is a moot point to this day whether, if
they had chosen to stand out, a sufficient number of Peers
would have been created to swamp the House of Lords ;
and even supposing that they would have been, it is a
question after all whether it may not sometimes be wiser
to endure the worst than to yield to intimidation. The
blow can rarely be repeated ; the intimidation, when once
found to answer, can always be renewed.

In taking our leave of the Georgian Era, as we fitly may
with the Duke of Wellington's Administration, it is proper
to call attention to some of the salient points in which the
old *régime* differed from the new, and to some of the un-
foreseen consequences which the latter has entailed on us.

One very important distinction is this, that while, by the rivalry of the two great parties which then contended for the mastery, the Crown was of necessity a gainer, by the rivalry of those which now maintain a similar struggle it is sure to be a loser. It seems to me incontestable that, from 1714 to 1811 the Crown had been steadily gaining ground, and that from 1811 to 1830 it at least did not retrograde. George II. was more powerful than George I., and George III. than George II. Had George IV. been a man of more character, he might perhaps have been more powerful than his father. The reason is that, in those days, it was impossible to exercise that pressure upon the will of the Sovereign which it is possible to exercise in these. If the Pelhams, the Russells, the Gowers, and the Montagues, loved place and power, they loved something else better, and that was themselves. They never dreamed of calling in the people to help them in displacing a rival. They never said practically to the Sovereign, If Your Majesty does not pass this measure, you must expect a revolution. They never even dared to stop the supplies, foreseeing, doubtless, that such a step might necessitate further measures, injurious in the long run to their best interests. It was better that one-half of the aristocracy should be out of office than that the whole aristocracy should descend from its vantage-ground. The special interests of party were postponed to the common interests of the whole order. And the consequence was that neither party could push the Sovereign beyond a certain point. If he dared them to do their worst, they could practically do nothing; and as this became more and more apparent the Crown became more and more powerful.

But when, after an exclusion from office which lasted nearly fifty years, the Whigs at length made up their minds to abandon this system, and called in the democracy to aid them in their struggle with the Tories, they established a precedent obviously fatal to prerogative, though neither party in the State has had the moral courage to denounce it. It is always an easy thing to persuade the people that some great change, no matter what, is essentially necessary to their welfare. A cry is raised throughout the country. A general election is of course favourable to its authors. And now the Crown, if adverse to the policy proposed, is no longer in an attitude of opposition to a political party only, but, as it is capable of being represented, to the whole people. The difference is enormous; and the pressure brought to bear upon the Crown is of course irresistible. The habit once adopted of calling in the people as thirdsman, by whichever party wants their aid, may have become a second nature; but it is to this, much more than to any loss of influence by the destruction of the old boroughs, that the weakness of the Crown since 1832 is to be attributed. It is the disproportion of the means employed to the end to be obtained that is the real danger of England at the present day. If the weight of the people and the threat of revolution is always to be thrown into the scale against a rival party when other means of action fail, we scarcely see how either monarchy or parliamentary government is to be preserved. It is like using the Constitution for fire-wood to furnish out a single meal. The aristocracy in former times had too much regard for their own interests to act upon any such system. It was better, they thought, to go without official meat than to strengthen and encourage the democratic element, by raising it to the position of arbiter in their own intestine quarrels. Since this prudent course has been abandoned—

Non equitem dorso, non frenum depulit ore.

Another point to which it is necessary to call attention is, the difference between the *idea* of government which was uppermost fifty years ago and that which is fashionable now. It is not because Lord Liverpool was able to carry all his measures, and to resist pressure from without, that he has been described as the last Minister who "governed" us, but because something more than measures were expected of him. The tradition still lingered in the lifetime of Lord Liverpool that one of the functions of Government was to form and to control opinion. And it was owing to the influence of this idea that the coercive policy of 1817 met with that sympathy from the public the existence of which even Sir G. C. Lewis does not openly deny. But this conception of Government cuts two ways. If it gave the Administration a firmer *locus standi* in the repression of popular demonstrations, it likewise placed popular demonstrations on a more logical and intelligible footing. In proportion to the difficulty of making their wants known through Parliament was the justification of the people in seeking other channels of publicity. These two opposing forces were correlatives of each other; and while Government still remained invested, in the public eye, with the imperial attributes aforesaid, the use of public meetings was not likely to be in excess of the popular necessities. The difference between that state of things and that in which the present generation has grown up is that, while Government has tacitly abandoned those regulative or directorial functions which it exercised in the Ministry of Lord Liverpool, the people have pushed still farther than before the practice of external agitation.

Between 1832 and 1868 we have had rebellions, riots, and seditious meetings to a most aggravated extent, all intended to intimidate a House of Commons which had recently been placed on a distinctly democratic basis. Are we to expect that a similar extension of the representation will be followed by a similar development of this lawless and aggressive spirit? The very contrary effect is the one that we have a right to anticipate. As Parliament becomes more popular, public meetings should become less frequent. The people should learn to acquiesce at least in the decision of the people's House. If they do not; if they only see in the relaxed authority of the executive an incitement to further interference, instead of a reason for abstaining from it; if they resent the jurisdiction of an assembly returned by household suffrage; most sensible men will come to the conclusion that they would rather have been governed by Lord Liverpool than administered by any of his successors.

The third and last point to be noticed is the great increase of power secured to individuals under the new *régime*. The feudal system had its own checks on arbitrary power; but they were of too summary and violent a character to suit a settled state of society; and it is not improbable that if the Black Prince had lived, and the Lancastrian Revolution been avoided, the Plantagenets might have anticipated the Tudors in establishing pure monarchy. However this may be, the feudal monarchy was a mixed system, under which the Sovereign was to be controlled by the aristocracy. The time came when the aristocracy split up into factions, destroyed its own power by internecine warfare, and made room for the ascendency of the individual. For the next two hundred years our government was one in which the sovereign power was lodged in one person. The defeat of Charles the First was only the defeat of one man : it left the principle untouched ; and it was represented in the person of Cromwell more fully than in the person of Charles. The victory of the Parliament was only an apparent one; and the first attempt to arrest or modify the growth of personal government in the seventeenth century was a failure. The second was more successful; and it must be allowed that when the Revolution settlement once got into fair working order it did certainly present such a distribution or division of the sovereign power as made the personal pre-eminence or despotism of any one man all but impossible. Walpole was far from being the perpetual dictator which it was the fashion at the time to represent him. He was absolute in his own sphere; but that was only because he was the servant of the Whig aristocracy. The great " Revolution families," with their boroughs and their moneyed interest, always had a bit in the mouth of the Prime Minister, and could check him when they thought fit either for their own benefit or for the public good. Within these limits, indeed, Walpole did govern with such absolute sway as apparently to justify to the full the invectives launched at him by Bolingbroke. But all the time there was in the background the check upon him which we have described. The Whig aristocracy, who represented the principles of the Revolution and the sanctity of Parliamentary government, could call him to immediate account if they believed him to be endangering either.

Ultimately he lost their confidence, not on political but on personal grounds; and forty years elapsed before an equally powerful Minister appeared upon the scene. In the meantime a new political force had been resuscitated in the Constitution in the shape of the Royal prerogative, which from the accession of George the Third constituted a further check on the personal will of the Prime Minister.

Whether this was used well or ill is nothing to the purpose; for it might obviously have been used in either way. Contemporaries supposed the King to be using it very well in preventing Mr. Pitt from repealing the Roman Catholic disabilities. In a self-governed country the opinion of the people must be considered: and here we have a distinct and conspicuous example of the use of his prerogative by the Sovereign to prevent the consummation of a policy which he knew to be unpopular with his subjects. Thus we see that the mixed form of government which existed in the country from 1688 to 1832, supplied very substantial checks on the personal authority of a Prime Minister. His Parliamentary majority, being largely composed of nominees, was always liable to be withdrawn, or at least seriously impaired, if he ran counter to the wishes of the higher nobility, among whom, in the opinion of many Liberal writers, the most enlightened intelligence is to be found.* On the other hand lay the Royal prerogative, still further circumscribing his independence. It may very well be that if Pitt or Canning had been emancipated from these restraints it might have been all the better for the public. That is a matter of opinion. All we are concerned to show is that under the old *régime*, that really mixed form of government which Hobbes condemned, not only were the forces of the State exerted with great success and glory, but also that a check was secured against the abuse of power by individuals stronger than we ever had before, or perhaps may ever have again.

But the aristocracy quarrelled again, as they had done centuries before, with a result which, though apparently the exact reverse of what occurred in 1485, may hereafter

* E. G. Lecky. *History of the Eighteenth Century*, vol. i. p. 175.

be found to have been really not very far removed from
it. The Reform Bill of 1832 was a good deal more than
a Reform Bill, as that term is generally understood. It
was an entire change of system : an advance out of one
zone of politics into another : a political revolution not
less pregnant or far-reaching than the deposition of an
ancient dynasty. Power was formerly distributed between
the Crown, the aristocracy, and the people, in not very
unequal degrees. There was then no one element of which
it could be said with certainty that in the event of a
struggle it must necessarily come off victorious. Previously
to 1688 the Crown was such a power. Subsequently to
1832 the people has become such a power. But in the
intermediate period we had a really mixed government,
which, though of comparatively short duration, as was
the case at Rome, and therefore to some extent justifying
Hobbes's opinion of it, did, nevertheless, great things for
this country, and did certainly prevent or greatly modify
the ascendency of individuals. The Reform Bill, however,
has emancipated the Prime Minister from the influence of
the borough proprietor, which was always at hand and
ready to act at a moment's notice. It has, to a great
extent, emancipated him from the control of the Crown,
if, as we are assured, no Sovereign could ever venture to
dismiss Ministers who were supported by a majority of the
House of Commons, or retain Ministers who were not.
And though this assertion may be somewhat in excess
of the exact truth, it cannot be doubted that the power of
the Crown to prevent a Minister with a majority from
doing what he likes in Parliament, which was really possessed to some extent during the Georgian epoch, has
now all but disappeared. For these two checks, which, as
we say, were immediate, instant, and direct, he has now

only to fear the unorganized and divided influence of public opinion acting at considerable intervals, and in the nature of things less curious about the privileges of Parliament and less jealous of the power of individuals than those who enjoy the one and are directly overshadowed by the other. The majority which supports him in Parliament is *his* majority; it consists, for the most part, of men absolutely devoted to his person, and returned by constituents who care for little else but the supremacy of their own party. As long, therefore, as he has their votes at his command, he may set all opposition at defiance. The time may come, of course, when he ceases to have their votes at his command. Every despotism is tempered by the fear of insurrection; but it is a despotism all the same.

This is the consummation in which the long-sustained clamour against electoral inequalities and aristocratic influence has finally landed us. Democracy has always been favourable to the power of individuals; and the progress of democracy in Europe during the nineteenth century corroborates this statement. Why, then, should England be an exception? It is useless to complain of the inevitable. We have knocked away the barriers by which the power of the Minister was restrained, and what right have we to be surprised if he takes advantage of his freedom? Such a Minister is only the chosen representative of a self-governed people—the exponent of the popular will, which has been made supreme. And what more can we want?

The Duke of Wellington's Foreign Policy may be described briefly as a policy of no nonsense. When he said non-intervention he meant non-intervention, and would not allow the principle to be violated in favour of one side more than in favour of the other. The Whigs wished to carry out the doctrine with a distinctly democratic bias. Wellington was determined to hold the balance even. This is the key to his policy on the Turkish Question, and to his policy on the Portuguese Question. At the death of Mr. Canning, in August 1827,* the Regent Isabella, daughter of the late King, who died in 1826, was in quiet possession of the Portuguese Government, and the English troops which had been sent to her assistance were recalled. Don Pedro, her brother, now Emperor of Brazil, had resigned his rights to the crown in favour of his daughter Donna Maria, on condition that she married her Uncle Don Miguel, second son of John VI., the leader of the Absolutist Party, she herself being the head of the Constitutionalists. Miguel, however, whom Pedro had appointed Regent instead of Isabella in 1827, was shortly afterwards proclaimed King, and restored the Absolute form of government. Portugal was, therefore, in a state of civil war, the conditions of which extended necessarily to all her dependencies and colonies ; and existed as much in the Azores as on the banks of the Tagus or the Douro. As Canning had refused to let a hostile force equip itself in Spain for the service of Don Miguel, so did the Duke, when Prime Minister, refuse to let a hostile force equip itself in England for the service of Donna Maria, the rival claimant of the throne. That she was the legitimate heiress and Don Miguel a usurper would give us no more right to interfere than the French would have had to interfere between Charles the First and Cromwell. Besides which, a variety of engagements entered into by Don Pedro in connection with his daughter's succession had not been

* *Vide supra*, p. 152.

kept,* while it was also maintained that the letter of the Constitution was on Don Miguel's side.† A number of Portuguese refugees who had assembled at Plymouth, with a view of passing over to the island of Terceira, where the Queen's party still maintained itself, were ordered off, and were furthermore prevented by an English frigate from landing at Terceira. Against these proceedings Lord Palmerston protested. But he should have seen that in principle it in no respect differed from the intervention of 1826. If Portuguese deserters and refugees were not allowed to make Spain a basis of operations against Portugal, *a fortiori*, they could hardly be allowed to make England. He says,‡ "Miguel had been permitted by our Government to send an expedition to conquer Madeira." Yes: but not an expedition organized in England, and starting from an English port. The Duke of Wellington was clearly of opinion that the people of Portugal preferred Don Miguel, and that we had no right to assist Don Pedro by force. In August 1828 Lord Strangford was instructed to tell Don Pedro of "the almost unanimous decision of the Portuguese in favour of Don Miguel."§

Even so late as April 1833 we find Lord Palmerston himself writing to Mr. Temple at Naples, in characteristic language, that "As to the contest between Pedro and Miguel, it is anybody's race yet." And, what is much more to the purpose, in the debate on the King's Speech, November 2, 1830, Lord Althorpe, then the leader of the Liberal party in the House of Commons, declared that the recognition of Don Miguel, who had for three years been King *de facto*,

---

* For a full account of Portuguese affairs from 1827–29, see *Despatches*, vol. v. pp. 358, 409 ; vol. viii. p. 375.

† *Quarterly Review*, July 1833.

‡ *Life of Palmerston*, vol. i. p. 302.

§ *Supp. Despatches*, vol. viii. p. 375 ; *Ellenborough Diary*, vol. i. p. 189.

ought not any longer to be delayed. Liberal historians, writing of this period, are in the habit of expressing themselves, with regard to this and other public questions, as if it was totally impossible there could be two sides to them. Yet here, for instance, we find the leaders of both political parties in the House of Commons, both Lord Althorpe and Sir Robert Peel, concurring with the first soldier of the age in their views of the Portuguese civil war; and this view the Tory view. It is evident, therefore, that parties in Portugal must, to say the least of it, have been very evenly balanced; and that there was no such marked collision between national opinion on one side and brute force upon the other as to bring the case within the limits of the principle laid down by Canning.* The Duke of Wellington was clearly of opinion that the two parties should be left to fight it out, care being taken that no other State interfered in favour of either. This, I firmly believe, would have been the view adopted by Mr. Canning had he then been alive. Lord Palmerston, with the zeal† of a newly-made convert, pleased himself with the idea of a combination in favour of Liberalism in the West of Europe to balance the combination against it which existed in the North.‡ But I very much doubt if in so doing he was treading in the footsteps of his master.

The Duke of Wellington believed that Lord Grey's Government had been guilty of very serious breaches of neutrality in their treatment of the Portuguese question, and his reasons for thinking so are given in a memo-

---

* Cf., p. 155. "England could be no party to forcing Absolutism on a reluctant nation."

† This did not last for ever.

‡ Life, vol. ii. p. 188.

randum of July 1832. The party of Don Pedro had openly raised troops in London. The vessels with these troops on board were allowed to sail from England to a French port, where their armament was completed by supplies furnished from England. Ships, manned by British seamen, under the command of British officers, and with the British flag flying, blockaded Madeira, and afterwards pursued and captured several Portuguese vessels. All this time, be it remembered, Don Miguel, against whom these operations were directed, was *de facto* King; a point which the Whigs, if anybody, were bound to respect, and which Lord Palmerston was the first to respect in the case of Louis Napoleon. Well might the Duke ask if this was neutrality. It was certainly not Canning's idea of neutrality; it was certainly not the neutrality which England would have ventured to exercise in the war between the Northern and Southern States of America. In June 1833 the Duke of Wellington brought forward a motion of censure in the House of Lords, founded on the above circumstances, and also on the capture of Miguel's fleet by Napier in May, and inflicted a defeat upon the Government which very nearly caused their resignation. But the House of Commons immediately passed a vote of confidence, and the storm blew over. Sir Robert Peel was just as strong against the Government as the Duke of Wellington. But the Ministerial reply rather evaded the real point at issue, which was not whether it was lawful or customary for individuals to engage in foreign service, or for English merchants to sell munitions of war to be used against a friendly Power, but whether the equipment of regular expeditions in the ports of a neutral country for the purpose of taking part in hostilities against the allies of that country, and operations of this character conducted under protection of its flag, were or were not a breach of international law.

On this question the debates on the Foreign Enlistment Act of 1819 may be consulted with advantage. It was easy for the Opposition to quote precedents against this measure. In the sixteenth and seventeenth centuries Englishmen, Scotchmen, and Irishmen had freely entered the service of Foreign States and fought against Powers with whom this country was at peace. Down to a late period in the eighteenth century the Government of Holland retained Scotch regiments in its pay. These were notorious facts. But this was a very different thing from English adventurers fitting out expeditions of their own in this country against a friendly Power, sailing under the British flag to the assistance of her rebel subjects, and taking forcible possession of her property. In the second place, it was quite clear that international relations no longer permitted of such freedoms as, under a looser system of public law, had been formerly tolerated. Besides, the Whigs themselves, in the reign of George the Second, had actually passed a statute making it felony for a British subject to enter the service of a foreign State ; and the only thing which made it necessary to supplement it by the Act of 1819 was the fact that the rebellious Colonies were not technically " States." The Whigs, in 1833 and 1834, attempted to repeal these Acts ; but the House of Lords refused its consent. And a pretty position we should have been in at the time of the American Civil War if the Tories had not stood firm ! This is another great service which they performed to their country immediately after the Reform Bill.

The Portuguese question was settled for the time by the Quadruple Alliance of 1834 between England, France,

Spain, and Portugal, securing the thrones of the two Peninsular kingdoms to Donna Maria and Donna Isabella, to the exclusion of Don Miguel in the one case and Don Carlos in the other. The Duke of Wellington disapproved of this settlement, as he did of the whole train of circumstances which led to it, believing them to have established a precedent which England hereafter might find extremely inconvenient to herself, and to be a direct violation of those principles of international law to which this country was pledged, and which afforded, in his opinion, the best guarantees for the peace and happiness of Europe.

In a very interesting letter, published in the *Croker Correspondence*, dated September 30, 1833, the Duke supplies Croker with a very clear statement of his own views on the Belgian question, which Croker afterwards expanded in the *Quarterly Review*. The Duke was of opinion that the union of Holland and Belgium was more likely to secure the latter from falling into the hands of France than the creation of an independent Belgian Sovereignty. But he seems to have underrated the difficulties attending the restoration of the Kingdom of the Netherlands, while the continued existence in Belgium of a disappointed and rebellious faction would have been a standing temptation to the French Revolutionaries. At the same time it must be remembered that, whenever there is a war in Europe, Belgium at once becomes a source of great anxiety to England; and that this could hardly have happened had the original arrangement been maintained. France might incorporate Belgium; but she could hardly have appropriated the whole united kingdom which was created at the Peace.

The Duke's opinions on the Eastern Question from 1825–31 are fully unfolded in his *Supplementary De-*

spatches, especially in a memorandum of November 1830, comparing the Protocol of April 1826 with the Treaty of July 1827,* and in a letter to Lord Aberdeen, October 11th, 1829, on the Treaty of Adrianople.† It had been Mr. Canning's object, in which the Duke heartily concurred, to prevent Russia from becoming the ally of Greece, and therefore to fix the terms for a settlement of the Greek question, to which the contracting Powers should be obliged, under any circumstances, to refer, *before* war should break out between Russia and Turkey. This object was successfully accomplished by the Duke in the Protocol negotiated at St. Petersburg in the spring of 1826. But he thought its provisions were endangered by the Treaty of London, into which the Protocol was converted by Mr. Canning in the following summer, and to which His Grace was no party. It introduced the element of force into a question which had hitherto been kept free from it, and precipitated some of those very consequences which the Protocol had been intended to avert. He pointed out very clearly, the difference between the two. The Protocol was founded on a request from one of the belligerents. The treaty was forced on the contending parties from without. The complaints of piracy might be true ; but then all the pirates were Greeks.‡ And if the existence of piracy forced "burdensome measures of protection" on the neutral Powers, what maritime war in the world, asked the Duke of Wellington, had not had that effect. The other nations of Europe, from 1801–1805, might just as well have insisted on England making an armistice with France. But the culminating absurdity was that, while the pretext for the armistice was piracy, it

---

* Vol. vii. p. 335.   † Vol. vi. p. 212.
‡ Finlay's *History of Greek Revolution*, vol. ii. p. 178.

was enforced against the Turks, who were not pirates, and not against the Greeks, who were. A Turkish squadron was destroyed by the Greeks while the armistice was actually in force, without the Allied Powers taking any notice of it. The battle of Navarino, which, by depriving Turkey of the command of the sea, left the coast route open to the Russians in the war which followed, was one of the direct results of this policy, an event which did not seem untoward only to the Duke of Wellington or the Tories, but was lamented by Lord Grey himself, who thought the Turks were abundantly justified. " Let us make the case our own," he said, " and consider how we ourselves should have acted."[*]

After the battle of Navarino, October 26, 1827, the Sultan, who had never finally agreed to the Treaty of London, refused to discuss it any further ; and the Ambassadors of the three Powers—England, France, and Austria—quitted Constantinople.[†] In August 1828 a French force compelled Ibrahim to evacuate the Morea ; and after languishing four years longer, the war was finally concluded in 1832. In February 1828 war had broken out between Russia and Turkey unconnected with the events in Greece; and the insurgents received considerable assistance from the Russians, who connived at the perpetration of the most frightful horrors by their co-religionists. The Treaty of Adrianople, September 1829, compelled Turkey to accept the Treaty of London, and shortly afterwards she evacuated Eastern Greece.

On the war between Russia and Turkey, the Duke's remarks are very striking. In the letter which I have mentioned, after pointing out that Russia, at the outset of the campaign, had declared her intention of adhering to the terms of the Treaty of London, and of seeking no territorial advantage from the results of the war, he comments very severely on the terms of peace, and the great territorial advantage which, in spite of her disclaimer, Russia had actually extorted ;* and, seeing in these conditions the virtual destruction of Ottoman independence, thinks " it would have been more fortunate, and better for the world, if the Treaty of Peace had not been signed, if the Russians had entered Constantinople, and the Turkish Empire been dissolved." In that case the great Powers could have decided on the distribution of its spoils, so as to prevent Russia from taking the lion's share, which hereafter they might find more difficult.

Of the Duke's Foreign Policy in general the principles were Conservative but not despotic. They were the principles of one trained in the stern school of revolutionary warfare to look with suspicion on all popular violence, and long accustomed to place sentiment and philanthropy lower in the scale of obligations than respect for public law and equal dealing between nation and nation. It was these which he thought were threatened by the Liberalism of the age in which he lived, and he knew the Courts of Europe too well not to know that the louder they talked of Christianity and humanity, the more likely they were to be contemplating some fresh inroad on the rights or liberties of their neighbours. It was from no want of sympathy with the Greeks that he shrank from the policy of enforcing the armistice required by the Treaty of London, but because he could not bring himself to disregard, under any circumstances, the treaties which existed between England and

* *Despatches*, vol. vi. pp. 167, 212.

Turkey, treaties described by Mr. Canning, in words which we have already quoted,* as " of very ancient date, and of uninterrupted obligation, which the Turks had faithfully observed." And he thought that, in the long run, mankind would suffer more from the breach of such engagements as these than from modes of government which, perhaps, seemed harsher than they really were, and which time and civilization were constantly tending to ameliorate.

His object was to act on fixed principles founded on considerations of general policy and justice, and accepted as a basis of action by the other great Powers of the world. That sympathy with any given people in a particular struggle should be allowed to interfere with the operation of these general maxims was contrary to his conception of statesmanship. If they worked in the long run for the good of all, they must not be neglected in the interests of one, whoever it might be, prince, people, or both together, who sought to be exempt from their control. In a word, he wished to see the intercourse of nations subject to the authority of law, and not to the caprice of passion. That cases of injustice and oppression must occur under all systems of human law, whether affecting the rights of individuals or the rights of nations, seemed to him no reason for dispensing with them. Civilization, with all the wrongs which the worst laws are capable of inflicting, is better than barbarism with none at all. And Europe under a general code, which might occasionally favour despotism, was better than Europe abandoned to the dictates of impulse, and unable to invoke any recognized principle or common bond against the march of ambition. Wellington's personal sympathies may have leaned in one direction and Canning's in another. But sitting on the

* Canning to Greek Deputies, 1825. *Life*, vol. ii. p. 444. *Cf.* p. 164.

bench, both were equally prepared to administer impartial justice according to established rules.

In judging of the Tory foreign policy, moreover, we must never forget the extreme views by which it was confronted, which hardly, indeed, stopped short of the propagandism of the French Convention. England, said Sir James Mackintosh and Sir Francis Burdett, was charged with a great mission towards the nations of Europe. The French Revolution was the counterpart of the German Reformation, of which Queen Elizabeth took the lead; and what she in her day did for Protestantism, England in their own was equally bound to do for Liberalism. Canning had no difficulty in disposing of that argument. Elizabeth, he said, was herself among the revolters from the Papacy: England, in the nineteenth century, was not among the revolters from Absolutism. We had fought that fight; we had taken our station. Our situation was what Elizabeth's would have been " had the Church of England in her day already been established in uncontested supremacy, acknowledged and unassailable by the Papal Power. Could anyone suppose that in that case she would not have played a very different part?" England, therefore, had nothing to do with revolution, or with wars of opinion. Her only mission was mediation. This was the position which the Tory Party, whether by the mouth of Castlereagh, Canning, or Wellington, were strenuous in defending, and which the Whigs were in such a hurry to abandon. As soon as they were seated in office, they became avowed partisans; and though Lord Grey privately protested, Lord Palmerston's energy prevailed, and lent a stimulus to the revolutionary movement throughout Europe which he lived to regret, and which cost us far more valuable friendships than any which it gained for us. In their haste to reverse the policy of their predecessors, the Whigs created a coldness between England and her old allies, which, had Sir Robert Peel been able to maintain himself in power in 1835, he would probably have removed, but of which, as it was, we long continued to feel the effects, if it did not virtually entail upon us the burden of the Crimean War.

CHAPTER V.

SIR ROBERT PEEL AND THE " GREAT CONSERVATIVE
PARTY." 1835 AND 1885.

IT is now just half a century since the dissolution of
the first reformed Parliament had shown how rapidly and
strongly the tide of reaction was setting in against the
Radical tendencies of the first Reform Bill. On the 29th
of January 1833, the Tory Party which took 'ts seat on
the Opposition benches counted only one hundred and
forty-nine members. On the 19th of February 1835, they
numbered two hundred and fifty. The General Election
in January had given them a hundred seats, while the
large number of Moderate Liberals inclined to keep Sir
Robert Peel in office reduced Lord John Russell's majorities, on more than one critical occasion, to a very low ebb.
As comparisons have been very freely instituted between
the condition of the Tory Party in 1835 and its condition in 1885, I shall make no apology for treating the
earlier part of Sir Robert Peel's career with some brevity,
that we may be able to dwell more fully on those incidents
of his life which appear to bear more particularly on the
political situation of the present day. Could the founder

of the great Conservative Party, and the author of the Tamworth Manifesto, rise from the dead at this moment, what would he have to say to Lord Salisbury, Lord Iddesleigh, Sir Michael Hicks-Beach, and Lord Randolph Churchill ?

Sir Robert Peel was born on the 5th of February 1788, near Bury in Lancashire. He was educated at Harrow and Christ Church, and took a double first in Michaelmas Term 1808. In the following year he entered the House of Commons as member for Cashel, and in 1811 became Under-Secretary for the Colonies. From 1812 to 1818 he was Chief Secretary for Ireland, in which office his anti-Catholic proclivities were so conspicuous that he acquired the soubriquet of "Orange Peel." O'Connell attacked him so violently that Peel was forced to send him a challenge, and the duel was only prevented by the interposition of the police. He had early won for himself a reputation on commercial and financial subjects, and in 1819 was appointed Chairman of the Bank Committee, which led to the resumption of cash payments. In 1817 he had been chosen to represent the University of Oxford, and in the same year he made his great speech against the Removal of the Roman Catholic Disabilities, which Mr. Charles Butler and Mr. Grattan both thought the ablest argument ever delivered on that side of the question. No wonder that after this he became the recognized leader of the Protestant interest, as it was absurdly called, in the House of Commons. In 1818 he retired from the Government, but re-entered it again as Home Secretary in 1822, when Canning, the leader of the Roman Catholic interest, became Foreign Secretary. Then was witnessed the curious spectacle of the two leading members of the Cabinet in the same House of Parliament replying to each other on the most critical public question of the day.

Down to 1825 no impression seems to have been made on the powerful and compact body which represented the anti-Catholic section of the Tories, and, as there is no reason to doubt, the majority of the English people.* Resolutions in favour of the Roman Catholics had been carried more than once by the combined votes of the Whigs and of the Tories who represented Mr. Pitt; but it was not till 1825, when Sir Francis Burdett moved and carried a Resolution to the same effect by a majority of thirteen, that rumours began to circulate regarding the firmness of Lord Liverpool. Lord Liverpool told Lord Colchester that there was no ground for such reports; but it is certain that, for some reason or other, Mr. Peel at this time was desirous of resigning, and that correspondence on the subject passed between himself and Lord Liverpool. It has been conjectured that in some inclination on the part of the Government to take the question into consideration is to be found the solution of the mystery which so perplexed the House of Commons in 1846, when reference was made to a speech of Sir Edward Knatchbull in 1829, from which it appeared that, in announcing his change of views to Parliament in that year, Mr. Peel had mentioned that he had begun to waver on the subject as early as 1825; and the *Edinburgh Review* (1829) declared that, while assuring Mr. Canning, in 1827, that his sole reason for not acting with him was his unchanged opinion on the Catholic Question, Mr. Peel had in his desk at home a copy of a letter written to Lord Liverpool

---

* "The Catholic question," said Canning, "must win, not force, its way."

in 1825, confessing that he doubted if the Roman Catholic Disabilities could be much longer maintained. There seems little doubt that in 1829 Mr. Peel did say something of the kind, though he denied all recollection of it in 1846. The words attributed to Sir E. Knatchbull are to be found in the *Mirror of Parliament*, though not in Hansard, and could not have been invented, nor did Mr. Peel challenge them. It has been thought, therefore, that when it first became known to or suspected by the Home Secretary that Lord Liverpool entertained the idea of yielding, he at once tendered his resignation, and that on this intention being combatted by his chief he may have written a letter consenting to remain in office, and making admissions capable of being construed into a qualified assent to the consideration of the subject by the Cabinet. This is the ingenious hypothesis put forward by the late Mr. Maddyn in his *Chiefs of Parties*, a book that deserves to be better known, and I confess that I know of no other solution of the difficulty equally consistent with acknowledged facts and with the character of Sir Robert Peel.

But the reconciliation of his speech in 1846 with his speech in 1829 is not necessarily a defence of his behaviour to Mr. Canning. Whatever view may be taken of the progress of his own opinions, it will never hereafter be believed that they constituted the sole bar to his junction with his former colleague. They may have constituted the only objection that was based on public grounds, the only one that could be taken into account in a Parliamentary explanation of his conduct. But the General Election of 1826 had been favourable to the " Protestant interest." On the 6th of March 1827, the House of Commons, which, in 1825, had passed Sir F. Burdett's Resolution by a majority of thirteen, threw it out by a majority of four.

16

Things were not as they had been two years before. It was by no means certain that the present system might not last for many years. Would it be well for Mr. Peel to compromise his position as leader of this great party, and to surrender the only distinction which gave him a station of his own in the House of Commons, and placed him on a footing of equality with Canning himself? It might be true enough that it was only the Roman Catholic question which prevented him from joining Mr. Canning. But it was the Roman Catholic question with a circumstance—as it affected the prospects of Mr. Peel.

It may be said, upon the other hand, that his personal interests only coincided with his public duty: that he was very properly unwilling to throw up the leadership of a great cause until he was convinced that it was hopeless; and that a doubt of its ultimate success was no reason for surrender while a chance still remained. For Sir Robert, be it remembered, was never converted to the principle of Roman Catholic Emancipation as he was converted to the principles of Free Trade, and this is a distinction which is too often lost sight of. To the last he entertained the same opinions as he had expressed in 1817. He simply bowed to the inevitable. The real question is, at what precise point in the history of the question he first made the admission to his own mind that it *was* inevitable. This we shall probably never know; yet it is the one thing that it is necessary to know before we can pronounce any final judgment on his conduct. If he had arrived at this conclusion before the retirement of Lord Liverpool, the verdict would certainly be against him; if not till 1828, he would be entitled to an acquittal.

But whatever the explanation of his own conduct, the

effect on his party was the same; and on this point I can add nothing to what has been already said in my chapter on the Duke of Wellington.

Sir Robert Peel, who succeeded to the baronetcy at the death of his father in 1831, was as little a convert to Parliamentary Reform as to Roman Catholic Emancipation. He shared all the Duke of Wellington's expectations of its probable results, which seem, after all, only to have been postponed; and his refusal to assist in the formation of a Tory Government in May 1832 must always remain, to my mind, a more ambiguous passage in his life than the affairs of either 1829 or 1846. It is a moot point to this hour whether at that stage of the contest any effectual resistance could still have been offered by the Tories. Lord Brougham thought that it could, and Lord Lyndhurst and the Duke doubtless thought so too. Croker was of the same opinion, and the main obstacle to the trial of the experiment was Sir Robert Peel, who, however, did not think it must necessarily be a failure. The Party came to the conclusion that if a Government could be formed, with a good man at the head of it in the House of Commons, prepared to bring in a moderate measure of Reform, the attempt might be successful. It was thought that the Duke was disqualified for the Premiership by his memorable declaration against all reform, which would prejudice the country against his Government before it had a fair trial. He did not consider for a moment what might be said about himself, but he saw that, for the public good, it was better Peel should be the chief. Sir Robert, however, steadily refused either to lead or to join a new Government which should recognize the principle of reform. And then for a season the Duke was accepted as the head. Again, however, his Reform pledges were thought to stand in the way; and finally the Speaker, Manners Sutton, with Peel's approval, agreed to take the Treasury, with Alexander Baring, afterwards Lord Ashburton, as Chancellor of the Exchequer. This arrangement seems to have broken down, not so much in consequence of Lord Ebrington's Resolution in the House of Commons, as through the astounding blunder committed by Mr. Baring himself, who, either suddenly losing his head, or suddenly repenting of his engagement, announced to a tumultuous and angry House of Commons that he regarded the resignation of the late Government as a great calamity, and that if they would consent to return and carry the Bill, without swamping the House of Lords, he, for one, would do nothing to interfere with them. This singular statement on the part of one who had just accepted high office in the proposed new Ministry, combined with symptoms of mutiny among the ultra-Tories, who cheered Sir Robert Inglis loudly when he protested against the adoption of Reform by any administration with which the Duke of Wellington was connected, was what really gave the *coup de grâce* to the last expiring struggle of the old Constitution; and not Lord Ebrington's Resolution, which was only the ostensible pretext for abandoning the field of battle. On this point Croker's evidence is conclusive. "We all agreed that Baring had been indiscreet, and that the proposal which he had made must end in the return of the Whigs. Inglis spoke so low that I did not well hear what he said; but Peel considered it fatal and conclusive against any Government to be formed by any class of anti-Reformers." It was all over. Troy was taken.

Danaique obsessa tenebant
Limina portarum nec spes opis ulla dabatur.

The Lords retired from the contest and the ancient *régime* was dead.

Was Sir Robert Peel, then, justified in his refusal to join the Duke of Wellington in a final effort to mitigate or avert this consummation ? This is, in my opinion, one of the most interesting questions which the great Reform Question has bequeathed to us. In the Croker papers we have a full record of the whole maze of negotiations and consultations which took place among the Tory leaders in that memorable month of May, and the only conclusion we can arrive at is that Sir Robert committed a grave error. Croker himself, be it premised, refused also to join in the attempt ; but then Croker, in 1830, had publicly declared that he would never again take office, and he considered himself more particularly bound by his connection with Lord Hertford. But he did not recognize the existence of the same difficulties in Peel's case, and the letter which he wrote to him on the 11th of May seems, to myself at least, unanswerable. Peel did not refuse because he thought any such attempt must necessarily break down, for he said that he thought that Manners Sutton might have succeeded. He refused, he said, because he was unwilling to play over again the part which he played on the Catholic Question, and the part which he was again to play on the Corn Law Question. But the part he was required to take in 1832, while not so damaging to his character as what he actually consented to do in 1829 and in 1846, was more urgently demanded by the public good, as Peel himself understood it. The sacrifice to be made was much smaller, and the object to be gained was much larger. Reform was a question of degree of more or less ; and though the King made a condition that the new Bill should be a real reform, he did not stipulate positively for the retention of Schedules A and B. Thus it was quite within Peel's power to introduce a measure which should have been comparatively Conservative; and surely any limitation whatever of a scheme which he considered so iniquitous would have better become a Conservative statesman than an attitude of absolute, and therefore impotent, antagonism which left it to become law with all its evils undiminished. To modify, moderate, or deflect what we have been defeated in our efforts to prevent, is not, under ordinary circumstances, considered any violation of consistency. Where was the difference in principle between bringing in a new Reform Bill and trying to amend the old one? A Conservative Bill would have been really only a Conservative amendment.

If Lord Grey returns [said Croker], see what must happen! the King enslaved, the House of Lords degraded, the Bill passed—the Revolution, I may say, consummated. And what will be your consolation then? The poor and negative one that you have maintained an apparent consistency in not having touched, even with a view of diverting it, the fatal instrument of the mischief. But the consistency will be only apparent. The real consistency would be that, as you did all that was possible to avert the danger, so now, when it is inevitable, you should exert every effort to mitigate and diminish it.

This reasoning was so conclusive that even Peel, it is said, was for a moment staggered. But he still held out. "He was," he said, "peculiarly circumstanced; he had been obliged to arrange the Catholic Question by a sacrifice of his own judgment, and he would not now perform the same painful abandonment of opinion on the Reform Question. He talked of the advantage to the country that public men should maintain a character for consistency and disinterestedness, which he would for ever forfeit if a second time he were on any pretence to act over again anything like his part in the Catholic Question." But if Sir Robert Peel had said virtually to the

public, It is true I am as much opposed to Parliamentary
Reform at this moment as I was on the day it was proposed; but we have been beaten in a fair fight, the people
have unmistakably pronounced in favour of it, and I am
willing to try, therefore, whether something rather less
sweeping, and retaining more securities for the stability
of the Constitution than the Bill introduced by Lord Grey,
may not find favour with the country,—could anyone have
reproached him with dishonesty?

Peel himself thought he was in a worse position for
changing front in '32 than he had been in '29. I cannot
see it. "I was then," he said, "in office. I had advised
the concession as a Minister. I should now assume
office for the purpose of carrying the measure to which,
up to the last moment, I have been inveterately opposed." So far from being able to follow this reasoning,
I should rather say that his position in 1829 made
matters worse instead of better. He does not seem to
have seen that between carrying out a policy to which we
have previously been opposed, after it has been floated
by others, and is practically irreversible, and being ourselves the initiators of it, while we have still the power
to prevent it, the difference is enormous. To embark
upon a bad system is one thing; to endeavour to make
the best of it, when its original authors have already
carried it so far that it is more dangerous to recede than
to advance, is another. A statesman suddenly entrusted
with the vessel of the State under these circumstances must
make the public interest his sole guide, and bring himself
to see that there may be a higher consistency in adhering
to this rule of conduct than in clinging to convictions of
which the progress of events has made the application impossible. When certain great points have been surren-

dered others may become questions of expediency; and principles which worked for good as long as they could be maintained in their integrity, it may be better to abandon altogether than to preserve in a diluted form, or when neutralized by measures of counteraction. Statesmen, however, cannot decide these questions till they are absolutely in possession of power, and can take a comprehensive survey of affairs from the higher elevation which it affords. They may then discover that they can do more for the public interest, in the long run, by remaining in power to carry out what they have formerly opposed than by leaving the work to others, who would only take advantage of the credit of these particular measures to push forward others of a more sweeping and subversive character. This was the opinion of the Duke of Wellington in 1832, and again in 1846, a man whose sense of duty has almost passed into a proverb, and whose personal honour and disinterested patriotism are equally unimpeachable. In acting as he did, Sir Robert, as I have elsewhere stated, was straining at the gnat after having swallowed the camel.

Lord Beaconsfield is of opinion that all the inconsistencies in his career will yield to one master key, and that is, his secret anxiety to escape from the section of the Tory Party to which he had attached himself almost as soon as he had joined it.

That age of economical statesmanship which Lord Shelburne had predicted in 1787, when he demolished, in the House of Lords, Bishop Watson and the Balance of Trade, which Mr. Pitt had comprehended, and for which he was preparing the nation when the French Revolution diverted the public mind into a stronger and more turbulent current, was again impending, while the intervening history of the country had been prolific in events which had aggravated the necessity of investigating the sources of the wealth of nations. The time had arrived when parliamentary pre-eminence could no longer be achieved or maintained by gorgeous abstractions borrowed from Burke, or shallow systems purloined from De Lolme, adorned with Horatian points, or varied with Virgilian passages. It was to be an age of abstruse disquisition, that required a compact and sinewy intellect, nurtured in a class of learning not yet honoured in colleges, and which might arrive at conclusions conflicting with predominant prejudices.*

Mr. Peel we are to suppose, in 1818, understood this, and saw that his colleagues did not understand it. He was anxious, therefore, to stand aloof for a while from men who were behind their age, to watch the course of events, and fit himself for taking a lead whenever the new dispensation should begin to evolve itself. " He broke loose from Lord Liverpool;† he retired from Mr. Canning; and believed, in 1830, that he had accomplished his emancipation from the Duke of Wellington." The hypothesis is ingenious; but we must remember that Lord Beaconsfield puts it forward only as a conjecture—a charitable mode of explaining conduct which must otherwise remain " ambiguous," not as a theory based on any actual evidence, but as one possible solution of a difficult problem, consistent with Sir Robert Peel's character, and deriving some confirmation from the later events of his life. But, to say nothing of the fact that many years afterwards he spoke of his long connection with the Duke of Wellington as the pride and glory of his life, it obviously cannot explain his anxiety to leave a Government, or his refusal to join a Government, containing men like Mr. Huskisson and Mr. Canning; nor, we must say, can we discover the slightest traces of any such political foresight as Lord Beaconsfield attributes to him, either in his speeches or his correspondence, or any of the innumerable anecdotes relating to him to be found in the memoirs of the period. Here he always appears

* *Coningsby*, bk. ii. ch. i.

† Peel resigned the Irish Secretaryship in 1818. But that was due rather to the quarrel with O'Connell than his discontent with the Government.

as the model Tory of the time; a wealthy and liberal country gentleman, an accomplished classical scholar, a lover and patron of art, with enlightened views on the currency and the criminal code; an excellent administrator, and a sound man of business, but a devoted adherent of the existing Constitution; less advanced than some of his colleagues in political economy; a Protectionist and a Protestant to the backbone; rather prone to Virgilian quotations than averse from them, and showing no outward signs of the "class of learning not honoured in colleges," which he is supposed to have been the first to appreciate. He may have meant much more when he shook his head at the Duke of Wellington, and shook his head at Mr. Canning. But if he did, it was a good many years before he let the public know it.

It has always seemed to me that pique played a considerable part in the decisions of Sir Robert Peel. When he tendered his resignation to Lord Liverpool in consequence of Sir Francis Burdett's motion being carried in 1825, it is difficult to doubt that he was influenced by some personal irritation. The last time such a measure had been carried he was not a member of the Government. He was annoyed at the King's decision in 1827; and it seems almost certain that in 1832 he had taken offence at something. Grenville, in his Diary of October 26, 1832, records in his own words what he picked up from Mr. Arbuthnot relating to the May negotiations when he met him at Downham in the autumn. Peel had "put Sutton up" to demanding the Premiership.

On Saturday the great dinner at the Conservative Club took place, at which a number of Tories, principally Peers, with the Duke and Peel, were present. A great many speeches were made, all full of enthusiasm for the Duke, and expressing a determination to support his Government. Peel was in very ill humour and said little; the Duke spoke much in honour of Peel, applauding his conduct, and saying that the difference of their positions justified each in his different line. The next day some of the Duke's friends met, and agreed that the unanimous desire for the Duke's being at the head of the Government which had been expressed at that dinner, together with the unfitness of Sutton, proved the absolute necessity of the Duke's being Premier, and it was resolved that a communication to this effect should be made to Peel. Aberdeen charged himself with it and went to Peel's house, where Sutton was at the time. Peel came to Aberdeen in a very bad humour; said he saw, from what had passed at the dinner, that nobody was thought of but the Duke, and he should wash his hands of the whole business; that he had already declined having anything to do with the Government, and to that determination he should adhere. The following Monday the whole thing was at an end. I am not sure that I have stated these occurrences exactly as they were told me. There may be errors in the order of the interviews and pourparlers, and in the verbal details, but the substance is correct, and may be summed up to the effect that Peel, full of ambition, but of caution, animated by deep dislike and jealousy of the Duke (which policy induced him to conceal, but which temper betrayed), thought to make Manners Sutton play the part of Addington, while he was to be another Pitt; he fancied that he could gain in political character, by an opposite line of conduct, all that the Duke would lose; and he resolved that a Government should be formed, the existence of which should depend upon himself. Manners Sutton was to be his creature; he would have dictated every measure of Government; he would have been their protector in the House of Commons, and, as soon as the fitting moment arrived, he would have dissolved this miserable Ministry and placed himself at the head of affairs. All these deep-laid schemes, and constant regard of self, form a strong contrast to the simplicity and heartiness of the Duke's conduct, and make the two men appear in a very different light from that in which they did at first! Peel acted right from bad motives, the Duke wrong from good ones. The Duke put himself forward, and encountered all the obloquy and reproach to which he knew he exposed himself, and, having done so, cheerfully offered to resign the power to another. Peel endeavoured to seize the power, but to shield himself from the responsibility and danger.

I think it probable, however, that in 1832 Sir Robert had too hastily come to the conclusion that the game was lost, and that no substantial improvement in the general character of the Reform Bill was any longer possible. I have already combatted this idea, but it swayed Sir Robert Peel without doubt, notwithstanding the fact that he said he thought a Tory Government might succeed under Manners

Sutton. He may, perhaps, have been willing that another should try the experiment from which he shrank himself; while he stood by without any responsibility for the result, secure of being called in if it turned out successful, and safe from the odium of the attempt if it proved a failure. This was said of him at the time; but I cannot say that I believe it. It seems to me that after 1831 he had made up his mind that further resistance was useless, and that the best thing to be done was to find some way of providing a breakwater against the wave of revolution flowing in upon us. The less resistance that was offered to the Reform Bill, when this conclusion had once been arrived at, the better.

The history of the first reformed Parliament is, I fancy, very little known. A good deal has been written about it, but it is not very much read. The Whigs had called into existence a new power which they were totally unable to control, and the Session of 1833 had hardly commenced ere Lord Grey found himself virtually in the same position in which Lord Palmerston found himself thirty years afterwards—compelled to rely for his existence on the support of the Conservatives. Neither the Irish Coercion Bill nor the Irish Church Bill could possibly have been carried had Sir Robert Peel chosen to oppose them; and his opposition to the Church Bill was only disarmed by concessions[*] which infuriated both the Radicals and the Repealers. The "tame and ineffective"[†] speech in which Lord Althorpe introduced the one, and the singular blunders which appeared in the draught of the other, did not tend to mitigate the unpopularity of either measure with a large section of the Liberals.

---

[*] Walpole's *History of England*, vol. iii. pp. 159–62.

[†] Lord Russell's *Recollections*, p 112.

If we were all of one mind [said Lord Holland], our course would be plain enough; but with Stanley's views on the nature of Church property, we are obliged to resort to fallacies to obtain his support to Liberal measures. Everything is in confusion. We dare not make public our measures before they are brought forward, lest we should alter them afterwards. There is no certainty in our councils, and I fear there will be no public confidence in them.

If the reader will turn to the correspondence of Sir Robert Peel with Mr. Croker, he will find abundant evidence that, partly owing to the actual incapacity of the Liberal Ministry, partly to the gulf which yawned between the Whigs and the Radicals, the probability of the Conservatives returning to office as early as 1833 was seriously entertained even by Sir Robert Peel himself. On Wednesday the 27th of February Lord Althorpe introduced the Coercion Bill, and for a full account of the debate we refer the reader to Lord Russell. But a few days afterwards Sir Robert Peel wrote the following letter :—

Now for the House of Commons. It is a good one to speak to, but that circumstance does not diminish my fear of it. It is not the suggestion of confidence and vanity, but it is the sober truth, when I tell you that on Friday night I could have moved it just the other way. Perhaps not Friday * night, but on Wednesday night, if I had chosen to follow Lord Althorpe, with his lame accounts of providing for Crown witnesses with good places in the police; of some man who had actually received a *threat* that his winnowing machine should be burnt; nay, of a clergyman who absolutely had panes of glass broken—if I had followed him, given an account of English crimes within the same period, and asked, as Perceval once asked of an excited House of Commons, in the language of true eloquence, " Will you hang a dog on such evidence ? " I could have trampled the Bill to dust. What does this show ? That there is no steadiness in the House ; that it is subject to any impulse, that the force of party connections, by which alone a Government can hope to pursue a consistent course, is quite paralysed. Three times already, with reference to three different measures, the Government has said, in the most childish manner, that if hot pressed they intend to resign.

My belief is that the Reform Bill has worked for three weeks solely from this, that the Conservatives have been too honest to unite with the Radicals

* Walpole, vol. iii. p. 154.

They might have united ten times without a sacrifice of principle. They might unite on twenty clauses of the Irish Bill.

And what is to happen then? The question is not, Can you turn out a Government? but, Can you keep in any Government and stave off confusion?

What must be the value of that change in the Constitution which rests for its success upon the forbearance and abstinence of parties? which intended to sacrifice the Tories as a party, which appeared to have sacrificed them, and which now appeals to them as a protection, almost the sole protection, from anarchy.

What are we doing at this moment? We are making the Reform Bill work; we are falsifying our own predictions, which would be realised without our active interference; we are protecting the authors of the evil from the work of their own hands. It is right we should do this, but I must say that it was expecting more than human institutions, intended to govern the unruly passions and corrupt natures of human beings, ought to calculate upon.

On the 25th of March 1833, Croker records a conversation with Sir Robert Peel, in which he found him

apparently resolved to accept office and make battle. He spoke with great firmness and spirit, said he would do his duty, and, if necessary, venture to attempt a Ministry. He would try whether Government could be carried on, and after a fair experiment he, at least, would have done his part. I gave him no encouragement, having no hope myself, but I could not deny that what he said was reasonable. He seemed to think there would be an entirely new combination, of which the Currency questions would be the basis. On that he was firm, but foresaw that Radicals and ultra-Tories would unite against him.

In the following April Sir John Key, one of the Members for the City, had given notice of an Amendment to the Budget, repealing the house and window tax; but before it came on Sir William Ingleby interposed with a resolution for abolishing one half of the Malt Tax, which was carried by a majority of ten, totally upsetting Lord Althorpe's financial calculations. This was on the 25th of April. On the 30th Croker wrote to Lord Hertford as follows :—

I told you that six weeks ago I dined at Lady Dysart's with Burdett, and that he was talking Conservative language, and of his own difficulties about *assessed taxes*. In the course of our talk I told him that I saw the chance of an earlier and more dangerous question than the *assessed taxes*—the *Malt Tax*. "Some fine evening," I said, "when no one expects it, Sir William

Ingleby will move the repeal of the Malt Tax and carry it by a small majority, and you will be all astonished next morning to find yourselves with a deficit of five millions and a half in your revenue, and reduced to a Property Tax, or, in other words, confiscation." Such were my very words, remembered by all the parties present; and, lo! on Friday evening, no one expecting it, Sir William Ingleby got up and moved the repeal of half the malt duty, carries it by a small majority, and throws the Budget, the Ministry, and the revenue, on their beam-ends. When the majority was declared, Althorpe, with that stupidity which has been called candour, declared that he " *bowed* to the decision of the House"; but his colleagues had soon sense enough to see that the bowing to the decision of the House was no such easy matter; that bowing to the loss of two and a half millions of malt would involve the loss of the whole five millions of malt, and the three millions of assessed taxes, for the repeal of which there is a motion pending for to-night, and that the loss of eight millions, with great doubts whether a Property Tax *can* be passed, was national bankruptcy. Their first thought, founded on Althorpe's silly readiness to bow, was to give up the whole malt and assessed taxes, and to try a Property Tax; their second, I believe, was to resign; their third was to endeavour to get the House to rescind Ingleby's resolution; and this they adopted—thereunto, I opine, much induced by an intimation which Peel sent them that he would support them in that course with all his strength.

The matter ended by Lord Althorpe proposing a Resolution declaring that the reduction of the malt tax and the repeal of the assessed taxes together would create a deficiency only to be met by a property tax, which it was inexpedient to adopt. This Resolution, with the help of the Tory Party, was carried by a majority of 198, and the Budget was safe. But it was abundantly clear that, but for the help thus afforded them by the Tories, the Liberal Government must soon share the fate of Actæon, and in the following year, when that help was withdrawn, their curse came upon them. The inherent weakness of all Whig-Radical Governments then for the first time became apparent; and as soon as the present one ventured to exceed the limits which the Opposition had prescribed, it tottered and fell.

The Church Bill of 1833, with the Conservative amend-

ments above mentioned,* had been accepted by Sir Robert
Peel as a necessary evil. It provided for the extinction of
ten bishoprics, of church cess, tithes, and first-fruits, the
income derived from the latter to be made up partly
from the income of the extinct sees partly by a tax
upon all benefices above the value of £200 a year.
The Appropriation Clause, enacting that any increase
of revenue accruing to the Irish Church from the im-
proved management of Church property might be appropriated to secular purposes, had been withdrawn on the
motion of Mr. Stanley, and the Bill was read a third
time in the House of Lords on the 30th of July. In
1834, however, the Appropriation question was revived in
the Tithes Bill introduced by Mr. Littleton, when Lord
John Russell thought it necessary to reaffirm the principle which had been surrendered in 1833. The confusion
which this sudden and unnecessary declaration carried
into the Whig ranks has been commemorated by an
historic metaphor. And, though the difficulty was got
over for the moment by the appointment of a Church
Commission, it appeared again directly, as soon as it was
announced that it should not be inconsistent with the
duties of that Commission to recommend the alienation
of Church property to lay uses. In the debate on this
subject, both Mr. Stanley and Sir Robert Peel spoke
strongly against the alienation of Church property; and
it is necessary to mention this more particularly because
it has been confidently asserted that Sir Robert Peel
assented in this speech to the secularization of the
Church property in Ireland. He did nothing of the kind.
He admitted, as Mr. Stanley did too, the right of Par-

* P. 252. The principal of these was the elimination of the Appropriation
Clause.

liament to redistribute ecclesiastical revenues within the pale of ecclesiastical purposes. But he never, either then or thereafter, swerved from his protest against any other application of them.

The Appropriation clause led to the resignation of the ablest man in the Ministry, Lord Stanley,* and with him of the Duke of Richmond, Lord Ripon, and Sir James Graham. This was followed early in July by the resignation of Lord Grey himself, in consequence of a split in the Cabinet on the subject of the Irish Coercion Bill. O'Connell had been led to believe, by some mistake of Mr. Littleton, the Chief Secretary for Ireland, that the Coercion Act of the previous year would not be renewed; and on the strength of this intimation supported the Whig candidate for Wexford. When, therefore, the Bill was introduced by Lord Althorpe, his indignation may easily be imagined. None saw more clearly than Lord Althorpe himself that the Ministry could never recover from this second blow. "The pig's killed," he whispered to Lord Russell, who was sitting next him. Being implicated in the statement on which O'Connell had relied, he at once resigned office, and Lord Grey, heartily glad to be released from a false position, immediately followed suit. Lord Melbourne was appointed in his place, and Lord Althorpe, being induced, with some difficulty, to resume his post in the House of Commons, the Ministry was patched up; and a modified Coercion Bill being accepted by the House entirely owing to the exertions of Sir Robert Peel, who persuaded his own Party to support it, the session came to an end without any further quarrels or complications.

On Lord Grey's resignation, the King had tried to bring

* He became Lord Stanley by the death of his grandfather in 1834.

about that coalition between the Tories and the Canningite
Whigs to which I have referred further on. Lord Melbourne declined the attempt, chiefly on the ground that he
could not ask the Duke of Wellington, Sir Robert Peel, or
Lord Stanley to concur in the Tithes Bill or in the Irish
Church Commission, and he accordingly kissed hands on
the 16th of July as Premier of a purely Whig Cabinet.
When, therefore, in the following November, the removal
of Lord Althorpe to the Upper House rendered necessary
a re-arrangement of the Cabinet, the King naturally felt
it useless to revert to his original suggestion, and, believing that the Whig-Radical Government was too weak
to last, resolved to fall back on the Conservatives. What
passed between His Majesty and Lord Melbourne on this
occasion only shows how necessary it is to be definite and
explicit in affairs of such delicacy and importance. In
the previous July Lord Melbourne had made the assistance
of Lord Althorpe in the Lower House an indispensable
condition of his own acceptance of office. Without it, he
said, he could not have formed a Government capable of
conducting efficiently the affairs of the country. So
said Lord Grey also. On Lord Spencer's death, the King
understood Lord Melbourne to say that the removal of
Lord Althorpe from the House of Commons destroyed
"the basis" on which the existing administration was
founded. According to his latest biographer,* though he
was now no longer of this opinion, he was too " proud " to
tell the King that he had changed his mind ; so that, when
he named Lord J. Russell as Lord Althorpe's successor,
His Majesty had good reason to doubt whether the experiment would succeed. He decided, no doubt in accordance

* Mr. W. T. M‘Cullagh Torrens.

with his own inclination, that it would not, and at once sent for the Duke of Wellington.

The attempt was premature. The King had over-estimated the force of the Conservative re-action at that particular period. He made a mistake which probably neither George the Third nor Mr. Pitt would have made. He did not allow the Whigs quite rope enough to hang themselves, nor public opinion quite time enough to ripen. But the attempt very narrowly missed of complete success. And the King's perfect right to act as he did has been so successfully established by Sir Robert Peel, that it is unnecessary to say more on that head. I see one reason, and one only, to regret it. The interference of the King checked the reaction for the time, and prevented its fruits from being reaped till 1841 ; whereas, had the Conservatives come back with a majority in 1836 or 1837, their leader would not have been so deeply committed to Protection as he was five years afterwards, and his adoption of Free Trade might have occurred under more favourable circumstances.

Sir Robert was at Rome when the news reached him, and, travelling night and day, he reached London on the 9th of December. His first offers were made to Lord Stanley and his friends, who declined to join the Government for reasons which Sir Robert himself did not think unsatisfactory. On the 17th of December, after the Government was formed, Sir Robert read out to his colleagues the celebrated Tamworth Manifesto, of which "they entirely approved,"* preparatory to the dissolution of Parliament which took place on the 1st of January. To this most important, and now historical State Paper,

* *Memoirs*, vol. ii. p. 58.

some few general remarks must be devoted before proceeding with our memoir.

The Tamworth Manifesto, says Lord Beaconsfield, was "an attempt to construct a party without principles," but he owns that "at an epoch of political perplexity and social alarm the confederation was convenient." It seems to me that Sir Robert Peel had no alternative. In December 1834 a Liberal Government had been in office exactly four years, and within that period, though they had passed two great measures, they had, between the effects of alarm and disgust, forfeited two-thirds of the political capital with which they commenced business. The extravagant revolutionary doctrines broached by many of their supporters, which they dared not disavow, had frightened* the more moderate Liberals who had supported the

---

* See Lord Melbourne's answer to Derby Address, December 2nd, 1834:—
"It would detain me too long, and my strength would hardly suffice, if I were to enter, in any detail, into the causes of the late events. You will not consider me as employing the language of complaint and discontent, but rather that of friendly admonition and advice, if I enumerate amongst them the want of confidence which has often been expressed in quarters from which we expected support, the strong condemnation which has been pronounced upon some of our measures, which I conceive to have been absolutely necessary—the violent subversive opinions which have been declared, and particularly the bitter hostility and ulterior designs against the Established Church, which have been openly avowed by several classes and bodies of Dissenters. When I mention this last opinion, I beg leave to say that I do not condemn those who conscientiously entertain it. It is not my opinion; but I mention it now with reference to its actual effect upon the course of public affairs. These sentiments and this conduct occasioned great alarm in high and powerful quarters; they terrified the timid, they repelled from us the wavering, they rallied men around the institutions which they conceived to be attacked, and they gave life, spirit, and courage to our political adversaries, who, you will recollect, after all, form a very large and powerful party in this country—a party powerful in number, powerful in property, powerful in rank and station, and, allow me to add, a party of a very decided, tenacious, unyielding, and uncompromising character."

Reform Bill, and who now saw in the violence of the Radicals a justification of the worst fears which had been expressed by the Conservatives ; while at the same time the practical incompetence displayed by the Whig Ministers in the House of Commons contrasted with the incontestible superiority of the Opposition leaders, had made their followers ashamed of them. Sir Robert Peel, in his address to the public, had to consider that he was appealing not only to the Conservative Party, but to the whole nation ; and that his object was to attract to himself as many of those Liberals as possible who would have been cordial supporters of the ex-Ministry had it not so miserably falsified all the expectations that had been formed of it. It was useless for him to attempt anything else with a view to real power. And if he did not mean to make a serious bid for power he ought not to have taken office at all.

Sir Robert Peel addressed himself to the new depositaries of power in the only language they could understand : he appealed to their Conservative instincts, their business-like habits, their tenderness of public credit, their respect for property, their love of order and respectability, their dislike of violent innovation, and, above all, to their appreciation of administrative ability. If he was to obtain a majority it could only be by these means ; and though he failed in his immediate object, so strong was the distrust created among all independent Liberals by the demands of the Radicals and the weakness and disunion of the Government, that the practical majority in the new Parliament on which the Ministry could rely was not more than thirty or forty.*

* In the trial divisions which preceded his resignation, Peel several times counted on his side more than 300 votes, *i.e.* on Speakership and Amendment

Sir Robert's ultimate object was to build up a great middle-class barrier, combining popular progress with constitutional principles, against the Radical revolution which seemed imminent; and in this, in my opinion, he entirely succeeded. It is a simple truth that from 1835 to 1865, a period of thirty years, the country was governed throughout on Conservative principles. The revolution was stayed: and that it was so was due, not exclusively, but in a great measure, to the policy of the statesman to whom fell the task of reconstructing the Conservative Party after the great crash.

Peel's position, however, was a much stronger one; the materials at his disposal more abundant and more solid: than might have been supposed from his Parliamentary following. Not only had he contrived to catch up and appropriate to himself, with wonderful tact and readiness, the spirit of the new constituencies—the sentiment of that numerous class which, though bent upon improvement, had never intended that improvement should extend to the overthrow of existing institutions—he represented also what, till within the last three years, had been the dominant system of the country for more than half a century. Long habit, prescriptive right, vested interests, hereditary sympathies, and the reflected glories of the great war were all upon his side. The old faith had been only superficially shaken by the hurricane of reform. It still retained its hold on large masses of the nation. The ideas and traditions of a lifetime were not to be uprooted in a day. When the intoxication of the moment passed off, and England woke up to look reality in the face, she

to Address, and in the three divisions which finally decided the contest the Whig majorities were 33, 25, and 27: and this in a House where the nominal strength of the Conservatives was only 250.

instinctively reverted to the party of order and prescription. Three years, in a word, had been far too short a term in which to consummate a social revolution commensurate with the constitutional revolution which took place in 1832. It had been comparatively easy for the French nation to throw off an upper class which had no connection with the lower, and lay on the surface of society without any anchorage at the bottom. In England the ancient *régime* was entwined with the roots and fibres of the national life, and bound to the hearts of the people by a thousand cords of association, which the revolution had doubtless loosened, but had by no means eradicated.

We see that so late as 1830, to say nothing of an earlier date, it is all but certain that the people would have been contented with a very slight change in their existing system: a change which should only lop off the excrescences without touching the trunk. We know that down to 1829 they would gladly have retained even all the excrescences could they only have purchased immunity from Roman Catholic Emancipation. Neither the temper of mind, nor the political convictions of which these attachments were the offspring, though turned aside for a time by the presence of a great popular movement, could, when the strain was taken off and the Reform Bill an accomplished fact, be prevented from resuming their sway. The time would come when the social change might be co-extensive with the political change. But it had not arrived in 1835. The change in the English people had been much slighter than was supposed; and though enough of the Reform spirit still lingered to enable the party managers to secure a Liberal triumph for the moment, yet it was only nominal; and many years were yet to elapse before the

Radical hopes, created by Lord Grey's measure, were to approach within measurable distance of fulfilment.

On the other hand, Sir Robert came to his task under some disadvantages from which the Conservative Party at the present moment is exempt. It had undoubtedly been a leading principle of the old system that the country was to be governed by the landowners, that our Constitution was what Lord Beaconsfield called it in 1843, "a territorial Constitution"; and there is much to be said in favour of this principle.* But the plan adopted for perpetuating it, when the old machinery was destroyed, was in some respects unfortunate. The Chandos clause was intended by the landed aristocracy to counteract the loss of influence which they had sustained by the destruction of their boroughs. They created a new class of clients in the tenant-farmers. The result was that Sir Robert Peel found it impossible to resume the thread of the Free Trade policy, indigenous to the Tory Party, where Canning and Liverpool had dropped it. This was a great misfortune, for it supplied the wedge which was soon afterwards to be driven into that great combination of " the landed, commercial, and manufacturing interests,"† —the *conglutinatio partium*—which Peel, like another Cicero, had for a time succeeded in effecting.

Could a similar combination be effected at the present day, in defence of credit, property, the national empire, and all that is dear to a commercial as well as to an aristocratic community, there is no such rock ahead to mar its future fortunes. The task may be more difficult, but the work, when once accomplished, would not contain within itself the seeds of its future dissolution. In Peel's

---

* See Chapter on Lord Beaconsfield.
† Wellington. Letter to Croker. Sept. 30, 1833.

case, indeed, even the dissolution of his party did not involve the immediate destruction of his work. And that should be an encouragement to Conservatives at the present day to persevere in his footsteps. It is not necessary to obtain a majority in order to win a practical victory. The result may be ensured both before the majority is won and after it is lost, if only a school of statesmen and a school of thought shall have been formed adequate to so great an undertaking.

From the Duke of Wellington's letters published in the last chapter it is clear that his apprehensions of any immediate change had begun to subside by the year 1834. But he still thought that it was only postponed for a little while. We have some reason at the present day for sharing in the Duke's convictions. But an opportunity was lost in 1835, perhaps fraught with fairer promise than even the opportunity of 1827, and which, if offered again, we trust will not again be lost. In the natural course of events, or, perhaps we should say, regard being had to the natural development of party, a new arrangement of political forces should have taken place after the Reform Bill. A broad and intelligible line divided the Whigs from the Radicals, while, on the other hand, all the questions had been settled which originally divided them from the Tories. At all events, the only one that remained was completely in abeyance, and not likely to be revived as a party battle-cry in that generation. Parliamentary Reform was done with. After the legislation of 1828 and 1829 no Government could have been compelled to re-open the question of Religious Disabilities. The Moderate Whigs need not have been divided from the Tories on the subject of Ireland. On questions of foreign policy it is not very likely that Lord Palmerston and the Duke of

Wellington would have long continued at variance. The Reform of the Poor Law and of the English Municipal Corporations need have created no difference of opinion between the two parties whom the force of events had made almost equally Conservative. By rights, the Radicals, the Repealers, and the more advanced among the Whigs, should have taken their seats on the Opposition benches, and the Canningite Whigs and Tories have been welded together into a powerful and popular Government, representing Conservative reform. We should then have perpetuated our Party system on a healthy basis : two parties, with a real distinction between them, instead of three, a scheme which almost necessarily places the casting vote in the hands of the weakest, and leaves the most important issues to be decided by the will of the minority.

The difficulties in the way of a Coalition in 1834 were purely practical. Between Melbourne, Palmerston, and Stanley on one side, and Peel, Wellington, and Lyndhurst on the other, there was no difference of principle. Lord Melbourne had drifted into an Irish policy which he felt bound in loyalty to support, but with which he had very little sympathy. That once out of the way, there was nothing to have prevented the union which the King suggested : nothing, perhaps, but some personal jealousies and rivalries which it might not, indeed, have been altogether easy to compose. But in 1885 there are no practical difficulties of any kind standing in the way of a union between the Moderate Liberals and the Conservatives. The Duke of Argyll has taken special pains to record his conviction that the cause of social improvement is as safe with the Conservatives as with the Liberals.*

* Speech in House of Lords, June 10th, 1885.

The middle classes have far more reason to be alarmed now than they had at the General Election of 1835. The Radical menace is darker and more threatening now than it was then. The rights of persons and the rights of property are more openly struck at. The great struggle between numbers and property has moved infinitely nearer. The flood is even now creeping under our doorways. Have we not ten times the motive to do what our fathers did in another generation, and rally round the party which promises peace, economy, and liberty, together with security for the tranquil enjoyment of all those personal rights, the prospect of possessing which is the best incentive both to intelligent industry and legitimate ambition ?

It may be said, of course, that for another Conservative reaction like that of 1835 we want another Tamworth Manifesto. But that is to mistake the true nature of the crisis. In 1835 Sir Robert Peel had to clear his party from all suspicion of a retrogressive policy. All that was then remembered of the Tories was their opposition to the Reform Bill. It was necessary to convince the people that a Conservative Government was as ready for social reform as a Whig Government. That is no longer necessary. The public know very well that the opinion I have quoted from the Duke of Argyll's speech is strictly true. The Conservatives have proved that they possess both the power and the will to undertake those domestic measures which the circumstances of the time require. And there is a further incentive to exertion on the part of both the middle and the working classes, which was wanting to the supporters of Sir Robert Peel. Our maritime supremacy is now at stake. Our vast Asiatic territory, our colonies and our commerce, that great English world beyond the sea, where our countrymen can find another home under the same flag, the same sovereign, and the same institutions, which they have known from their infancy, are all in peril. Sir Robert Peel offered us peace, retrenchment, a more secure foreign policy, and a long series of social reforms. The Conservatives can offer us all these, and the salvation of an empire to boot.

Parliament was dissolved on the 30th of December 1834, and re-assembled on the 19th of February 1835. The elections were favourable to the Government, though they fell short of returning a Conservative majority. Sir Robert, as we have seen, gained about a hundred seats; and, in addition to these, he could calculate on the votes of some fifty independent Liberals, of whom Lord Stanley seems to have been the leader, on most questions to which they were not already pledged. With this hand he determined, in the language of the card-table, to see the House. He thought it just possible that his measures, being judged upon their merits, might gradually commend themselves to the country, and that he might in time detach from the Whig ranks many who only wanted a reasonable excuse for supporting a Conservative Administration. He might thus form an independent majority, which would answer all the purposes of a purely Party majority; and if it had not been for the obstacles which Lord Melbourne had foreseen he would probably have succeeded. But the two Irish measures to which the whole Liberal Party stood pledged, i.e. the Irish Church Commission, and the Appropriation Clause, were insuperable. And the leader of the Opposition, knowing that on these his Party must support him, held the Government in his hand. Some consciousness, perhaps, of the desperate nature of the struggle to which he would be committing himself, if the decisive battle * was fought upon the Appropriation question, constrained the Whig leader to try other modes of attack before having recourse to this. But Sir Robert, though defeated on the Speakership by a majority of ten, and on an amendment to the Address by a majority of seven, did not think that either of these divisions required him to resign office. The Debate on the Address,† which lasted nine nights, always valuable as a piece of Parliamentary history, is, at the present moment, peculiarly interesting and instructive. Sir Robert Peel himself and other speakers on the same side, in justifying the acceptance of office by the Conservatives, laid especial stress on the internal dissensions of the late Government which entirely neutralized their large nominal majority, so much so that Sir Robert could point to half-a-dozen instances recorded in the pages of *Hansard* in which they had been kept in power entirely by his own exertions. How, then, could they have gone on? or how could any Government formed out of the same materials succeed any better?

No other Government could be formed without a selection of individuals from each of these numerous parties, which, though they are now acting in concert, have been, but a few short months ago, and may be in a few short weeks again, in bitter hostility to each other.‡

He entirely confirmed the King's view of the removal of Lord Althorpe, describing him as "the corner-stone" of the Whig Cabinet, and quoting the words of Lord Grey

---

* The Irish Church Bill had been passed, without the Appropriation Clause, in July 1833. The question now was whether the Tithe question should be settled without this principle being recognized. The contest lasted three years longer, and ended in a compromise, by which the Whigs abandoned the Appropriation Clause, and the Tories withdrew their opposition to the Irish Municipal Corporations Bill.

† *Hansard*, vol. xxvi. pp. 150-250.

‡ *Ibid.*, p. 241.

himself to the effect that the Government entirely depended
on him. I offer you, he said, peace, economy,* "*the
restored confidence of powerful States,*" and reforms both
civil and ecclesiastical which should remedy acknowledged
evils without the violation of principles to which only two
years ago even the leader of the Opposition had professed
an inviolable allegiance.† Do not, he said with conscious
power and dignity, lightly refuse these offers. He was
there, he said, by no act of his own. The disunion of
the Liberals had forced him into his present position.
But he was determined to maintain it to the last; and if
compelled to quit it before he had been allowed fair
play, he felt he could rely with confidence on the justice
and generosity of the public. On the subject of foreign
politics occurs the following remarkable statement :—

The Government (his own Government) state that they entertain con-
fident expectations of being able to maintain the blessings of peace. They
already see a tendency to increased confidence in the British Ministry on
the part of some of the Great Powers of Europe. . . . It has been argued
on the other side that it is an ill omen, a positive evil, that the military
Governments of the Continent should have any confidence in the Ministry
of England. There might be some foundation for this if the Ministers had
contracted any engagement with those Governments which could bind them
to depart from the true principles of British policy, and from their dis-
inclination to interfere with the internal affairs of other countries. We have
contracted no such engagements, but we are proud of the confidence of
foreign Powers, and wish to maintain their good-will.

The above remarks are, of course, an allusion to the
over-active foreign policy of Lord Palmerston, who, with
more zeal than discretion, had given deep offence to our
old German allies.

The Amendment was carried by a majority of seven;
but Sir Robert still hoped to be allowed time to bring
forward his measures. They included a Dissenters'

* The estimates for 1835 were lower than they had been since 1815.
† *Cf.* Lord J. Russell's speech on Church Temporalities Act.

Marriage Bill, an English and an Irish Tithes Bill, a Church Discipline Bill, and an Ecclesiastical Courts Bill,* and measures were promised founded on the Report of the Municipal Corporations Commission. It was not the policy of the Whigs, however, to allow Sir Robert time to take root, or for his measures to make their natural impression on the public mind. Lord John Russell, finding other attacks fail, at once brought up his reserve; and moved, on the 2nd of April, that the House should resolve itself into a Committee on the Irish Church. This was carried by 322 votes to 289. On the 6th he revived the Appropriation Clause by a resolution affirming that the surplus revenue of the Irish Church should be applied to the education " of all classes of Christians." This was carried by 262 votes to 237: and, finally, on the following day, he moved that no Tithe Bill could be considered satisfactory which did not embody the foregoing Resolution. This was carried by 285 votes to 258: and then at last Sir Robert yielded; not, however, without inflicting a parting castigation on the Whigs, which, if wanting in the brilliant sarcasm of one Tory leader, and the stinging irony of another, has a propriety and emphasis of its own which must have left a lasting impression on the House. Three years afterwards he had an ample revenge on the statesman who abandoned the Appropriation Clause after it had served its purpose, and enabled him, by representing it as indispensable, to turn the Tories out of office.

On the Ecclesiastical Commission, however, which had been issued by Sir Robert in the previous February, as it has been violently attacked by Churchmen, some further observations may be necessary. The Ecclesiastical

* Brought in when he again became Prime Minister.

Commission only raised the old question of the exercise of the royal supremacy through the medium of a non-religious House of Commons. It would hardly have been maintained by Keble, or Pusey, or by any of the warmest opponents of the Judicial Committee of the Privy Council, that it was not within the power of the Crown before 1828 to make those changes in the internal economy and financial arrangements of the Church of England which Peel proposed to effect by means of a Royal Commission, or that such exercise of power by the temporal Head of the Church was likely to be injurious to the first estate. If there is any real objection, it is to be found in the new character imparted to the House of Commons by the legislation of 1828-9. It certainly appears to me that the admission of Dissenters and Roman Catholics to Parliament was a reason rather for restricting than extending the jurisdiction of the House of Commons in matters ecclesiastical. The conditions of the alliance between Church and State agreed to in 1534 were virtually broken by the State when the temporal power passed into the hands of an assembly not necessarily connected with the Church.* I think, therefore, that the Conservative Government of 1835 was, perhaps, theoretically wrong in the appointment of the Ecclesiastical Commission, though it is clearly unjust to saddle Sir Robert Peel with all its consequences. He did not pass the Act of 1840, dealing with the capitular estates; and the management of episcopal estates, which was taken over by the Commissioners with the consent of the Bishops, might, I have heard, be resumed by them if they thought it expedient so to do.

On the other hand, we have to consider, not only the

* Keble, *Papers and Reviews*, p. 207.

great difficulties of his own situation, but also the precarious position of the Church herself, and the possibility that the inroads on her freedom committed by the Tories of that day saved her from a worse fate at the hands of her adversaries. This was not the view taken by the High Churchmen of the period, who seem to have thought that it would be better to run all risks. And there appears to be little doubt that it was the issue of this Commission that sowed the seeds of that distrust of Sir Robert Peel which alone made the Young England Party possible. In a very remarkable book which was published in 1843, and attributed at the time to Mr. Gladstone himself, we find the discontent of the High Church Tories with the Conservatism of Sir Robert Peel very strongly expressed.

An Ecclesiastical Commission has been created which has broken up the outward system of the Church, violated its oaths, tampered with its independence, destroyed the rights of private property, dried up the sources of individual endowments, mutilated those Cathedral Corporations which should have been restored and revivified to have become the chief arms of its strength, and annihilated episcopates for money.*

These are the words of no hot-headed partizan; not one of the advanced Tractarians, not one even of the old port-wine Tories who regarded every atom of mortar in the edifice of Church and State as inviolable, but of the late Rev. William Sewell, a man who had thought and read deeply, and who took precisely the same view of the subject as we find in *Coningsby*. Men of this way of thinking believed that so long as the Tory Party, so to speak, retained its ἀρχή, there was always a hope of rallying the people to the old banner, but that if the Tories themselves by their own act and deed signed away their inheritance, then, indeed, it was lost for ever. Those,

* Hawkstone, vol. ii. p. 362.

however, who reason in this manner are too apt to forget
that statesmen must look upon the Constitution of the
country—that great fabric of laws, customs, and institutions
which England has gradually built up for herself—as a
whole; and that as a general rule they can only consider
the relative, not the absolute, value of the parts of which
it is composed. What the Conservative Party conceived to
be threatened in 1835 were those fundamental principles
which hold this great system together: the principle of
property, the principle of authority, the hereditary principle, and certain well-known international principles
essential to the security of our empire. The only party
which could maintain these principles, after the destruction of the ancient *régime*, was a party of compromise, a
party which should include the bulk of the middle classes,
who had the most to lose by revolution, but who at the
same time were decidedly hostile to privilege. Now a
privilege, whether of divine or human origin, is still
a privilege, and the question which Sir Robert had
to ask himself—analogous to that which Conservatives
in all similar situations have to ask themselves—was
whether the Church of England might not fairly be
called upon to abate somewhat even of her just claims
—temporal claims exclusively—for the interest of the
whole system.

All forms of polity grow old and wither with time. No
human wisdom can preserve them in their integrity for
ever. But the stronger our faith in their moral influence
and the quality of national character which they are calculated to produce, the greater will be our anxiety to defer
their doom as long as possible; and this by any sacrifice
short of the very attributes or possessions which constitute their capacity for good. At what point the sacrifice

becomes too great, and defeats its own object, requiring us to give up the kernel for the sake of preserving the shell, *et propter vitam vivendi perdere causas*—must always be a difficult and anxious question for a statesman to decide; and some indulgence and allowance may fairly be claimed by everyone who, if he decides it wrongly, has at least decided it honestly. I believe that Sir Robert Peel was honestly trying to do the best he could for what all Conservatives had at heart; nor should the fact, if fact it is, that he was wrong in any particular concession, lead us to forget that in the main he was successful, and stayed the plague for one generation. In 1868 it reappeared.

It will be seen that I have used the words Tory and Conservative indiscriminately to denote the Constitutional Party which sprang up after 1832. I have done so on purpose, because, while anxious to preserve to the Conservative Party the original title which it inherits from the eighteenth century, denoting functions and principles which, if dormant, are not extinct, it seems to me idle to deny that its duties are now very much what they were in 1835, the defence, that is, of our existing social order against the headlong and destructive spirit which every political revolution generates in turn. Fifty years ago the danger passed away, and men wondered that they had ever been afraid of it. They forgot the means by which the Conservative instincts of the English people had been rallied and organized; and the public spirit which had led Conservatives of all denominations to forget obsolete distinctions, and to combine for the benefit of the Commonwealth. What has been done before may be done again. But it can only be done by the exercise of the same virtues, and the recognition of the same truth,

18 *

namely, that with every new point of departure in our political history, parties, if destined to be permanent, must assume a fresh character, and incorporate with themselves the new ideas and new elements of power which time periodically ripens.

CHAPTER VI.

SIR ROBERT PEEL—(*continued*).

" ' PEEL, in or out, will support the Poor Law,' said Lord Marney, rather audaciously, as he reseated himself after the ladies had retired. ' He must '; and he looked at his brother, whose return had, in a great degree, been secured by crying that Poor Law down.''* I was anxious, in my last chapter, to carry forward the history of Sir Robert Peel to the end of the Tory Administration of 1835. We must now retrace our steps to consider very briefly what was the attitude of the Tory Party on the most important question which at that time occupied the attention of the public. I mean the new Poor Law. Of the bitter hatred with which the new system was regarded by the agricultural poor at, and long after, the date of the above conversation (1837) the present writer has a clear recollection. He remembers, as a child, being puzzled at hearing the workhouse called the "bas-tyle" by the village labourers, with a strong emphasis on the second syllable ; and he has always believed that it was the first thing which disturbed, to any serious extent, the old relations of amity and loyalty

---

* *Sybil.*

between the peasantry and the gentry. The chief objections to the Act were the creation of a Central Board, the formation of parishes into unions, and the transference to the overseers of the powers formerly exercised by the magistrates. The total abolition of out-door relief, which was originally contemplated, was found to be so far in advance of public opinion that a compromise was adopted, by which, while the old system of "allowances" was given up, the Commissioners were authorized to grant out-door relief in special cases; and owing to the efforts of the Tory Party, the power taken away from the Justices by the original draught of the Bill was partially restored to them by retaining the right to order out-door relief when they could certify of "their own personal knowledge" that the case was one of destitution. But in spite of these amendments, a blow was struck at the influence of the country gentlemen from which it has never entirely recovered.

What were called allowances were sums of money paid to able-bodied labourers whose wages were insufficient to support them, and had first been sanctioned by an Act passed in 1795,* at a time when the distress of the agricultural population was attracting universal attention. It was just at this time that the labourers were feeling the combined effects of the enclosure of wastes and commons which had proceeded very rapidly in the early part of the reign of George the Third and of the great rise in prices which followed the American war. Mr. Wilberforce and other country gentlemen took up their cause very warmly. They introduced the allotment system; and we may probably trace the hand of Wilberforce in the comprehensive and very remarkable measure for improving the condition

* 36 Geo. III., cap. 23. Dec. 24, 1795.

of the peasantry, which was drawn up by Mr. Pitt himself, though, owing to the pressure of foreign affairs, he was unable to carry it any further. It was proposed by the great Tory Minister that industrial schools should be established in all the villages of the kingdom, and that the parish officers should be empowered to levy the necessary rates. He also went the length of recognizing the claims of the poor, whether they were paupers or not, to a distinct maintenance out of the produce of the soil ; and part of his plan was that any person entitled to parish relief might receive a lump sum in advance to enable him or her to buy a cow or a pig, or pay the rent of a small plot of ground. Like all Mr. Pitt's measures, his Poor Bill bears the stamp of a great and generous mind, capable of rising above mere hackneyed conventionalities. It was a vastly different scheme which the Liberal friends of the poor man now concocted for him ; and though it may be that the system adopted in 1834 was the wiser of the two, it seems to me that, if the principle of out-door relief was to be recognized at all, it was better to carry it out to its logical conclusion, as Mr. Pitt did. However, the Tory Party, in 1834, were not prepared to suggest any such alternative, and contented themselves with condemning the centralizing tendency of the Poor Law Board, the invasion of the parochial system, and the destruction of the old machinery which had worked so well for centuries. It was not a system to be abolished with a light heart, Mr. Canning used to say ; and he attributed the peace and prosperity of England, and the loyalty of the people during many very trying periods, mainly to the existence of the old Poor Law, which gave them a hold upon the land, attached them to the gentry, who were really relieving them out of their own pockets, and recognized

their *right* to a maintenance which raised it above the
level of charity.

I am not aware that the peasantry in those days were a
peculiarly abject race, or deficient in independence and self-
respect.   On the contrary, I should be inclined to think
that they would contrast very favourably in these points
with the labourers of to-day, and that their horror of
" coming on the parish " was even greater than we find
in their descendants.   Many people thought that all that
it was necessary to do was to repeal the Act of 1795,
before which time no complaints had been made either of
the mode in which the law was administered, or the influence which it exercised on the people.   There is no
doubt that to some extent the Act of 1834 went beyond
the necessities of the case, and was a covert attack upon
the authority of the rural proprietors, whom it was attempted to bring into odium by making them answerable
for abuses with which they had nothing to do.   But there
is a complete answer to this imputation.   Lord Brougham
himself admitted that the country gentlemen had discharged their duties most admirably.   The Whig-Radical
Party, however, through the new Poor Law and the
Municipal Corporation Act, saw their way to a combined
assault upon the Church and the gentry, undermining the
influence of the one in the towns and of the other in the
counties, which circumstances made it peculiarly difficult
for the Tory Party to repulse.   The abuses of the existing
system were so flagrant, the demoralization wrought by
them so widespread, and the actual pecuniary burden
entailed by the poor-rate so intolerable, that the country
gentlemen and farmers were only too glad, perhaps, of any
scheme that relieved them from it, however mischievous
some of its provisions might be found.

The Duke of Wellington supported the Central Board principally on the ground that it was impossible to obtain uniformity of administration otherwise. But uniformity of administration has not been secured under the new system ; and I think the Tory leaders ought not to have allowed the jurisdiction of the country gentlemen to be transferred to the overseers, or the old parochial system to be abolished, without a more determined protest. The Board of Guardians was the creation of the new law. Under the old one, out-door relief was granted on a magistrate's order ; and this created a close and intimate connection between the landed proprietors and the poor, which had existed for centuries, and which it should have been the first object of Tory statesmen to defend. This is not the only occasion, however, on which the Tory Party has been blind to its own interests in the matter of local administration. But, in regard to the condition of the peasantry, if the question is no longer to be settled on the principles of political economy, as was intended by the reformers of 1834, the Tories cannot do better than revert to the principle of Mr. Pitt's proposal, which is what Lord Carnarvon and others are now attempting. Pitt himself, be it remembered, was a disciple of the economists, though he saw that their laws were not necessarily of universal application. He, moreover, contemplated nothing in the shape of robbery or confiscation. The founder of modern Toryism upheld all the rights of property ; but he believed that the poor were entitled to be maintained by the land, and that in a manner which should not entail the degradation of pauperism.

Sir Robert Peel did not oppose the more objectionable provisions of the new law as energetically as he might have done. But a new era was at hand, when the rights of labour were again to be recognized by the last great Tory statesman whom it is my purpose to pourtray, and who always endeavoured, as far as modern conditions made it possible, to tread in the footsteps of Mr. Pitt.

The new Bill became law on the 14th of August 1834, and soon afterwards followed the great fight of 1834–5, which has already been described. The victory of the Whigs, and their retention of office during the next five years, was due to what has been called the Lichfield House compact, by which the Repealers and the Radicals bound themselves to keep the Whigs in power in return for concessions which it is doubtful if the Whigs themselves did not know to be impossible. Ireland was to have the Appropriation Clause. But if the Whigs could not carry the Appropriation Clause in the Parliament of 1832, what chance had they in the Parliament of 1835? As much may be said of the Radical demands, the abolition, namely, of Church rates, and the admission of Dissenters to the Universities. A Bill for the commutation of Church rates, charging them on the Consolidated Fund, had been introduced by Lord Althorpe, and rejected by the Dissenters themselves on perfectly intelligible grounds. But the Whigs knew well enough that nothing further was possible; and when, in 1837, a measure for the abolition of the rate was introduced by the Chancellor of the Exchequer to propitiate his Radical allies, it was obliged to be withdrawn. The Appropriation Clause shared the same fate in 1838, so that it became pretty clear to both the Home Rulers and the Radicals that the famous transaction which has now passed into a proverb had ended only in the Whigs keeping the oyster and the allies receiving the shell. Nothing was done towards opening the Universities to

Dissenters, and the latter party found themselves treated by the Whigs of 1835 exactly as they had been treated, just a hundred years before, by the Whigs of 1735. They had secured a majority for Walpole, and when they asked for their reward they were told that the payment was impossible. They had secured the triumph of Lord Melbourne, and received practically much the same assurance. Their disappointment led immediately to the defeat of the Government on the Jamaica Bill, the resignation of Lord Melbourne, and the celebrated Bedchamber Plot.

Before discussing the part played by Sir Robert Peel in this affair, we must notice his opposition to the English and Irish Municipal Corporation Bills, and the great speech which he made on the Irish Church Bill in 1835. In connection with Municipal Reform Lord Lyndhurst steps upon the scene, and we are reminded of the rumour that he had his eye upon Sir Robert's place. Certainly he cut up the English Municipal Reform Bill in the House of Lords in a style which Peel did not attempt in the House of Commons, probably because he knew it was no use. It is also true that he resented very warmly a remonstrance that was addressed to him for having struck out clauses which the leader of the party had supported. "Peel! What is Peel to me? Damn Peel!" are words, certainly, which do not go far to rebut the charge which has been brought against him. Sir Robert, too, at this particular moment, happened to have left town, and the world said he was "sulking at Drayton." But, however this may be, he reappeared in the Commons to support Lord Lyndhurst's amendments, and succeeded in saving some of the more important ones, which were accepted by the Government rather than endanger the Bill or necessitate a second crisis.* "They'll

* The Bill received the Royal assent on the 9th September 1835.

take the Bill as it is," said Lyndhurst, "for it will do their work."　So thought Lord Melbourne also.

" You may not," he said, "see all the consequences of this to-morrow : but you have given by law a permanent power in all the centres of industry and intelligence to the Dissenters which they never had before, and which they could never have had otherwise. These are the classes who will really gain by the change, not the mob or the theorists ; every year their strength will be felt more and more at elections, and their influence on the legislation. Depend upon it, it is the Established Church, and not the hereditary peerage, which has need to set its house in order "*

Both Lyndhurst and Peel laid great stress on an amendment intended to exclude Dissenters from exercising the ecclesiastical patronage vested in some of the Corporations. The difficulty was evaded by a clause enabling these bodies to sell their ecclesiastical property ; but it has always seemed to me that Lord John Russell was right in his argument that this privilege having already been conferred upon Dissenters by the defeat of the Test and Corporation Act, it was too late to exclude them from it then. The second concession wrung from the Government related to the rights of freemen, both proprietary and political rights, which the Bill would have extinguished altogether. In pleading for the retention of the Parliamentary franchise by this class of electors, Sir Robert argued that the abolition of it was a direct violation of the engagements contracted by the Reform Bill ;† and he expressed, at the same time, his great anxiety to retain even this modified connection between the working-classes and the House of Commons, showing that the extinction of popular franchises by the Reform Bill was a real ground of complaint with the sober-minded Tories whom Sir Robert represented,

---

* *Life*, vol. ii. p. 156.

† This was frequently referred to by Mr. Disraeli in the Reform Debates of 1859 and 1867.

and was no mere after-thought, invented by imaginative politicians in their enthusiasm for Tory Democracy.

To the Irish Municipal Reform Bill the objection was of a different character. The unreformed Irish corporations represented the principle of Protestant ascendency in its most naked and oppressive form. But that was no reason, said the Tory Party, why we should change it for the principle of Roman Catholic ascendency in its most naked and oppressive form. They would not consent to the overthrow of one form of religious exclusiveness merely to set up another; especially when the one to be abandoned was part of the ancient Constitution, and had been expressly guaranteed by the Act of 1829; while the proposed substitute was described by O'Connell himself as " a normal school for teaching the science of political agitation." It is, indeed, perfectly true, and this should always be remembered, that Protestant ascendency in Ireland was not the work of the Tories. The idea of governing Ireland by means of a Protestant colony acting as a Protestant garrison originated exclusively with the Whigs. The Tories, finding the system in existence, continued to maintain it; but the great statesman, the second founder of the Tory Party, contemplated, without doubt, its gradual abrogation. Mr. Canning also did the same; and even Sir Robert Peel, in the debate on the Church Bill, to which we have already referred, declared that he should prefer the endowment of the Roman Catholic clergy and establishment of the Roman Catholic Church, to the policy propounded by the Whigs.

I have said that the principle of the Appropriation Clause was revived in the Government Tithe Bill.* In 1838, however, the clause was abandoned on the under-

* Church Bill.

standing that the Conservatives should withdraw their opposition to the Irish Municipal Corporation Bill. Hitherto
the Tory Party had held out for an alternative scheme,
abolishing the existing Corporations and creating new
governing bodies, the members of which should be appointed directly by the Crown. This was the policy of
Sir Robert Peel, and subsequent events have clearly
demonstrated its wisdom. But the Whigs, of course,
would not listen to it, and, to ensure the withdrawal of
the Appropriation Clause, Peel consented to discuss the
details of the Corporation Bill. These, however, were
obstinately contested for three years longer, when the
main point contended for by Sir Robert—the fixture, that
is, of the Municipal Franchise in the smaller towns at a
ten-pound qualification—was ultimately conceded, and the
Bill became law in August 1840.

It seems, however, that on this subject, as on others,
his opinions developed very rapidly ; for we are assured
by Mr. Disraeli that he had not long been in office, after
1842, before he changed his mind on the Irish Question
as completely as he did upon the Corn Laws. The Maynooth grant, together with the " Godless Colleges " and
the Charitable Bequests Act, were only fragments of a
great scheme which was floating in Sir Robert's mind for
the complete reconstruction of the Irish Constitution, social,
political, and ecclesiastical, and reaching as far as that
very endowment and establishment of the Roman Catholic
Church which, in 1835, he denounced as "rash, unwise,
and impolitic." The prosecution of O'Connell was to terminate the reign of agitation. The Devon Commission
was to justify the reconstruction of the Land Laws. And
before he finally quitted office, he had undertaken to place
the Irish Municipal Corporations on the same footing as

the English. We are assured by the same authority that it was only the escape of O'Connell which deterred Sir Robert Peel from entering on this large scheme. Lord George Bentinck himself was avowedly in its favour; and so, we may shrewdly suspect, was his illustrious biographer.

Sir Robert Peel's speech on the Irish Tithe Bill, in July 1835, was practically a speech on the Appropriation Clause; and one of the ablest he ever made in the House of Commons. It was exactly suited to the level of his audience, and convicted the other side of such absurd arithmetical blunders, that no wonder their waning reputation as financiers was nearly extinguished by it. Discarding for the time being all arguments drawn from the sanctity of Church property, Sir Robert declared his intention of meeting his antagonists on their own ground, within their own ring, so to speak, and proving that, on their own premisses, their proposal was utterly indefensible. He took their own estimate of the incomes which were necessary for the proper support of the Irish clergy, and then showed that if their Bill was carried there would not only be no surplus to devote to secular purposes, but a considerable deficiency for the State to make good. It is in this speech that he made the statement to which I have referred, though in language which I wish had been different, relating to the endowment of the Roman Catholic Church. There were, he said, "three courses" open to any Government on the subject of the Irish Church:—To leave it as it was; to make the Roman instead of the Anglican branch the Established Church of Ireland; or to do what the Government was doing— impoverish the one without profiting the other. The second of these three modes of treatment would, he thought, be "pregnant with fatal consequences." But it would be infinitely preferable to the third. I quite agree with Sir Robert Peel; it was the proper policy of the British Government to treat Ireland like Scotland, and the Roman Catholic Church had a better claim to establishment than the Presbyterian. The Tories of that day, however, were not equal to such a stroke of genius as this; nor would Sir Robert Peel have found it answer his immediate purpose so well as the policy which he adopted. In fact, it would have broken up his party; but had "the descendants of the Cavaliers," as Lord Beaconsfield called the English country gentlemen, when addressing them on this very subject, only plucked up a little spirit, and followed the example of their ancestors, what a world of misery and misfortune, past and probably to come, this country might have been spared!

But the secularization of the Church property in Ireland was both a crime and a blunder of the deepest dye. It was a crime, because the Church lands were clearly the property of the Church, and if one branch of it did not seem to be turning them to good account, they should have been entrusted to the other. It was a blunder, because an endowed and established Roman Church, drawing its priesthood to some extent from the upper classes, and imbued with the tastes and feelings of educated gentlemen, would have changed the face of Ireland in a moment, and have made rebellion and separation impossible. Such a measure would have saved England, and have saved Ireland. It would have enlisted Ireland on the side of our national institutions; and the Church and the Monarchy, personal freedom and the rights of property, would have been as secure in this country now as they were throughout the eighteenth century. It was Sir

Robert Peel's misfortune to be too late on several important public questions. Had he only seen the Roman Catholic question in its proper light in 1829, he need never have made his celebrated speech against Repeal in 1834.

It may be said, perhaps, of Sir Robert Peel's Maynooth Bill, that it deserves exactly what he said himself of Lord Melbourne's Tithes Bill—that it was an outrage on Protestant feeling without doing any real good to the Roman Catholics : " the difference between three in a bed and two," as Mr. Disraeli said of the proposal to increase the endowment from £23 a head to £28. The Maynooth Bill, judged merely on its own merits, was, indeed, one of the most pitiful incidents in the whole history of Toryism. The beggarly amount of the grant itself, and the price at which it was purchased in the shape of Conservative sentiment, make one glad to hurry over it with as few words as possible.

In noticing the Ecclesiastical Commission of 1835,* I have mentioned the Capitular Estates Bill, or, as it is called on the Statute Book, the Ecclesiastical Revenues and Duties Act. To this Sir Robert Peel gave his full support, though he was not answerable for its details ; and as the Archbishop of Canterbury, Dr. Howley, did the same, we may reasonably suppose that it did not deserve all the reproaches which were heaped on it, by Sir Robert Inglis in the Lower House, and the Bishops of Winchester and Rochester in the Upper. Sir Robert Peel argued that the willingness with which the Church had consented to the redistribution of cathedral revenues had done much to reinstate her in the good opinion of the country ; and no doubt the man who knew how to submit with dignity

* See previous chapter.

and good temper to the exactions of a highwayman may
sometimes have risen in *his* good opinion too. It does
not follow that the Bill was right because it was popular ;
or that it was not robbery because the victims submitted
to it with a good grace. A better defence is the plea of
necessity ; the probability that if the Church had not
submitted to this operation at the hands of her friends,
she would have had to submit to a much ruder one at the
hands of her enemies.

The Whigs, as we have already seen, had alienated
both the Radicals and the Repealers ; and in 1839, on the
question of the Jamaica Constitution, they were left in
the lurch by the Radicals, and escaped defeat only by a
majority of five. They at once resigned. The Duke was
summoned to the Palace, and the young Queen was advised
to send for Sir Robert Peel. Then followed the scene
described with such inimitable truth and humour in the
pages of *Sybil*. The Tory leader was afraid of the Whig
Ladies of the Bedchamber, and perhaps with reason. " I
have no small talk," said the Duke of Wellington, " and
Peel has no manners." However this may be, Peel stood
out for what he believed to be the letter of the law, and
required the dismissal of nine out of the twenty-five ladies
who had the misfortune to be Whigs. He expressly tells
Croker that the Queen was *not* under the impression that
he wished her to discharge them all,* but only the Ladies
of the Bedchamber ; and he appeals to the reign of Queen
Anne for precedents to justify his conduct. All this
comes out in the *Quarterly Review*, heavily shotted with
italics and notes of admiration. But, after all, it seems
to me that Sir Robert was making a mountain of a mole-
hill. He could not have gone on with that Parliament,

* *Croker Papers*, vol. ii. p. 345.

nor yet with a new one, unless he had obtained a clear majority; and if he had got that, the ladies might have done their worst.

I have only one word to add on this memorable transaction, and that is that the term " unconstitutional " is more easily applied than defined. The Constitution, I know, has its unwritten laws and general understandings which, with rare exceptions, are as binding as an Act of Parliament : but have we any authority for saying that the duty of the Sovereign to appoint the ladies of her Court according to the will of the Prime Minister, was, at the accession of Her present Majesty, one of them ? In the negotiations between Lord Moira on the one side, and Lords Grey and Grenville on the other, in 1812, the Whig leaders made the dismissal of the Prince Regent's household a condition of their acceptance of office. But Lord Moira replied that, though the Prince had never intimated the slightest intention of retaining those officers about his person, he could not allow that an incoming Minister had any constitutional right to demand their resignation. The officers of the household were fully prepared to retire ; but the Whigs insisted on their right to compel them to retire, and this right was explicitly denied and the claim peremptorily rejected. Sir Robert quoted the Whig demand of 1812 as a precedent in favour of himself. But I hardly see how the disallowance of a claim can constitute a precedent for reviving it.

Towards the end of the session of 1840 the Whigs had ceased to command a majority in the House of Commons, but, after repeated defeats on the question of Irish Registration, they still remained in office, relying on the results of a dissolution. In 1841 Lord Melbourne tried the experiment of a declaration in favour of Free Trade ; that is

19 *

to say, of an eight-shilling fixed duty. But it came too
late. It was everywhere looked upon as a last bid for
popularity, and a dishonest repudiation of principles which
the leaders of the party had to the last moment emphatically maintained. Their Budget also was a failure, one of
its cardinal provisions being rejected by a majority of
thirty-six. On this evidence of the state of feeling in the
House of Commons Sir Robert Peel spoke. On the 27th
of May he moved a vote of want of confidence, which was
carried by a majority of one. The Ministers dissolved ;
and the General Election gave the Tory Party a majority
of ninety.

We now enter on a new phase of Sir Robert Peel's Parliamentary career, the last and the best known, but not,
perhaps, the happiest or the most dignified. I have always
thought that the seven years which elapsed between the
autumn of 1834 and the autumn of 1841, form the brightest
and most honourable period of his chequered and eventful
life. Universally looked up to both by friends and enemies
as the foremost public man of his age ; the aberration of
1829 condoned or forgotten, and nothing regarded but his
consummate Parliamentary ability, his mastery of debate,
his knowledge of affairs, his capacity for business ; the
leader of " the country gentlemen of England "—a position which he would not exchange, he said, for the confidence of sovereigns ; in the prime of life ; in perfect
agreement with his followers ; with nothing to conceal
or to retract : he occupied a station than which I can
imagine few more worthy to be envied, by those, that is,
who seek the good of life in the prickly domain of politics.

Addressing his supporters in the back drawing-room at
Whitehall Gardens, holding a chair between his hands,
and resting one knee upon the cushion, as his custom was,

he had no misgivings and little anxiety about the future. His real career was still before him ; and, as he well knew, the hour could not be long delayed when he must enter on his heritage. Not even when playing on the House of Commons like an old fiddle* was he seen to more advantage. Handsome, gracious, if at times a little stiff or pompous ; proud of himself and of his followers, his reception at the great Conservative banquet of 1839 was, if he had only known it, perhaps, the culminating point of his felicity.

Sir Robert Peel's second administration will probably be known to history chiefly for that great reconstruction of our fiscal system which was Sir Robert's contribution to the cause of national progress. But if his intentions towards Ireland have been rightly described by Lord Beaconsfield, who had no reason for misrepresenting them, he is as much entitled to our admiration for what he intended to do, as for what he actually did. If Sir Robert Peel had really made up his mind towards the close of his career to inaugurate a new system in Ireland ; to take up the ecclesiastical policy of the Tory Party where Mr. Pitt had been obliged to drop it : to anticipate an agrarian revolution by a wise and Conservative reform of the Land Laws, which should leave untouched where they existed, and create where they were absent, those relations between the people and the aristocracy which prevail in England, and which Mr. Gladstone professed, at one time, to wish to see naturalized in Ireland : if this was the policy which Sir Robert Peel was contemplating in 1844, it is one to entitle him to the respect of all true Tories, far more than the reform of the tariff, though here, too, be it remem-

* *Life of Lord George Bentinck.*

bered, he was only following in the footsteps of his Tory predecessors, Bolingbroke, Pitt, Liverpool and Canning. Circumstances, however, threw Sir Robert Peel into a different groove. In 1843 he was obliged to introduce an Arms Bill. In 1844 came the prosecution and escape of O'Connell ; and before he could recover himself, the Potato Famine, and Free Trade, followed by the necessity for further repressive measures in Ireland, brought his Government to the ground, and put an end for ever to the visions which he is said to have entertained. There can be no doubt that the vote of June 1846 on the Irish Coercion Bill was, on the part of the Conservatives, a vindictive vote. Retributive justice they would probably have termed it ; but its only excuse is that it was the act of men smarting under a recent sense of injury, and too angry to listen to prudence. It was an exact repetition of the vote of 1830 on the Civil List ; and, it is hardly too much to say, has been followed by analogous consequences.

The Irish Question—like the Goodwin Sands—has swallowed up many a gallant vessel : but of all the wrecks which lie buried in it, none has been so complete and so disastrous as the destruction of the Tory Party in 1846. No doubt the repeal of the Corn Laws had left the vessel in a perilous condition, and may be said, with truth, to have been the final cause of the catastrophe ; but it is possible, I think, that if no opportunity of defeating the Government had occurred till men's passions had begun to cool, and more and more members had come to see what the Duke of Wellington saw then, and what Lord Derby acknowledged afterwards, the mistake of 1829 might not have been repeated, and the Tory Party might have recovered from the shock. The Duke has been severely criticised * for his advice on this occasion, to the effect that the maintenance of a good Government was of more consequence than the Corn Laws. But is it not perfectly true ? Are not constitutional questions of infinitely greater moment than questions of taxes and tariffs ? Those who choose to answer the question in the negative are, of course, at liberty to do so. But I cannot understand such an answer being given by any real Tory or Conservative.

For a complete account of Sir Robert's financial measures, and the Whig struggles which preceded them, I must refer my readers to the admirable volume of Lord Iddesleigh.† It is interesting to know that more than forty years ago Sir Robert Peel justified his imposition of the income tax by saying that we had " nearly reached the limits of taxation upon articles of consumption," words which, when uttered the other day by a Tory Chancellor of the Exchequer, were received with a storm of protestations, as if they invited our assent to some novel and dangerous heresy. Whether the statement is true or false, it was made deliberately by Sir Robert Peel in 1842; and it was on this conviction that he founded the financial system which has since been developed by successive Chancellors of the Exchequer, both Whig and Tory. Whether it may not have been carried too far by the eminent financier who has so long been the ornament of the Liberal Party is a question for history to decide. But the doctrine that the English people must " live cheaply " was one that was very early imbibed by Sir Robert Peel ;

* Mr. Disraeli's *Life of Lord George Bentinck*; Mr. J. McCarthy's *History of Our Times.*

† *Twenty Years of Financial Policy.* By the Right Hon. Sir Stafford Northcote, M.P. London, 1862.

and the working classes should, in common gratitude, remember to which Party it is that they owe the introduction of a system which has benefited the poor at the expense of the rich to an extent, perhaps, hardly reconcilable with justice.

The name of Sir Robert Peel has long been so exclusively associated with domestic affairs that we are apt to forget the important foreign questions with which he was brought in contact : the. Portuguese and Spanish civil wars ; the Union of the two Canadas ; the Syrian question in 1840 ; the Spanish marriages ; the Revolution of 1848 ; and the now half-forgotten quarrel with Greece about the claims of Pacifico. On all occasions he adopted to the letter those views of English foreign policy which were held by the Duke of Wellington ; and it is remarkable and interesting to find him, in 1835, laying down precisely the same doctrine, in regard to the " continuity of our policy," as was recently expressed by Lord Salisbury.* After the Whigs returned to office, in 1835, the Spanish Government, being hard pressed by the Carlists, applied to England for assistance. The Whigs agreed to suspend, by Order in Council, the Foreign Enlistment Act of 1819, so as to permit of troops being raised in England for the service of the Queen of Spain. Even if this strong measure was justified by the Quadruple Treaty,† the Quadruple Treaty itself was a violation of the public law of Europe, as laid down at Aix-la-Chapelle and elsewhere, and was regarded with extreme disfavour by the Tory chiefs. Lord Mahon, the late Lord Stanhope, brought the question before the House of Commons in a remarkably able speech on the 24th of June, 1835, in which he con-

* Speech at Mansion House, July 29th, 1885.
† Sir Robert Peel expressly denied that it was.

tended that the Order in Council was a clear violation of neutrality, in the spirit if not in the letter. Now, it happened that the Quadruple Treaty had been negotiated by the Whig Government in 1834, but was not formally concluded when they left office. England, however, was morally pledged to its provisions, and, when laid before Sir Robert Peel and the Duke of Wellington, both felt bound to adhere to them. Referring to this in the debate on the Spanish Legion, Sir Robert Peel said : " He considered nothing of such vital importance to the character and interests of this country, as that the engagements entered into by one Administration should not be disturbed by another of opposite political principles." The public will judge for themselves whether the pupil of Sir Robert Peel or the pupil of Lord Beaconsfield has been more faithful to the doctrine here proclaimed.

In all the difficulties which arose with foreign Powers during the fifteen years that lie between his first Ministry and his death, we find Sir Robert Peel invariably true to those principles of policy which I have already described in the fourth chapter of this volume. They are all summed up in his great speech in the Pacifico debate on the 28th of June 1850, in which he protests, almost with his dying breath, against the encouragement of European democracy. The whole speech is much more an answer to Mr. Roebuck than an attack on Lord Palmerston.* He upholds to the full the doctrine of non-intervention, as embraced by the Duke of Wellington, the same doctrine, he assures us, which was held by Castlereagh, Liverpool, and Canning ; and lays down most emphatically that whether despotism or democracy

---

* Lord Palmerston did not represent Whig principles of Foreign Policy, as they were understood by the Whig families down to 1830.

is the aggressor, English interests are the sole guide by which an English statesman is to regulate his conduct. This is the doctrine which we have the authority of Sir Robert Peel for saying was handed down from Mr. Pitt himself, through the succession of statesmen we have named, and which has been by him transmitted, through Lord Derby and Lord Beaconsfield, to Her Majesty's present Administration.*

What I have desired to point out clearly is that Sir Robert Peel was, in all essential respects, a genuine Tory. In foreign policy, in ecclesiastical policy, in constitutional policy, he had no sympathy whatever with the views of either Whigs or Radicals, though he might occasionally support their measures. His support of the Royal Prerogative in 1834 followed only the example of Mr. Pitt in 1783 and Mr. Canning in 1827. The State, he said, was bound not merely to do justice, but to show favour, to the Church of England. Such popular franchises as the Reform Bill had spared were to be jealously protected and maintained. Freedom of trade was one of the oldest Tory principles. He may not always have found it easy, as leader of a great party after the Reform Bill, to render a literal obedience to these principles; but he always strove to act in the spirit of them; and those who try to represent him as a seceder from Toryism, and towards the end of his career as virtually a Liberal, have not looked for his opinions where he himself would have most wished them to be studied, in the pages of Hansard.†

In the history of politics Sir Robert Peel occupies a place for which his natural disposition and his political

---

* See Lord Salisbury's speech at Brighton, October 15th, 1885.

† The remark of Mr. Greville, that Peel ought to have been a Whig, shows only that Greville did not understand what it was to be a Tory.

education pre-eminently qualified him. His mission was not so much to originate as to moderate, control, and instruct. He represents the period which lies between 1832 and 1867, between the first Reform Bill and the second, during which the peaceable evolution of middle-class ideas was repeatedly threatened with interruption by democratic violence. Sir Robert Peel secured for it a fair field, and enabled it to run its course. He was the great Minister of the middle classes who, by rallying them round the reformed Constitution, was able to save both his own order and theirs from the revolution which seemed to menace both. This was his work in politics—to secure an orderly and Conservative development of the great series of reforms which the changed conditions of England after 1815 rendered necessary, and which had begun in the life-time of Lord Liverpool. And this mission he most successfully fulfilled. His spirit dominated English politics for exactly one generation, during which this work was being accomplished. It lived after his death, not only in the little knot of statesmen who bore his name, but in the whole tone and temper of our public life, among both Liberals and Conservatives, and in the country at large as much as in the House of Commons. His very name seems a synonym for all that is safe, judicious, business-like, sound, and practical. In spite of the two great schisms of 1829 and 1846, we cannot help looking back upon him as a man whom any party would have been wise to follow. We cannot help it. Nor can I doubt that if he had been spared, his old followers would again have fallen under the spell, and again have mustered under his banner. He could not have found a better name than Conservative for the particular phase of Toryism with which his name is most intimately con-

nected : nor do I see what better one could be found for
the party which in the present day has again to oppose
that spirit which Sir Robert laid, but which has once
more left the "gates of darkness," and is moving to and
fro upon the land.

Sir Robert Peel was a popular man in private life,
with the few persons whom he really liked, or loved.
But in anything approaching to *bonhomie* or geniality,
he is said to have been singularly deficient.   Even to
the ordinary courtesies of Society he was sometimes incapable of conforming; and the squires and the rectors
who were invited to meet him at great country houses,
were often mortified by a demeanour which was needlessly
frigid and repellent.   I have heard that while the guest
of a well-known baronet in the midland counties, the
clergyman of the parish, an old gentleman of most venerable appearance, ventured to ask him some question
about public affairs, and was answered only by a
freezing stare, which speedily drove him off to the more
congenial society of the whist-table.   Lord Beaconsfield
or Mr. Gladstone would have smiled and put the question by.   I have been told another anecdote of Sir Robert
which it is not quite so easy to believe.   He had invited
a London friend, a professional man of high standing, to
visit him at Drayton.   In riding round the neighbourhood the gentleman, who belonged to that district, passed
the house of an old acquaintance, and he proposed to Sir
Robert that they should call.   Peel agreed : they were
shown in; and regaled with an excellent luncheon.   But
from the moment he entered the house to the moment he
left it, Peel never spoke a single word.   Among his Parliamentary supporters the same infirmity was apparent ;
and when contrasted with his leading contemporaries,

Palmerston, Stanley, Melbourne, or the Duke of Welling-ton, who was the soul of frankness and simplicity, it told much to his disadvantage. There are many men who, in trying to be dignified, only succeed in being pompous, and create difficulties for themselves in trans-acting the affairs of life, which those who are more natural escape. But Sir Robert Peel, according to all tradition, must have done more than this, and have relied often upon downright rudeness to protect himself from possible familiarities.

He was, as I have said, a keen sportsman and an excellent shot, and he and Lord Eversley used to be considered, at one time, among the two best game-shots in England. In cover-shooting Sir Robert Peel, who, perhaps, did not like pricking his legs, usually took the outside, while the Speaker preferred walking with the beaters. He was a scholar, and fond of scholarship, though, perhaps, too much given to quotations which had " previously received the meed of Parliamentary appro-bation." One of these, which I always thought very happy, though it came a little oddly from Peel, was in answer to a Whig, during the Reform debates, who wished Mr. Canning had been there. " I wish to heaven that he was," said Peel :

" Tuque tuis armis, nos te poteremur, Achille."

But I found that Canning himself had quoted the same line in reference to Mr. Perceval. Sir Robert Peel was a man of fine taste, and a liberal patron ; and with all his faults, and they were neither few nor slight, was a worthy specimen of the class to which he belonged—a class peculiar to England, and to which England is deeply indebted—the untitled territorial aristocracy.

CHAPTER VII.

LORD DERBY.

The eight years that followed the death of Sir Robert Peel were a blank in domestic legislation. The great Exhibition, the *Coup d'État* in France, the Crimean war, and the Indian Mutiny diverted the public mind from Constitutional and administrative questions, and made Lord John Russell's revival of Parliamentary Reform, in 1852 and 1854, almost ridiculous. But with the return of the Tories to power in 1858, the Radical Party re-opened their batteries ; and from that moment may be dated the commencement of Mr. Disraeli's education of his party.

Conservatism, however, down to the death of Lord Palmerston, was, so to speak, in commission. It was represented on both sides of the House. Lord Palmerston was a disciple of Mr. Canning, and as much opposed to the progress of democracy as his master. In his foreign policy, if at one time, when he was fresh to the work, he had transgressed the great principles which Mr. Canning and the Duke of Wellington had laid down, he had in later life recurred to them, and made English interests the sole measure of his actions. But he was badly served by Lord Clarendon and Lord Russell ; while the Peelites were taking a line of their own, and beginning to import into our foreign policy considerations by which neither Wellington nor Peel would have allowed it to be influenced. As Lord Palmerston returned to the Tory view the Peelites drifted away from it, and for many years were a source of great embarrassment to the Premier in promoting the interests of this country. The motley character of the Government, and the appearance of vacillation which it frequently imparted to their counsels supplied abundant fuel for the orators of the Opposition who, incensed at the coalition which had driven them from office both in 1852 and 1859, were little inclined to spare the authors of their downfall. The coalition between the Whigs and Radicals, and the singular foreign policy of Lord Russell, were unfailing topics of sarcasm in both Houses of Parliament. But the country, on the whole, was governed on Conservative principles, and in the most vigorous sallies of the Opposition there always seemed to be a flavour of unreality. The country was willing to take its Conservatism from Lord Palmerston, and a considerable section of the Opposition preferred it to their own.

Such was the period during which the Tory Party was led by the brilliant and impetuous noble who gained the name of the Rupert of Debate; and who, if the game of politics could be decided by a series of successful charges, would have been the most powerful of modern statesmen. But in politics, as in war, it is by combination and calculation, by patience and perseverance, and the long and careful study of all the problems of the age, that permanent triumphs are attained; and for these the late Lord Derby had little or no inclination. In the then temper of the public mind, a Conservative Government should properly have been in office. Yet the Tories were obliged to look on while the Liberals occupied their place, and carried out their principles in disguise. Lord Derby loved the excitement of politics, but not the cares of office, or the trouble and fatigue of training. He played the game like a great patrician who took it as one of the natural incidents of his position, and not as an earnest statesman, to whom it is all in all. He "drank delight of battle with his peers." He revelled in the *gaudium certaminis*, but he cared nothing for the stakes. Not that it is meant that Lord Derby was a man of no convictions. The very reverse was the truth. In certain subjects he took a deep and abiding interest from the first hour of his public life to the last. He was a religious man and a sincere Churchman. He was one of the most zealous champions of the "Protestant Constitution of these realms." His sense of duty was one of the most marked features in his character. But it suited him better to promote these objects as the leader of the Opposition than as the head of the Government. He could not interest himself in the minute details which are necessary to the success of Parliamentary campaigns, or apply himself to the management of men, and the conciliation of obstinacy or stupidity It was just as easy for the Tories to have governed England from 1855 to 1865 as for the Liberals ; and the only thing that prevented it was that Lord Palmerston possessed just those qualities in which Lord Derby was deficient.

Lord Derby was naturally the abler man of the two. During the earlier part of his career nobody would have dreamed of comparing them together. Mr. Stanley was regarded as the natural successor of Lord Grey ; and not either Lord Palmerston or Lord John Russell. The ease with which he mastered the most complex questions, when he chose to give his mind to them, was only equalled by the talents for business which, whenever he allowed them fair play, excited the admiration of men who had passed their lives in counting-houses. As an orator, a scholar, and a man of letters, Lord Palmerston made no pretence of competing with him, yet in the practical conduct of politics he beat him out of the field, and kept the Tories on the Opposition benches till he died of old age.

The name of Lord Derby is connected principally with three great questions, the Irish Question, the Reform Question, and the Corn Law Question. His maiden speech was on the Irish Church, and almost the last words he uttered in the House of Lords were on the same subject. He made his mark in the House of Commons by his advocacy of the first Reform Bill, and the last act of his last administration was to develop the principles of the great measure which was carried by Lord Grey. It was idle to taunt Lord Derby with inconsistency, whatever might be said of others, in taking up the question of Reform ; while the saying which is often imputed to him as a proof that he was actuated by purely party motives never fell from his lips. His alleged boast that he had " dished the Whigs," was invented by the Whigs themselves.

The fourteenth Earl of Derby was born at Knowsley in Lancashire on the 29th of March 1799. He was educated at Eton and Christ Church, where he won the Chancellor's prize for Latin verse, the subject for that year being Syracuse. His family belonged to the old Whig connection ; and in 1821 he entered Parliament as member for Stockbridge, a nomination borough belonging to the Grosvenors ; and in 1824 he addressed the House of

Commons for the first time on Mr. Hume's motion for an inquiry into the state of the Irish Church. He then said he believed that "the four great evils under which Ireland laboured were the want of a resident gentry, the want of capital, the want of employment, and the want of education, and that all these wants would be aggravated by diminishing the means of the clergy."

When the Whigs came into power Mr. Stanley was made Chief Secretary for Ireland, and it was in this capacity that he earned for himself the reputation of being the only man of whom O'Connell was afraid. The Whigs found it necessary in 1833 to introduce a Coercion Bill, and the conduct of it devolved upon Lord Althorpe, who made such a miserable figure in introducing it to the House, that when he sat down, even Ministers themselves began to despair of its success. Stanley retired with the papers for about an hour, thoroughly got up the case, and, returning to the House, delivered so brilliant and forcible a speech that it turned the fortunes of the fight, and ensured the safety of the Bill. But if he earned the hatred of the Repealers by fiery scorn and pitiless logic which he poured upon their heads, he ought to have earned the gratitude of Ireland for his Education Act. The measure was founded on the Report of the Select Committee appointed by the Tory Government in 1827, and was carried through the House of Commons in July 1833. The following year, however, saw the beginning and the end of his connection with the Whig Party. The Appropriation Clause which has already been explained, was so entirely contrary to his ideas of the rights of property in general, and the sanctity of Church property in particular, that, having first succeeded in eliminating it from the Church Bill of 1833, he resigned when it was restored in the Tithe Bill of 1834. In the explanatory speech which he delivered on the 2nd of June, he lays down in the clearest language the grounds which made him quit the Ministry and dread the future. " This doctrine of proportion," said he, " is pregnant with danger as applied to Ireland, and, if once admitted, is certain to be applied to to England. If you once admit the doctrine that the majority in every parish is the religion of the State, you acknowledge at once that the State has no religion."

Mr. Stanley, who, in 1834, by the death of his grandfather, became Lord Stanley, was joined in his retirement by Sir James Graham, Lord Ripon, and the Duke of Richmond. The seceders did not at once join the regular Conservative Party, nor did they become members of the Tory Government of 1834. But when the Whigs now evinced their intention of adopting a more Radical policy, and giving their sanction to attacks on the Constitutional status of the Church of England, Lord Stanley and his friends crossed over to the Opposition benches and worked steadily and successfully with Sir Robert Peel, till another and more fatal schism in turn tore asunder the Conservatives, and dispersed them upon every coast. In Sir Robert Peel's Ministry of 1841 Lord Stanley was Colonial Secretary, and proved himself a most able coadjutor in the work of that illustrious statesman. But with the year 1846 came that unhappy rupture which undid the whole work of the last fourteen years, and left it to be done over again by a hand no less skilful and a brain more subtle and daring than Sir Robert Peel's. Had Lord Stanley at this time sat in the Lower House of Parliament, it is probable that the political history of the last twenty years might have been very different. But in 1844 he had been raised to the House of Lords by the title of Baron Stanley of

Bickerstaffe, and in his absence the large majority of the
Conservative Party who had revolted from Sir Robert
Peel were left without any leader in whom they could place
implicit confidence.   They were yet to learn that they
still possessed one within their ranks who would equal,
if he did not even leave far behind the fame of Sir Robert
Peel, as he was in originality of mind, in genuine eloquence, and in dauntless courage undoubtedly his superior.
But at that time his great capacity was unsuspected, and,
to the public eye, the bulk of the Party in the House of
Commons showed to great disadvantage beside the little
constellation of which Sir Robert was the centre.   Removed
to the House of Lords, Lord Stanley did all he could for
his Party; he gave them the immense moral support of
his great name and rank, and his high character.   But he
could not do for them what he could have done in the
House of Commons.   Perhaps upon the whole it was as
well for the Party that this was so.   Had they ever returned to office as avowed Protectionists, which must have
been the case in 1846, 1847, or 1848, it would have been
worse for them in the long run.   Even as it was, they had
not in 1852 entirely shaken off the taint, and it was this
and nothing else which prevented them from securing a
majority at the General Election.

On the merits of Free Trade and Protection, regarded
as an abstract question of political economy, it would be
waste of time to expend another syllable; nor was it ever,
in fact, a genuine note of distinction between political
parties.   The real question which underlay the controversy
of 1846 was this : what was the value to the nation at
large of a prosperous domestic agriculture, and a great
and independent landed interest ?   What price, if any,
would a wise man be prepared to give, in order to retain

these interests as a constituent and a preponderating part of the body politic. No doubt a man might give a different answer to *this* question according to whether he was a Radical or a Conservative; for the Whigs, be it remembered, down almost to the last moment, had as little thought of interfering with the Corn Laws as the Tories. A man must be mad to think of such a thing, Lord Melbourne said. Eventually, however, the whole Whig-Radical Party, and a section of the Tory Party, became ranged on one side, and the bulk of the Conservatives on the other. The latter said that Protection was necessary to British agriculture, and the former denied it. The Protectionists said that the agricultural interest and the territorial system were too valuable to be sacrificed, even if the support of them did entail a slight additional burden on the people—a condition, however, which they disputed. The Free Traders said *fiat justitia ruat cœlum*. Let Free Trade triumph, and let the consequences take care of themselves. Thus the reader will see that the question was divided into two parts—first of all, whether a duty on foreign corn was really essential to the permanent welfare, or, in other words, to the existence, of agriculture as one of the great industries of the country; and, secondly, whether, if it were, the article was worth the price. Was it worth while to make the consumer pay an additional farthing for his loaf, in order to keep up throughout the country a wealthy, intelligent, and respectable class of tenant-farmers, and a body of resident landed gentry discharging all those local duties and functions on which Mr. Gladstone himself has pronounced so eloquent a panegyric, or was the saving of the additional farthing worth all these advantages combined? If rents fell so low that country gentlemen could not live on their estates, and land came to be divided between a class of small impoverished cultivators, and rich absentees who valued it only for their amusement, and bought and sold it like other articles of luxury; if all the old hereditary ties and reciprocal obligations, which distinguished English rural life and softened the contrast between rich and poor which frowns with such ominous severity in our large cities, were to be destroyed; if all these consequences were to be the price of Free Trade; would the country on the whole be the gainer?

The answer to the first of these questions is more doubtful now than it was thirty years ago. Then it was thought that the fluctuations in price which accompanied the old system were more injurious to the farmer than a lower average subject to fewer vicissitudes. But then it was never contemplated that wheat should fall to thirty shillings a quarter. Given all the conditions of the market as they existed in 1845, and the Free Traders may have been perfectly justified. Whether they would have carried their point had things been as they are now, and in the face of the American competition which threatens to swamp even our dairies, is another question altogether. The possibility of such results was, indeed, pointed out at the time.* But it was treated with indifference, and now that they have come upon us, the wisest are disheartened and perplexed; unable to reject the evidence of their senses, yet equally unwilling to admit the possibility of a revival of protective duties.

Of the proper answer to the second question I entertain no doubt whatever. It is one in which the pecuniary interest of the agricultural labourer is but small; for whether he has higher wages and dearer bread, or lower

* See Lord Beaconsfield's speech in the House of Lords, March 28, 1879.

wages and cheaper bread seems not to be a matter of
great importance. But his moral interest in the existence
of a flourishing tenantry and a resident aristocracy is
immense, and, other things being equal, would decidedly
turn the scale, *sua si bona norit.* And if we take the
community at large, the same truth will hold good. Lord
Beaconsfield, who looked on this question with the eye
of a born statesman, always refused to accept the economical argument as conclusive.

I take [he said] the only broad and only safe line, namely, that what we
ought to uphold is the preponderance of the landed interest; that the
preponderance of the landed interest has made England; that it is an
immense element of political power and stability; that we should never
have been able to undertake the great war on which we embarked in the
memory of many present; that we should never have been able to conquer
the greatest military genius which the world ever saw, with the greatest
means at his disposal, and to hurl him from his throne, if we had not had
a territorial aristocracy to give stability to our Constitution. . . .*

Your Corn Laws are merely the outwork of a great system fixed and established on your territorial property, and the only object the Leaguers have
in making themselves masters of the outwork is that they may easily overcome the citadel.†

The comparative advantages of a territorial and a commercial aristocracy is a matter of opinion: but that the
object of the Leaguers was to erect the latter on the ruins
of the former is a fact. Cobden said so himself. He said
that Free Trade was the only way of undermining the
influence of the governing and feudal classes. He wished
to see a class of great commercial statesmen "thrusting
aside the nobles," and creating "a new policy adapted to
the ends of a great trading community."‡ It is evident
now that this was the ulterior design which underlay the
Free Trade agitation. Nobody can doubt it after reading

---

* Speech at Shrewsbury, 1843.
† Speech in the House of Lords, March 28, 1879, *et passim.*
‡ Mr. Morley's *Life of Cobden*, vol. i. p. 134, vol. ii. pp. 396, 482.

Mr. Morley's book, even if he did before. And whatever we may think of the merits of the question, it clearly imparts a very different aspect, and a much more interesting character, to what has usually been regarded as a purely economic controversy. Here we have the two great theories of national greatness brought face to face; and the combatants in such a strife, to whichever party they belonged, must be accredited with something beyond purely selfish motives or class interests. Cobden wished to transfer to his own class the power of the landed aristocracy. The landed aristocracy wished to keep it where it was. It is absurd to say that the one was either more or less selfish than the other; nor is it a matter of course that the one system was better calculated than the other to promote the interests of the public. England is something more than " a great trading community." The nation certainly would not wish to see every great question decided by reference only to trading considerations. History does not tell us that empires built exclusively on commerce have been the happiest or the most durable or the greatest benefactors to the world. At all events, the question is still a moot point in political philosophy, and what I now wish to impress upon the public is that, in resisting the Free Traders, Lord Stanley and the Tories were fighting for a political theory much more than for a lucrative advantage: that they understood what the Leaguers really wanted; and that both sides were contending for something of infinitely greater importance than a Corn Law considered only as an end in itself.

Both Protectionists and Free Traders may have been wrong in believing that the repeal of the Corn Laws would help to ruin the landed aristocracy. Sir Robert Peel did not think so. And probably both the one side and the

other exaggerated the consequences likely to result from
Free Trade. But it will hereafter be acknowledged that
the real struggle of 1846, though comprehended by the
leading statesmen engaged in it, was not rightly understood at the time by the great body of the people; and that
to appreciate the motives of Lord Stanley and Mr. Disraeli,
no less than those of Mr. Bright and Mr. Cobden, we must
look a good deal further than the mere price of wheat,
and see that it was distinctly a struggle for pre-eminence
between two rival classes, in which the poor man's loaf
played, in reality, a very secondary part.

Lord Stanley, who, in 1842, on the discussion of the
Canada Corn Bill, had recommended Sir Robert Peel to
adopt Free Trade with the Colonies and Protection against
the rest of the world, did not take an altogether unstates-
man-like view of the position; but he declined the unlimited
Free Trade—" free imports against hostile tariffs "—to
which Sir Robert Peel had become a convert, and there
was nothing left for him but to become the leader of the
Opposition, an office which his sense of duty did not permit him to decline, but which certainly he was far from
coveting. It was the Duke of Wellington who finally persuaded him to take the lead, in order that there might
still be an organized party left for the Constitution to fall
back upon. But he did so in no sanguine spirit, and, as
we know from the memoirs of Lord Malmesbury, betrayed
at times an apparent want of confidence in his own supporters which events showed to be unwarranted, and which,
at times, wounded them deeply. Had he possessed the
same knowledge of mankind as Mr. Disraeli, he would never
have made such a mistake. But he could not bring himself
to believe that with the young and untried soldiers, who were
all that he had at his command, it was possible to confront,

with success, the veterans who had fought round Peel, or
had been trained to affairs under Liverpool. He did them
a grievous injustice, which he did not discover till it was
too late, and when the fairest opportunity that ever came
to the Conservative Party, while he was at their head, had
been allowed to pass.

Lord Stanley, who had now become Lord Derby, declined to take office in 1851, on the resignation of
Lord John Russell; but seems to have had no alternative in 1852, when the Whig Ministry fell before the
vengeance of Lord Palmerston. His followers were impatient. The Crown was in difficulties; and finally he
accepted the Treasury without the aid of either Mr. Gladstone or Lord Palmerston, who professed to be afraid of
the odour of Protection which still clung to him. All
things considered, he is allowed to have acquitted himself
with credit. Exactly one generation ago, he proclaimed
the policy of the Conservative Party to be one of social
improvement, and how well that pledge has been redeemed
we shall see when we arrive at the history of our own time.
But in spite of the good opinions which he won from all
classes, and though six months of office had encouraged and
organized his party, which, strengthened by the General
Election, now presented all the appearance of a regular
Opposition, formidable both by numbers and discipline, I
am still of opinion that, if the Tories had not been forced
to take office till after the beginning of the war, they
might have taken it and kept it probably for Lord Derby's
lifetime, and, in that case, the quarrel between Mr. Gladstone and Mr. Disraeli might never have occurred. In
1855 the Coalition Ministry fell amid a storm of public
indignation. Both Whigs, Peelites, and Radicals were
alike discredited. The Free Trade controversy was over.

The Reform controversy had not begun. The Conservatives would have come into office with their hands free. All the country wanted was a strong Government; and Lord Derby's Government would have been virtually, if not nominally, a strong one; for it would have been certain that, on the first appeal to the country, he must, after recent events, be supported by a large majority. Everything, in fact, was then in Lord Derby's favour. By what strange fatality was it that he only took office just when everything was against him? He accepted the seals in 1852, in 1858, and in 1866, when he was surrounded with difficulties; he refused them in 1855 and shrank from them in 1862, when he had the ball at his feet!

On the 3rd of June 1862 the House of Commons met to consider a resolution, proposed by Mr. Stansfeld, to the effect that " the national expenditure was capable of reduction without compromising the safety, the independence, or the legitimate influence of the country." Lord Palmerston met the resolution by an amendment, which was ultimately carried by 367 votes to 65. But Mr. Walpole had given notice of another amendment to be moved in substitution for Lord Palmerston's, which would have received the support of the entire Conservative Party, and of a good many Liberals besides. Referring to this amendment before the debate began, Lord Palmerston observed that " the question which the House would now be called on to decide was—whether gentlemen who sat on the Ministerial or the opposite benches were best entitled to the confidence of the House and the country." By this language he drew from Mr. Walpole a declaration that he would not, under those circumstances, take the responsibility of moving his amendment. It is not true, we believe, that he was acting by the advice of Lord Derby; but it can hardly be doubted that, if Lord Derby's reluctance to resume power had not been known to the Party, this opportunity of re-seating him would not have been deliberately lost.

What deep mortification was felt by Mr. Disraeli at the loss of these golden opportunities, when he saw all the fruits of his own careful and patient labour in the House of Commons completely thrown away, and the party which he had formed and trained with such consummate skill hard held in the moment of victory, who shall take upon himself to describe? In many respects it was impossible for the Conservative Party to have had a better leader than Lord Derby. In his high rank, his spotless character, and his great wealth, he was a second Lord Rockingham. In his intellectual force, his fervid eloquence, and his happy wit, he was a second Fox. Such a combination as this must have triumphed over all obstacles, had he in whom it was embodied been actuated by the ordinary motives of English politicians. But Lord Derby had neither the ambition nor the daring essential to the leader of a party circumstanced as the Tories then were. He shrank from responsibility; and instead of being annoyed by the successive defeats which three times turned him out of office, he welcomed each of them as a happy release, and flew back to his favourite pursuits—his books, his horses, and his gun—with the delight of a school-boy. He was even bored when he heard that his great lieutenant was asked to meet him in the country. "Now," he said, "we shall be obliged to talk politics."

It is easy to understand how, under a chief of this kind, the Tory Party were constantly on the verge of obtaining a majority, and yet never quite succeeded. His wit, his eloquence, his splendid abilities, his ancient birth, his great position, made him a leader whom any man would be proud to follow. But the sustained energy, the real love of political power as the finest field for the exercise of the human faculties, were always wanting. What he had not himself he could not infuse into his followers; and the Tory Party remained to the day of his death condemned to the punishment of Sisyphus, always rolling the stone to the top, and always finding it roll back again to the bottom immediately afterwards.

The defeat of Lord Palmerston on the Conspiracy to Murder Bill, in 1858, made way for Lord Derby a second time, and he was almost immediately confronted with the question of Parliamentary Reform, which had been again raised by Mr. Bright during a kind of progress through the northern counties in the autumn and winter of that year. What would the Derby Government do? Would they bring in a Reform Bill or not?—that was the question of the day. Toryism in the reign of George the Third had effected a compromise with the oligarchy, and would have been content to carry it out, if only the Whigs would have allowed them. But as soon as the latter found out that the death of the old King was to make no change in their position they began to look to another change in the Constitution for that restoration to power which they had expected from a new reign, but which, after the reconstruction of the Tory Government in 1822, seemed even more remote than ever. A wiser policy on the part of the Tory Government after the death of Mr. Canning might have modified the great change which undoubtedly, in some form or another, had become imperatively necessary before the death of George the Fourth. But they missed their chance, and the Whigs created the middle-class system which lasted from 1832 to 1867. This, too, the Tories would have let alone if the Whigs would have agreed to do the same. But as soon as it became apparent that the old game was still to be continued, and that whenever the Whigs were in difficulties a new Reform Bill was to be harnessed, like a leader, to their jaded cattle in order to pull them out of the mud, thus leading to the perpetual unsettlement of the Constitution, and the constant derangement of the Party balance, it became the duty of the Tory leaders to consider seriously how this system could be stopped.

Whether the decision at which Lord Derby then arrived was a really spirited and sagacious one, or whether it was prompted by a comparatively short-sighted ambition and superficial acquaintance with the state of public feeling, has been the theme of endless controversy and bitter recrimination. But our own opinion is that the policy of 1859 deserves neither the praise nor the blame that has been poured upon it. It was a simple necessity. If the Conservatives were ever to form a permanent administration, the Reform question must be got rid of by one means or another. As long as it was kept alive, the Whigs had it always in their power to turn the Tories out of office at their own good will and pleasure. And the consciousness of this truth was fatal to the usefulness of the Tory Party, even as an Opposition. How, then, was this problem to be solved? There were but two ways, either by passing a Reform Bill that should lay the question at rest for at least another generation, or by dividing the Whig Party as Pitt and Sir Robert Peel divided it, and bringing over the more moderate among them to the Conservative camp. No doubt the latter course was the one more agreeable to Conserva-

tive traditions, and to the personal sentiments of Lord
Derby. But the experiment had been tried ; Lord Derby
had ascertained beyond a doubt that there were none
among the Whigs prepared to play the part which the
Duke of Portland played in 1795, and which he himself
had played in 1835. Help from that quarter there was
none. There remained then but the other alternative,
unless the Tories were contented to remain in opposition
for ever, and to see all the prizes of public life, all the
rewards which stimulate a healthy ambition, all the
satisfaction which great minds derive from exercising
the art of government, monopolized by a small clique
who had nothing to give in return for this enormous
sacrifice.

This idea of a union with the Conservative Whigs
has always been a favourite one with all moderate and
reasonable Tories, and the difficulties in the way of it
are raised exclusively by their opponents. Whether we
are nearer to it now than we were twenty years ago
remains to be seen. But in a pamphlet published in
1860 an excellent judge of parties, as they then stood,
the late Lord Ormathwaite, while declaring that in a
union between the regular Conservatives and the more
Conservative-minded of the Whigs lay our best safeguard
against democracy, at the same time expressed his own
opinion to be that the Whigs would never come to that
agreement. Their party traditions, their jealousy of new
associates, the ambition of their leading families, which
nothing less than a monopoly of official honours would
be enough to satisfy, were, he thought, insuperable obstacles to any so desirable a result. It may be hoped that
during the last five-and-twenty years the Whigs may have
learned something and forgotten something, and that in

the verification of Conservative predictions regarding the
progress and tendency of Radicalism, they may see reason
for reconsidering their position.   It is greatly to the credit
of the Tory Party that they have never hesitated to make
overtures to their opponents, when the public service
seemed to require it.   Pitt, Canning, Sir Robert Peel,
and Lord Derby, all did this in turn, and proved by
their actions the Tory boast of being less exclusive than
their opponents, and less bound and fettered by connection.   In fact the old Tory idea was to form an
administration capable of carrying on the King's Government in a capable and constitutional manner.   The Duke
of Wellington said he did not know what Whig and
Tory principles meant.   The country must be governed;
order must be maintained;   the law must be obeyed;
changes in conformity with the Constitution must periodically be made : but he knew nothing of the divine
right of any set of men to a monopoly of administration.   Because Pitt, Canning, and Lord Derby invited
the Whigs to assist them upon this understanding, they
were not Whigs themselves.   The suggestion is simply
ludicrous.   Neither of them professed to give up any single
point which was essential to Toryism.   They asked their
adversaries to consider whether for the public good they
would not serve under that banner.   The time may come
when a real fusion of parties will be found absolutely
necessary, and then, no doubt, sacrifices may have to be
made on both sides.   But none were either offered or
suggested on the occasions we have named.

The two cardinal provisions of the Bill introduced by
Mr. Disraeli on the 28th of February were identity of
suffrage in towns and counties—the occupancy franchise
in the latter being reduced to ten pounds—and the restric-

tion of the forty-shilling borough freeholder, who had hitherto voted for the county, to a vote for the borough in which his qualification was situated. My own opinion of the Bill of 1859 is that its provisions might possibly have been found to work well, but that it did not make sufficient allowance for prejudices which held a high position among popular errors, and were sure to be turned to good account by the veteran tacticians opposite. It is quite true that, as the value of money is always changing, a purely pecuniary qualification would be always unstable; that a £6 borough franchise would have been just as arbitrary as a £10 borough franchise without any prescription in its favour; that it was sure to be assailed in turn, and that more quickly than the last; that it could be defended on no principle, that it held out no prospect of permanence, and that, at the best, it would but secure a temporary cessation of hostilities until the exigencies of the Liberal Party should demand the revival of the question. The £10 franchise had, at all events, borne the test of one generation. The people were accustomed to it. There was, indeed, no principle to support it, any more than the lower one, but there was prescription. The existing franchise might then possibly be sustained. But, if that were given up, there appeared to be only one alternative.*

Again, it was perfectly true that, from an abstract point of view, the townsman had no more right to vote for both the borough and the county than the countryman had to vote for both the county and borough. And, indeed, the principle of Mr. Disraeli's clause had been conceded in 1832, when all borough freeholds above the value of £10, which previously had given votes for the county, were shorn of that privilege. It was likewise quite true that

* See speech of Mr. Disraeli, July 15, 1867

uniformity of franchise between the towns and counties
would not have created identity of interests leading to
electoral districts if it had not existed there already; that
to seek to keep up an artificial distinction between town
and county by a difference in the suffrage, when all
natural distinctions had vanished, was futile; that if these
natural distinctions still survived, identity of suffrage would
be quite powerless to efface them, and that, if not, it
would be equally powerless to produce them. These arguments seem to us, as arguments, unanswerable, and if the
contest had depended upon logic the Government must
certainly have won it. But Mr. Disraeli should have
remembered that the idea of Reform had long been
indelibly associated in the public mind with the reduction
of the borough franchise; that the restriction proposed to
be placed upon the borough freeholders, however just in
itself, was capable of being placed in a very invidious light;
and that the hard and fast line which the uniform franchise would have drawn was sure to provoke exactly the
kind of alarm that was raised by Mr. Henley and Mr.
Walpole. It seems highly probable that if Government
had introduced a measure less scientific and more practical, if they had lowered the county qualification to £25
and the borough franchise to £8, leaving other things
pretty nearly as they found them, the Bill would have
passed, a ministerial majority would have been returned
at the General Election, and the Conservative Party have
continued to govern the country till Parliamentary Reform
was once more called into requisition by the necessities
of the Whig Opposition. But how long would that have
been? There would have been little peace for a Conservative Administration while the Reform League had a leg to
stand upon. The new franchise would, in a very short

time, have been made the butt of hostile demonstrations and Hyde Park orators. The battle would have had to be fought over again. And the Conservative Party must either have done what they did in 1867, without the same logical background, or proposed a simple scheme of further reduction, which their rivals would certainly have out-bidden. As it is, the first Conservative Reform Bill was the true justification of the second, and, whatever else Lord Derby's Government may be charged with, it cannot be charged with inconsistency.

Lord Hartington's vote of want of confidence in the Conservative Government, based chiefly on the inadequacy of their Reform Bill to meet the blazing necessities of the case, and their failure to preserve peace between France and Austria, was carried in a very full House by thirteen votes. Lord Derby again resigned, and made way for the second ministry of Lord Palmerston, who, by maintaining those Conservative principles which satisfied the majority of the nation, and using the Liberal phraseology which pleased the majority of the House, retained office to his death.

In the following year, 1860, Lord John Russell introduced a Reform Bill of the same kind as that which we have assumed that Lord Derby might have carried; that is to say, a simple reduction of the town and county franchise, without any lateral franchises, and a moderate measure of redistribution. This Bill, introduced on the 1st of March, was not read a second time till the 3rd of May, though it encountered no regular opposition. On one night of the debate the House was counted out. On the very next night a like catastrophe was with the greatest difficulty prevented. On the 4th of June a private member moved to postpone the whole question till the House had

before it the census of 1861. And in deference to the
feeling then displayed, Lord John Russell, a week afterwards, withdrew the Bill, announcing, with characteristic
courage, that he intended to prepare another. The assurance was listened to with a courteous smile by a House
too pleased to be sarcastic. Not a tear trembled on the
eyelids even of Lord John himself. And without a murmur
of regret the question, as a Government question, was
shelved for another six years.

In 1866, however, Lord Russell's Government, in which
the Radical influence had again become predominant, introduced a Bill for the extension of the franchise, reducing
the county qualification to £14 rental and the borough
franchise to £7, but unaccompanied by any scheme for the
redistribution of seats, which was to form the subject of
subsequent legislation. The Tory party at once objected
to this separation of the two branches of the subject, on
the ground that they could not consent to so large a reduction of the franchise till they knew what use was to be
made of it; and must decline to be committed to the first
and irrevocable step till they were aware in what direction
it would lead them. The speech of the present Lord Derby,
then Lord Stanley, in seconding the motion of Lord Grosvenor to the above effect, was then and has ever since been
considered unanswerable. The Government was saved from
defeat by the narrow majority of five, and a distribution
scheme was at once produced. But in committee on the
Franchise Bill Lord Dunkellin carried an amendment
against the Government, substituting a rental for a
rating franchise, on which Lord Russell resigned, and
Lord Derby returned to office.

Having tried and failed in the experiment of uniformity
of suffrage, Lord Derby willingly agreed to Mr. Disraeli's

proposal that a rating suffrage was the only firm ground beneath their feet. He was a convert to this opinion long before 1867; and when the time came he was fully prepared for the event. It is a pity, therefore, that he did not take firmer ground from the beginning. The real objection to the Franchise Bill of 1866 was exactly the same as the Conservative Reform Bill of 1859 had been intended to anticipate; and it is to be regretted that it was not resisted mainly upon that ground. The £10 franchise was a purely arbitrary franchise. It rested on no principle, and was only safe as long as it was not attacked. Nevertheless the £10 franchise had weathered many storms, and the Parliaments returned upon that qualification had done exceedingly good work. This was a very good reason for letting that franchise alone, but not for changing it to another of the same kind. Every syllable that Mr. Lowe said against changing the £10 franchise was still more fatal to a £7 franchise than it was to Household Suffrage. If the £10 franchise, which had so much in its favour, was unable to hold its ground, how long could a £7 franchise, with nothing in its favour, last?

Unfortunately, however, the Conservatives chose a middle course. Had they boldly declared that there was no alternative between maintaining the existing franchise and a descent to Household Suffrage, had public opinion been allowed time for reflection, and the instability of any intermediate resting-place been constantly set before it, we firmly believe that Mr. Gladstone's Bill would equally never have become law, and that the Conservatives would have been carried into office with a definite policy before them deliberately adopted by the nation. When we consider that Lord Derby himself had made up his mind upon the point; that Mr. Disraeli,

with a majority of the able men who served as his lieutenants, was of the same opinion ; that the feeling of the
rank and file against half measures was so strong that
they ultimately compelled Government to abandon the
scheme which had been adopted in deference to a section
of the Cabinet, and insisted on a bolder measure : when
we consider all this, it is certainly much to be regretted
that the Bill which ultimately passed was not produced at
once, without any vacillation or delay.

Our representative system having thus completed the
middle-class phase of its career, now, under the auspices
of the Tory Party, entered on the popular. The process
was so perfectly natural, the transition so obvious and inevitable, that the Tory Party made little or no difficulty
about the matter. One or two thought the change was
rather too abrupt, and might with advantage have been
postponed or graduated, just as certain of the Liberals
thought about the county franchise during Mr. Gladstone's
late Government. But, on the whole, they wisely came
to the conclusion that the transition period, inaugurated
in '32, having now run itself out, and other classes being
as fit for the franchise now as the £10 householders were
then, it was better to take that opportunity of settling the
question at once. Such was the opinion, among others,
of the veteran Tory Mr. Henley, who, having resigned
rather than assent to the measure of 1859, gave his warm
and undeviating support to the Bill of 1867.

It is curious that the question which alone prevented
Lord Derby from reaping the fruits of his Reform Bill
should have been the same which had always been a
stumbling-block in his path from the beginning, and which
had caused his retirement from office just thirty-six years
before : I mean the Irish Church Question. What were

the precise motives which determined Mr. Gladstone and
the Liberal Party to raise this question in the spring
of 1868 I am not called upon to enquire. Though other
circumstances had changed, the secularization of Church
property was no more defensible in 1868 than it had been
in 1834.* ' Whatever arrangement might have been made,
the property of the Catholic Church, whether Roman or
Anglican, should have been retained for the service of
religion. But concurrent endowment was rejected, and
the Tories vigorously, though uselessly, strove to keep the
ecclesiastical revenues of Ireland on their existing basis.
Mr. Disraeli, however, had not counted on the coalition
between the Roman Catholics and the Dissenters, which the
policy of Mr. Gladstone brought about; nor yet, perhaps,
on the strength of the general feeling which existed at that
time on the subject of the Irish Establishment. Numerous independent Liberals, who would certainly have supported the authors of household suffrage in the towns,
were obliged to vote against them when the Disestablishment of the Irish Church was thrust in between, and made
the first question for the jury. This was the result which
those who hoisted the signal for attack, of course, foresaw; and their tactics were perfectly successful. A large
majority was returned in favour of Mr. Gladstone in
December 1868, and for the third time Lord Derby, who
had resigned the office of Prime Minister in the spring of
the year, saw his Party driven back to opposition.

The closing scenes of Lord Derby's political career are
profoundly affecting. With the passage of the Reform Bill
his work as the leader of the Conservative Party was ended.
The appeal to a new constituency, and the introduction of
wholly new questions, formed an appropriate occasion for

* Cf. p. 256.

the inauguration of a new chief. And Lord Derby retired from office with a proud consciousness that he had, for twenty years of unusual discouragement and adversity, retained the unbroken loyalty of a great party, and repaid it with services of almost inestimable value. But Nature was more kind to him than Fortune. She spared him only to witness the disappointment of all those hopes which had been founded on his last great measure, and the overthrow of that national Church whose champion he had been from his entrance into public life. His speech in the House of Lords against the second reading of the Irish Church Bill will long be remembered with the warmest interest and sympathy. He spoke not with his accustomed energy, not with mocking irony, not with sparkling wit or vivid logic, but with a solemn gravity, a touching pathos, a deep and earnest conviction far beyond the arts of rhetoric to strengthen or adorn.

Few statesmen have taken their farewell of the political stage under circumstances so impressive and so solemn. And his parting reference to one of the most powerful scenes ever drawn by the hand of the master of modern fiction was not only one of the happiest strokes of a consummate orator, but the grave prophetic warning of a dying statesman, which did not fall unheeded on a nation's ears, and has borne fruit in those good works and redoubled exertions which promise to carry the Church of England through the storm which he foretold, and with which the horizon is already black.

Lord Derby was not in office long enough to exercise much influence on our foreign policy. But it is well worth remembering that, on two occasions out of the three when he was deposed by a Whig-Radical coalition, members of the Liberal Party lived to regret the vote which they had given. This was stated very strongly by Mr. Cobden after 1852. " I look back," he said, " with regret on the vote which changed Lord Derby's Government. I regret the result of that motion, for it has cost the country a hundred millions of treasure, and between thirty and forty thousand good lives." That is to say, that if the Tories had remained in power, England would have remained at peace, whereas, by handing over the reins to the Liberals, we were plunged into the Crimean War. This was Cobden's opinion, who was, if anything, an unwilling witness. Nearly twenty years afterwards, Mr. Disraeli said positively that he *knew* this to be the case. " I speak of what I know, not of what I believe, but of what I have evidence in my possession to prove—that the Crimean War would never have happened if Lord Derby had remained in office."*

The second occasion on which a member of the Liberal Party made a statement similar to that of Mr. Cobden was in 1859. It may be remembered that one of the principal counts in the indictment against Lord Derby, which was submitted to the House of Commons by Lord Hartington, was, that he had not only failed to prevent the war between Austria and France, but that, by professions of sympathy with the former, he had encouraged her to proceed to extremities. When the division was taken, incredible as it may seem, the dispatches had not been laid before the House; and members voted in ignorance of the only documents on which their decision ought to have rested.† Lord Derby was defeated by a majority of

---

* Speech at Manchester, April 3, 1872.

† It is stated in Lord Malmesbury's *Memoirs* that the Papers were printed and ready for circulation, but that Mr. Disraeli did not wish them to be produced. This is one of the mysteries of politics, which is not likely to be cleared up till the publication of Mr. Disraeli's own biography.

thirteen, and the Tory Government resigned. Yet as soon as the correspondence appeared it became evident that they were not to blame; that they had done everything that any Ministry could have done to avert war; and that they had given the Austrians no encouragement at all. Mr. Horsman was the member who then had the candour to confess that he deeply regretted his share in the overthrow of the Government.

Lord Derby, as an orator, had more variety than Mr. Gladstone, and more impulse than Lord Beaconsfield. His greatest speeches were undoubtedly those which he delivered in his contest with O'Connell. There was a *fierte* about these which he never exhibited quite in the same degree afterwards. In the later part of his career he probably never shone so brilliantly as during the second administration of Lord Palmerston. Those terrible summaries of the session, for which Lord Lyndhurst was so famous during the government of Lord Melbourne, were scarcely superior to those summaries of the recess with which, every February, Lord Derby used to regale the House of Lords. The merciless logic, the sparkling gaiety, the pungent sarcasm of these harangues will never be forgotten either by those who heard them or by those who read them. With singular uniformity, every succeeding autumn produced its crop of blunders to supply fresh materials to the orator. Now it was the cession of Savoy and the unique character of the communications between our Foreign Minister and our Paris Ambassador. Now it was the language held towards Russia on the subject of the Polish insurrections, the pompous hints of what England would do in case the Czar was contumacious, and the discovery that it meant nothing worse than calling him a very ill-bred man. Now it was a lecture sent to Denmark, dictating submission to the Germans; and now one addressed to the Germans, commanding them, on pain of our displeasure, not to touch Denmark. Now it was a prospect of assistance held out to the Danes, and then an expression of surprise that they should ever have relied upon it. Our quarrel with Brazil, our formation of an Anglo-Chinese army, our cession of the Ionian Islands, and last, but not least, our offer of Malta to the Pope—all, in turn, supplied Lord Derby with topics of the most congenial character, and were the source of some of his happiest efforts.

Lord Derby in private life was one of the most delightful of mankind; and as a great landowner and landlord, one of the most popular. In Lancashire, it is not too much to say that he was idolized; and the noble part which he played during the terrible crisis of the " cotton famine " will never be forgotten by the sufferers. He subscribed £10,000 for their relief, and cheerfully sacrificed what he probably prized more; his leisure and his favourite occupations, to the superintendence of the great scheme of charity which he had been mainly instrumental in establishing.

Among his own tenantry he was regarded as a sovereign with a divine right to their allegiance; and I have been told by one of his most intimate and confidential friends that, on asking a small Roman Catholic freeholder in Lancashire how he meant to vote at the forthcoming election, the man replied that if anybody else had asked him that question he would have knocked him down. " Who the —— should I vote for, but my Lord?" " But the priests?" said his interrogator. " D—n the priests!" roared this faithful subject of the House of Stanley. " I shall vote for my Lord."

Lord Derby, strange to say, was a vain man rather than a proud one; and in his own honse, and among his own friends and tenants, was the most easily accessible and the most familiar and colloquial man alive. He was not an indolent man, as has often been imagined. When in office his application was indefatigable; nor was he insensible to the dignity of power. But he did not love politics for their own sake; and when he took office, did so rather from an over-ruling sense of duty than from any liking for his task. But he never neglected business; and the quickness of his parts enabled him to master details in a much shorter space of time than would have been required by ordinary men. His heart, however, was not upon the Treasury Bench; nor had he any taste for those strategical manœuvres which are as necessary in politics as in war. The soul of honour himself, he was incapable of suspecting either falsehood or trickery in others, and was, perhaps, a little impatient of the precautions which are necessary to counteract them.

CHAPTER VIII.

As the history of Toryism approaches our own times, the
task of the historian becomes at once more easy and
more difficult. It is easier, because events are nearer,
and the record supplied by Parliament and the public press
more copious and accessible. It is harder, because, as
we cross the line which divides our contemporaries from
our predecessors, other sources of information, which afford
the most interesting materials for both history and biography, begin to fail us. The series of memoirs and
correspondence which extend from the middle of the
eighteenth to the middle of the nineteenth century probably leave little to be discovered hereafter by the most
curious investigators of the annals of English statesmanship. But though numerous works have been published
during the last twenty years in which the name of Mr
Disraeli, for instance, repeatedly appears, it is found only
in short notes or brief fragments of conversation, and we
may look in vain for any full or trustworthy narrative of
transactions supplied either by the principal performer,
or one who enjoyed his inner confidence.*

At the same time it appears to be highly probable that
in the case of Lord Beaconsfield the absence of such in-

---

* Neither the *Croker Papers* nor the last three volumes of the *Greville
Memoirs* are any exception as far as the subject of this article is concerned.

formation signifies less than in the case of any other public man whose career I have attempted to portray. We have, doubtless, much still to learn of the conduct of individuals and parties during the thirty years which elapsed between 1850 and 1880. But of the real political faith, the innermost convictions with regard to the problems of the present and the history of the past, which inspired Mr. Disraeli through his long Parliamentary career, he has himself left us the fullest and frankest exposition in the well-known trilogy comprised under the titles of *Coningsby*, *Sybil*, and *Tancred*. Combining the views therein set forth—the result, at all events, of independent study and reflection—with the effect upon his mind of long practical experience in the conduct of affairs, we are able to explain a great deal which is apparently contradictory, and to see that his policy, however externally different at one time from what it appeared to be at another, was always true in reality to the cardinal principles which he had adopted in his early manhood.

Lord Beaconsfield was one of the three great Tory Ministers of the last hundred years who have impressed a distinct character on the political creed which they either inherited or adopted, and have formed schools of statesmanship. The other two are Sir Robert Peel and Mr. Pitt, the founder of the new Tory Party which emerged from the great struggles of the eighteenth century, and which still represents, in most essential points, the principles of that great statesman. Each of the three is connected with a distinct phase of this system. Pitt virtually put an end to the quarrel between the King and the aristocracy, and reconciled the Tory doctrine of Monarchy with the Whig doctrine of Parliament. Peel accommodated Toryism to the new *régime* established by the Reform Bill, and his name will always be identified with the progress of middle-class reform. Lord Beaconsfield carried Toryism into the next stage, and made it the business of his life to close up the gap in our social system which, during the second quarter of the nineteenth century, had, as he thought, gradually been widening, and to reconcile the working classes to the Throne, the Church, and the Aristocracy.

As I have observed elsewhere, "no other English statesman who has risen to the same eminence has ever contemplated the English Constitution from the same external height, or brought to the consideration of political theories an understanding so absolutely unhampered by the shackles of political tradition." But the very freedom from prejudice, and from those *idola specus* in which the majority of his contemporaries had been educated, while imparting a freshness and raciness to almost every word that he uttered, and every act that he performed, interposed a kind of gulf between himself and his political associates which impeded his advance in public life. He never adopted with any heartiness the new *régime* which was established by the Reform Bill of 1832. Of ancient and illustrious descent, he could sympathise with a genuine aristocracy. A self-made man, whose escutcheon was his pen, and who had lived to some extent by his earnings, he could sympathise with labour. But with the great " middle man "—the great middle class so long regarded as the backbone of English life—his sympathies, I suspect, were small. Herein, I think, lies the key to his entire policy ; and both the strength and the weakness of his position. He never could acquire the confidence of those classes who worshipped the name of Sir Robert Peel ; and while they retained their predominance he struggled vainly to gain a firm hold of power. But he was the first to see that this predominance could not last. "I have no faith," he said in 1839, speaking of the throne of Louis Philippe, "I have no faith in a middle-class monarchy." He saw that the old aristocratic *régime*, with all its external anomalies, and all the fictions which he satirized, represented fixed principles and contained large elements of power. He believed the same of a great popular monarchy based on the love and loyalty of the people, such as he believed the monarchy of the Tudors to have been. But he evidently did not believe in the stability of institutions founded only on a compromise and appealing only to the selfish instincts of capitalists. Thus there was a large and most important element of Conservatism in this country with which he was never really in communion. And the explanation of his Parliamentary vicissitudes down to 1868 may be found in this circumstance alone. On the other hand, as the extension of the franchise and the admission of the working classes to such a share of political power as would reduce to a secondary position the classes enfranchised by the Reform Act of 1832 was, sooner or later, inevitable, it was a great advantage to Mr. Disraeli to have thus early identified himself with the interests and sympathies of the poor, so that his measure of 1867, and all subsequent legislation in their favour, seemed but the natural development of views which he had previously enunciated.

He was a young man in 1833, and not of an age to appreciate the true merits of Sir Robert Peel's policy, which was exactly suited to the transition period ushered in by the Reform Bill. Mr. Disraeli was too eager to look over and beyond this period. He did not see that Peel was doing all that it was possible for him to do at that particular time. He was impatient of the cautious, practical, compromising system which was then in reality necessary in order to prevent worse things. But his prescience was not at fault. Like Burke, he was only " right too soon." The Duke of Wellington, Sir Robert Peel, and many others believed that the Reform Bill of 1832 was destined, in the long run, to work sweeping changes in the Constitution. But Mr. Disraeli's mind, so to speak, went out before him to encounter them. After Sir Robert Peel's accession to office in 1835, and the demonstration of Conservative feeling in the nation at large which had all but kept him there, the same extreme measures, triennial Parliaments, vote by ballot, which he had at one time advocated as a means of enlisting the people on the side of the Tories against the Whigs, no longer seemed necessary : and Mr. Disraeli's warmest admirers can afford to admit that, on these points and some others, his youthful enthusiasm carried him into the region of extravagance. But the principle underneath was sound : the Toryism of the future must be popular Toryism or nothing. Sir Robert might preside with advantage over an interval of middle-class Conservatism, but the younger generation of Tories must look farther ahead, and be prepared for a different dispensation.

National institutions, when placed on a popular basis, must enjoy the confidence and affection of the people. It was useless to give power to the masses, and then to act as if you were afraid of them. The old system rested on supports not altogether dependent on the popular will; and public opinion supported the Government in resisting, if necessary by force, all that savoured of revolution. But with the great change of 1832 the monarchy and the aristocracy lost their independent position. When the people were entrusted with power, it was absurd to suppose they would not use it; and the only way by which our ancient order could be maintained was by making the people themselves its guardians and custodians. Hence the Conservative working-man. It might or might not be possible to create or discover such an entity; but unless it was, Conservatism was manifestly impotent. If the dominant class in the country was not Conservative, what could any other class hope to effect by professing such a faith?

For preaching these doctrines he was called a Radical in disguise, an unprincipled adventurer, and a fantastical dreamer. But through evil report and good report he clung to his original ideas, and before he died had the satisfaction of knowing that his countrymen had done justice to his motives. And do we not all now recognize the wisdom of his advice? His Radicalism had consisted in trying to make the working class Conservative. After the Reform Bill of 1832 our institutions were left dependent on the people; and the sympathies which once existed between the upper and the lower classes, but which had been gradually fading during the nineteenth century, must be revived by some means if these institutions were to be preserved. If this is Radicalism, I am afraid we must all take a leaf out of the same book.

More than this—he had made a study of the English people, and saw clearly that, while ministering to their material wants and adjusting the relations between employers and employed, so as to satisfy their legitimate demands, it was possible also to touch their imaginations by appeals to the greatness of their country and the splendour of her imperial traditions. He understood well that the highest and the lowest classes in every country are the

most susceptible to such emotions * and he felt certain
that the English working-men would heartily support him
in the generous foreign policy to which they had so long
been accustomed, and which had only recently been abandoned. It was this combination which he endeavoured to
carry, out during the only period of his life when he
wielded the real power of a Minister ; nor can it be said,
notwithstanding his final downfall, that his estimate of
the popular sentiment was proved to be erroneous. Down
to the last two years of his administration he continued to
be the favourite of the people ; and had a dissolution taken
place in 1878, there can be little doubt that he would
have maintained his majority in Parliament. The change
was due partly to circumstances over which he had no
control, partly, it is said, to differences of opinion which
prevented him from turning to the best account the burst
of patriotic enthusiasm by which the working classes
were stirred during the last Turko-Russian war. Had he
been free to do so, and taken the tide at the flood, he
might have more than realised his vision, and found himself as popular as the first Pitt, and perhaps more powerful
than the second.

The story of his entry into public life has been told so
often that, marvellous as it is, I shall not reproduce it
here. Not the wildest romance that ever entered into the
brain of poet, dramatist, or novelist, can equal the un-

* By this is meant that neither of these two classes is so nervous about
the chances of war as the intermediate class, the one having so much to lose
that it can afford to lose something, the other having nothing. Both, therefore, are more at liberty to feel the force of higher considerations than
members of a class engaged in making money, whose fortune and position
in life are likely to be very seriously affected by national disasters. I see
that Lord Derby the other day spoke with some contempt of appeals to the
national imagination. Chatham would not have spoken so, nor Chatham's
son, nor Mr. Canning.

varnished facts of that astounding history. Distinguished
by peculiarities singularly trying to English tastes and
habits; enjoying the rare bad fortune of being both hated
and ridiculed at the same moment and by the same persons; pelted with libels and caricatures; the object of a
thousand enmities which he took no pains to conciliate;
without money, without interest, without patrons, the
young man who replied to Lord Melbourne's good-natured
inquiry whether he could be of any service to him, that
"he wished to be Prime Minister," actually lived to
realise his heart's desire, to trample on the prejudice,
malignity, and jealousy which impeded his early rise, to
overcome obstacles which, in a country like England,
seemed absolutely insuperable,

> To mould a mighty State's decrees,
> And shape the whisper of the Throne,

and to die amid the universal lamentations of the English
people, who felt, perhaps with some twinges of self-
reproach, that they had recognized his greatness too late.
The only parallel that approaches at all to this wonderful
fulfilment of boyish ambition is Warren Hastings taking
possession of Daylesford, the ancestral hall which he had
vowed to himself he would re-purchase when lying a
penniless school-boy by the side of the little brook at
Churchill.

Mr. Disraeli's career as a party leader began with the
Session of 1849—the year after the death of Lord George
Bentinck. At this time the novels which gave the world
so startling an emendation of the received version of
English history from the Revolution to the Reform Bill,
had already been published, and did not recommend him
very highly to the veteran statesmen of the day. He
appeared among these as the young Napoleon appeared

among the grey-haired marshals of Germany, the upsetter of all the political maxims in which they had been trained from their youth. It was not to be believed that one with such antecedents as his could ever become a genuine English statesman. His first appearance in the House of Commons; the strange costume, the drooping curls, the unaccustomed language, the eccentric daring which then seemed like puerile conceit; the defiance of the House which then looked like theatrical bravado;* the imputed extravagance of his views on English politics; his very wit, humour, and sarcasm, even his birth and origin, were all remembered against him. The few who knew him well, and were competent judges of character, knew better. The two ablest heads on the Tory side of the House—Lord Lyndhurst and Lord Derby—soon observed his real genius; and it is highly to Lord Derby's credit that he always stood up manfully for his honesty, loyalty, and sincerity whenever he heard them called in question. When asked why no one trusted Mr. Disraeli, he would first of all deny that no one did. "*I* trust him," he would say on such occasions; and, if pressed further, would ask his interrogator if he knew why Mr. Canning was never trusted. "Because he was regarded as a *parvenu*," he would explain, nobody knowing better than Lord Derby that both Mr. Canning and Mr. Disraeli were better-born men than hundreds who affected to look down upon them, and who tried to find in the assumed lowness of their origin an excuse for sneering at principles which they were wholly incapable of understanding.

It may be true that it was not till Lord Derby came to know him intimately that he entertained so high an estimate either of his character or his genius. In the

* Maiden Speech, December 7th, 1837.

Croker Papers there is a letter from Lord George Bentinck, implying that Lord Stanley was not very friendly to Mr. Disraeli; and it is said in the new volume of the *Greville Memoirs* that in 1852 Lord Derby wished Mr. Herries to lead the House of Commons. But there is no allusion to any such wish in the *Life of Mr. Herries*; and, at all events, it is quite certain that if Lord Derby wished anybody else than Mr. Disraeli to lead the House of Commons then, he never wished it again. Through all this array of envy, hatred, and uncharitableness, Mr. Disraeli fought his way to victory, but not without receiving wounds of which the traces long remained, if, indeed, they ever totally disappeared. He had so long been contending with enemies whose remorseless and unscrupulous hostility seemed to justify recourse to every device and every manœuvre which party warfare renders possible, that he long continued to attach more importance to a party victory than it always, perhaps, deserved. This is only to say that he was human. But the effect was, perhaps, in some respects unfortunate; since it gave colour to the charge that during his leadership of the party he accustomed his followers to think more of putting their opponents in a minority than of any other object; a charge which closer investigation only very slightly justifies, and which, at the same time, is equally true of his adversaries, but which has nevertheless just that element of truth in it which confers plausibility, and is said to make misrepresentation more dangerous than unqualified falsehood.

But if we review Mr. Disraeli's career from 1849 to, at all events, 1869, we shall see that he was acting under circumstances which often seemed to leave him no alternative. At the commencement of this period he found himself at the head of a weak and dispirited minority, with all the first statesmen of the day, excepting Lord Stanley, in arms for his opponents. He was not in the position of Sir Robert Peel in 1833; for though the Parliamentary following of Sir Robert Peel was not more numerous than his own, the party was infinitely stronger in the country at large, and Peel himelf had sat in Parliament for twenty-four years, had occupied important ministerial positions for the greater part of the time, and had been Home Secretary and leader of the House of Commons for three years. In Parliamentary and official experience he was the superior of any man in that House. His own supporters, if some of them did not much like him, respected him for his proved capacity and unequalled talents for business. All these qualifications the leader of 1849 had yet to show that he possessed. He had to prevent the doubt, distrust, and dejection into which the Tory Party were plunged from sinking into absolute despair, and ending in practical dissolution. He had to keep up their spirits by any and every means that presented themselves; and the tactics for which he has occasionally been blamed had frequently their origin in this necessity, compelling him at times to fight battles without profit, and to take office without power, solely for the sake of stimulating the energies and reviving the confidence of his followers. Every general knows what it is to be at the head of a dispirited army, in the face of a superior force, weary of inaction, doubtful of the ability of its leaders, and deteriorating every day in discipline and self-respect. Then, if an opportunity offers of inflicting a sharp check upon a presumptuous adversary and of affording to his troops the excitement and encouragement of a successful battle, he knows that the moral effect of such a field will more than repay him for the effort, even though the issue bring him no material advantage. Such was often, though not always, the position of Mr. Disraeli during the first twenty years that followed the death of Lord G. Bentinck.

In 1849 his first business was to reconstruct the Party, and to bring back to the Conservative banner as many as he could of the original members who had strayed from it. In this attempt he was eminently successful. Accepting Free Trade as the decision of the country, he turned his attention to those burdens upon land which had only been justified by Protection ; and so judiciously chosen were the motions which, on this subject, he annually submitted to the House, that in the course of three years he was able to reduce the Government majority to only fourteen. In 1851 the distress of the agricultural classes was acknowledged in the Queen's Speech, and on Mr. Disraeli's motion calling on the Government to introduce some remedial measure in conformity with the recognition, the Ayes were 267 and the Noes 281. So far, therefore, Mr. Disraeli had shown himself possessed in an eminent degree of the talents proper to a party leader. He had raised the Tory Party from the ground, and given it once more the form and number of a powerful Parliamentary Opposition. The next step was to teach both the party and the public that it was fit for something more than this, and that it contained within its ranks men capable of conducting the business of the country should circumstances call on them to do so. Accordingly, when Lord John Russell resigned office, after his defeat on Mr. Locke King's motion on the 20th of February, Mr. Disraeli was anxious that the party should take office, if only for the above-mentioned purpose. He had got his instrument into good order and was anxious to put it to a practical test. To facilitate this object he was willing to resign the leadership of the House of Commons to Mr. Gladstone ; but, that gentleman and Lord Palmerston both declining Lord Derby's overtures, the negotiations dropped, and Lord John Russell resumed office.

In the following year, however, he resigned again, and then it became impossible for Lord Derby to avoid taking office any longer. Had he, however, been able to persevere in his refusal, it seems probable that a Coalition Ministry must have been formed in 1852. In that case there is no reason to suppose that events would have taken any different course from that which actually ensued, or that we should not have had the Crimean War, and the break-up of the Government just the same ; and I have already expressed an opinion that, in that event, Lord Derby would have been in a better position to take office in 1855, had he not induced the breach between himself and the Peelites by taking office in 1852. But, for the reasons already given, it was a matter of urgent necessity that he should take office at the earlier of those two periods, and neither he nor Mr. Disraeli were at all dissatisfied with the result.

The Government was defeated on the Budget, the principal features of which were the remission of half the malt tax ; the gradual remission of half the tea duty ; the assessment of income tax on one-third of the farmers' rental instead of one-half ; the extension of income tax to incomes of £100 a year of precarious income, and of £50 a year of permanent income ; the extension of the house tax to houses of £10 a year rateable value, and an increase of the assessment to 1s. 6d. in the pound on houses and 1s. on shops ; the whole produce being calculated at £1,723,000. It is easy to see that these proposals were not likely to command the assent of the new House of Commons, in which the majority was hostile to the claims of the agricultural interest. But it may not be so generally understood why the Chancellor of the Exchequer was obliged to introduce them. In the autumn of 1852, the agricultural depression of the last few years, though diminishing, had not yet entirely disappeared. The Opposition perceived that if the Chancellor could be forced to make his financial statement before the expiration of the year, instead of waiting until the usual time in the spring of 1853, it would be morally impossible for him not to propose something for the farmer, which, in all probability they would be able to use against him. What they foresaw came to pass. Being compelled to make his statement in December, instead of in the following April, the reduction of the malt tax and the alteration in the assessment of the income tax on agricultural incomes were forced upon him, and, to compensate for these remissions, he was compelled to resort to the house tax and the income tax. Four months later he would have been relieved from this necessity. But his opponents were aware of the fact, and forced his hand, as we have seen. The Government were defeated, on December 16th, by a majority of nineteen, and were succeeded by the Aberdeen administration.

They had scarcely expected to retain office. But the General Election had greatly increased their numbers. They had shown the stuff of which they were made. Except on one point, their measures had given general satisfaction : and they resumed their place on the Opposition benches with that confidence in their own resources and in the skill and genius of their leader which had been Mr. Disraeli's first object to inspire. That once done, the first and most important step was gained. Lord

Derby and Mr. Disraeli had done for the party in 1852 what Sir Robert Peel and the Duke of Wellington had done for it in 1835. It was once more a powerful and a practical Opposition; by which I mean that, in any regular attack which it might choose to direct against the Government, it would be supported by the consciousness that it was in a condition at once to take office, with every probability of a majority being returned in its favour at the first appeal to the people. The taint of Protection had turned the scales against it in 1852. But that was now washed out. The country was weary of the Whigs, and " England did not love coalitions." Everything was in favour of the Tories ; but, unfortunately, when the time arrived, through some want of prescience or moral courage on Lord Derby's part, the chance was missed, which never came again ; and the fairest opportunity between 1846 and 1874 of re-establishing in power a permanent Conservative administration was disastrously wasted.

Mr. Disraeli ground his teeth in silence under this heavy disappointment ; and well he might, for it consigned the flower of his manhood to the dreary work of Opposition, or the still more painful task of leading the House of Commons with a minority, and deferred the fruition of his hopes, and the power of giving effect to his own concep-tion of the political creed which he had adopted, for nearly twenty years ! When the golden fruit was at last plucked, his physical energies had already begun to fail him ; and, though his mental powers still shone with unclouded lustre, and his political genius was never more conspicuous than during his seven years of office, the indomitable will, intrepid self-reliance, and power of sustained exertion dependent upon bodily health, which had carried him triumphantly through so many struggles, were not what they had been. Years of hard work, repeated disappointment, and constant worry had done their work; and he had scarcely been two years in office before he found himself unequal to the ever-growing labours of the House of Commons, and was obliged to relinquish to another what, in all modern administrations, is the post of danger.

But it was not only on Mr. Disraeli himself that Lord Derby's decision in 1855 exercised this disastrous influence. Its effects were visible at once on the surface of the Conservative Party. They again began to lose heart, and, as a natural consequence, became querulous and mutinous. They had given a loyal support to the Government during the Crimean War. They had steadily kept aloof from any co-operation with the Radicals, though plenty of opportunities occurred. But when their legitimate reward slipped through their fingers they became hopeless and demoralized, and, if I may say the word, even factious. Mr. Disraeli also was now driven into a method of opposition which, brief as it was, has supplied his enemies ever since with a standing topic of reproach. Truth compels me to state that I cannot think the Vote of Censure on the Chinese War of 1857, or the opposition to the Conspiracy to Murder Bill in 1858, will bear very close investigation. The excuse for both is that it was necessary to do something to restore the *morale* of the party, disheartened as it was by seeing Lord Palmerston in the place which ought really to have been their own, and apparently seated there for life. More than that, neither Mr. Disraeli nor Lord Derby, nor the Conservative Party at large, were likely to forget that Lord Palmerston was kept in power by a confederacy between Whigs and Radicals more truly dishonest than anything which has been laid to the charge of the Tories either before or since. If the public wish to know what Mr. Gladstone thought of the chief whom he preferred to Lord Derby, they need only refer to the *Life of Bishop Wilberforce.* Mr. Disraeli always felt that the Tory Party had been "jockied," and was on this account less scrupulous, perhaps, in his method of avenging them than he otherwise might have been. But it is nonsense to assert that Mr. Disraeli "set the example" of this mode of warfare. The combination of the Whigs and Ultra-Tories to destroy Mr. Canning : the combination of the Radicals and the Tories under Sir Robert Peel to defeat the Jamaica Bill in 1839, were combinations essentially the same in principle as those of 1857, 1858, and of 1866.

The vote of 1857 was promptly condemned by the constituencies. But in the following year Lord Palmerston, abandoned by his own Parliament, at once made way for Lord Derby, who again failed in persuading Mr. Gladstone to join him, though how nearly he succeeded may be read in the volumes to which we have already referred—the *Life of Bishop Wilberforce.* It was clearly no principle of any kind which restrained Mr. Gladstone at this moment from joining the second Derby Ministry. His objections were exclusively personal. It is on record, therefore, and cannot be omitted in any history of Toryism, that down to the year 1859 Mr. Gladstone was a Tory.[*]

Of the connection of the Tory Party with the Reform Question, regarded as a question of statesmanship, enough has been said in the previous chapter. On Mr. Disraeli's conduct of it, from a party point of view, too much praise can hardly be bestowed. He early accustomed them to see in the subject of Parliamentary Reform

[*] He voted for the Reform Bill of 1859.

one of those great Constitutional questions which can become the private property of no one party in the State. As the Whigs, by the mouth of Lord John Russell, in 1852, had chosen to re-open the question, they had placed the Tories where they were before 1830, as free, that is, to handle the subject in their own way as they had been then. Lord Althorpe expected the Tories under Wellington to settle the Reform Question, and thought they might have done so without any dereliction of principle. When the subject was revived their right revived too. In 1858 they stood in the same relation to the Reform Bill of the future as they had done in 1828. The Bill of 1832 could place them in no worse position. Because the Whigs had carried a bad Bill was no reason why the Tories should not try to pass a better one. This was the line of argument which gradually prepared the Tory Party for the undertakings of 1859 and 1867, and caused these measures to be accepted without any of those party convulsions which occurred in 1829 and 1846. In one point alone I think Mr. Disraeli, or possibly Lord Derby, was at fault,* and that is in not declaring from the first, when Lord Russell's Government announced their intention of dealing with the subject, that, after the failures of 1852, 1854, 1859, and 1860, to discover any half-measure between the existing franchise and Household Franchise which the House of Commons would accept, they would either have the last or nothing. This was the resolution to which both Mr. Disraeli and Lord Derby had really come, and if they had boldly announced it in 1866, they must have succeeded either in "pricking the imposture," as Mr. Disraeli said of the Bill of 1859,

* See p. 324.

meaning that they had exposed the unreality of the cry, or else they must have carried the Bill of 1867, without any of the drawbacks which attended it.

It must not be forgotten that on this subject of Reform Mr. Disraeli had reason to feel very strongly. In 1859 one of the chief points in the indictment against the Tory Government had been their failure to deal with this question on a scale and in a spirit adequate to the requirements of the nation. On this platform Lord Palmerston and Lord John Russell had united all sections of the Liberals. In 1861, Lord Palmerston and Lord John Russell threw over the Reform Question after it had served its purpose, just as three and twenty years before Lord Melbourne had thrown over the Appropriation Clause after it had served its purpose. Mr. Bright declared that the humiliating position of Lord John Russell reminded him of the bankrupt tradesman who, having carried on business for many years on fictitious credit, at length called his creditors together, glad of an opportunity of getting rid of his obligations. And a Liberal historian, writing on the same transaction, describes it as follows:—

Whatever doubts may be entertained with regard to the wisdom of the course pursued by the Government in reference to this question, there can scarcely be any difference of opinion with regard to the political morality of their conduct in this respect. Lord Palmerston, after having succeeded in obtaining the support of all sections of the Liberal Party to enable him to expel the Derby Government from office, on the ground that the Reform Bill they had introduced was not sufficiently effective to meet the wants of the nation or the requirements of public opinion, now threw overboard the question altogether ; and his colleagues shared the blame that attached to such conduct by continuing to hold office under a Minister who had been capable of such palpable inconsistency.*

After this I think that both Mr. Disraeli and the Tory Party may have felt that their hands were completely

* Molesworth's *Hist. Eng.*, vol. iii. p. 243

untied, if they had ever been tied, on the Reform Question; and that for the Whigs any longer to claim Parliamentary Reform as something belonging to themselves which the Tories had no right to touch, was too monstrous an outrage on common sense for even the bewildered and mystified British public to continue to submit to.

There can be no doubt that the ultimate effect of the Reform Bill of 1867 on the fortunes of the Conservative Party has been decidedly beneficial. Had they not introduced Household Suffrage, to put the question on the lowest ground, their opponents would have done so; and the Conservatives would have incurred all the odium of resistance to a popular measure, without avoiding any of the Constitutional dangers with which it was supposed to threaten us. But I am prepared to deny that they would have gained even the barren honour of consistency by standing out either for a smaller measure, or for none. Sir Robert Peel himself had always regretted the extinction of popular franchises by the first Reform Bill,* and in the eyes of that eminent statesman it would never have seemed inconsistent with Tory principles to endeavour to redress the wrong, if the Whigs themselves insisted on re-opening the question. As soon as they did so Mr. Disraeli seized the opportunity of declaring that the Conservative Party now held themselves free to deal with the question as they chose; and declined to be shackled by any kind of engagements or tacit understandings to the contrary, founded on an erroneous conception of Tory principles, and in ignorance, even, of very recent circumstances in the history of the Tory Party. During the

* See p. 284.

struggle over the first Reform Bill, Lord Aberdeen suggested household suffrage to the Duke of Wellington without exciting either surprise or opposition.

The Reform Bill of 1867, notwithstanding the unfavourable result of the first appeal to the new constituencies which it created, was the making of the Tory Party, according to Lord Beaconsfield's conception of its history and its destinies. It gave them the position which they required for dealing with the social problems of the age; and let the Radicals sneer as they may at the Toryism of the people, they have felt its weight, and know that in the popular instincts to which Lord Beaconsfield appealed they have an enemy not to be despised. The Act of 1867 puts the coping-stone to Mr. Disraeli's reputation as a Party leader. But the excellent judgment which he displayed in declining to take office in 1873, and the excellent reason which he gave for it, proved that he knew how to play a waiting game as well as a forward one. Beaten by a majority of three on Mr. Fawcett's Dublin University Bill, Mr. Gladstone at once tendered his resignation to Her Majesty, who, without a moment's delay, sent for Mr. Disraeli. The Conservative leader, while informing Her Majesty that he should have no difficulty in constructing an Administration, stated at the same time his reluctance to attempt it in the existing House of Commons. The event justified his foresight; but even had it not, nobody can deny that he was right and Mr. Gladstone wrong on the question of Parliamentary conduct. To say, as Mr. Gladstone did, that, when a Minister is defeated and resigns, the leader of the Opposition is bound to take office in his place, is to say that no leader of Opposition who is not ready to take office ought to press his resistance so far as to defeat the Government. Now, as a leader of

Opposition can, in the nature of things, only be in this condition under circumstances which occur at rare intervals, it follows from Mr. Gladstone's doctrine that during the greater part of their tenure of office Prime Ministers shall be virtually absolute ; exposed only to abstract criticism, which is never to be carried to any practical result.   There were members of the Tory Party, we believe, who, though they did not doubt the correctness of Mr. Disraeli's theory, doubted the soundness of his judgment in not taking office at once and dissolving when he had the chance. And it is impossible to say even now what might have happened if Mr. Gladstone had given himself the chance of another Session, and had conjured up some other great question with which to dazzle public opinion.   The probability is, however, that nothing of the kind could have been done in the existing House of Commons.   The energies of the party were distracted and exhausted, Government was beaten and demoralized, and it is probable that Mr. Gladstone's best chance lay in doing what he did, and trying for a new House of Commons with a smaller majority kept in order by the danger of a powerful and sanguine Opposition.   Mr. Disraeli justified himself to his supporters in words of memorable import:—

I believe that the Tory Party at the present time occupies the most satisfactory position which it has held since the days of its greatest statesmen, Mr. Pitt and Lord Grenville. It has divested itself of those excrescences which are not indigenous to its native growth, but which, in a time of long prosperity, were the consequences, partly of negligence and partly, perhaps, in a certain degree of its traditions. We are now emerging from the fiscal period. . . . But there are other questions. . . . which must soon engage the country. The attributes of a Constitutional Monarchy—whether the aristocratic principle should be recognized in our Constitution—whether the Commons of England shall continue an estate of the realm, or degenerate into an indiscriminate multitude—whether a National Church shall be maintained—the functions of corporations—the sanctity of endowments, the tenure of landed property—all those institutions and privileges which have made this country free and famous, and conspicuous for its union of order and liberty, are now impugned, and in due time will become great and burning questions. I think it is of the utmost importance that when that time arrives, which may be nearer at hand than we imagine, there shall be in this country a great Constitutional Party which shall be competent to lead the people and direct the public mind. And, Sir, when that time arrives, and they enter on a career which must be noble, and which I hope and believe will be triumphant, I think they may perhaps remember—and not, perhaps, with unkindness—that I at least prevented one obstacle from being thrown in their way, when, as the trustee of their honour and their interests, I declined to form a weak and discredited Administration.

We may here take our leave of Mr. Disraeli as a party leader. The result of the General Election placed his party in power with a clear majority of fifty. And we may now regard him as having realised in his old age the dream of his youth, and the more practical conceptions of his riper years, in the establishment of the claim of the Tory Party to be the " popular political confederation of this country." Some people attributed the Tory victory to the wrath of the licensed victuallers, irritated by Mr. Bruce's Licensing Bill, some to a religious panic, some to both ; and " Beer and the Bible " was a favourite taunt which the defeated Liberals hurled at the heads of their antagonists. But, though no doubt these exasperated " interests " did swell the Tory majority, a deeper and more permanent feeling than anything which these wrongs could have produced was the mainspring of the movement. The people had begun to recognize in the Tory Party the existence of qualities which, however obscured during their more recent history, had never been totally extinguished, and had once been their distinctive badge. They felt, in a word, that under all the objectionable policy attributed to Toryism, supposing the imputation to be true, there lay a fund of national sentiment and loyalty to English ideas not equally discernible in their rivals. Great revulsions of popular feeling are seldom attributable to specific grievances. These may fire the train, but more general causes must have laid it.

Turning to Mr. Disraeli as a statesman, we have to consider the shape which Toryism assumed in his hands under the three heads of Constitutional Principles, Social Legislation, and Foreign and Colonial Policy. He seems to have been the first to see what is now very generally acknowledged, that one result of the Reform Bill of 1832 and of the further extensions of the Franchise which were sure to follow, must be to enhance very greatly the power of individuals. Events have certainly justified his sagacity so far. The *Spectator** thinks we may be tending towards a Republican Dictatorship. Lord Beaconsfield hoped the tendency might lean towards a monarchical revival. His ideal scheme† for the future embraced a vast extension of local self-government, with a corresponding limitation of the functions of Parliament, a well-educated people, and a free press attracting to itself the best intellects in the country, and supplementing, if not superseding, the representation of the people by the House of Commons. Has not the extraordinary development of the political press, to which the foremost statesmen of the day are proud to contribute, and which has already eclipsed to some extent the interest of the Parliamentary debates, gone far to justify one part of this conception? Is not local self-government even now about to be expanded on a great scale, and to be entrusted with the settlement of numerous important questions hitherto reserved for the Imperial Legislature? And

* December 7, 1878.

† "Let us propose to our consideration the idea of a free monarchy, established on fundamental laws, itself the apex of a vast pile of municipal and local government, ruling an educated people, represented by a free and intellectual press."—*Coningsby*, book vii., chap. ii.

shall we have long to wait for that spread of education which was another condition of the system which he thought might be established. The growth of the power of individuals which he foretold in 1844, has gone hand in hand with that decline in the efficiency of Parliament which he predicted at the same time: and is not the correspondence between the circumstances of the present moment and these remarkable suggestions, which were thrown out more than forty years ago, one of the most striking instances of political prescience on record ?

What he said of the House of Commons then the leaders of the Liberal Party are saying now. What he then predicted is now seen to have occurred. The tendency which he discerned in its cradle is now becoming so strong and so rapid that the ablest men of the day are alarmed by it. Under such circumstances it is at least pardonable to consider whether the most ancient institution of the country, which has gathered around it the love and the homage of thirty generations, is incapable of supplying us with the required antidote. This, no doubt, is the leading suggestion, the architectonic idea, of *Coningsby* and *Sybil*; and surely we have as much right to speculate on the cure of a great political evil by strengthening one part of the existing Constitution, as by setting up a new one in its place. If the people of this country are satisfied with the working of the House of Commons as it at present exists, with its omnivorous yet sprawling activity, its ignoble and ceaseless altercations, with its lower level of principle, and with the gilded dulness which, according to Mr. Lowe and Mr. Gladstone, has now established her reign in those halls of ancient eloquence—so be it. The machine may jog on for a time, and all these speculations and reflections may seem en-

tirely superfluous; or, on the other hand, if, by some
great agitation of the public mind, the evil spirit should be
exorcised and the House of Commons rise once more to
its former level of moral and intellectual greatness, in
that case, of course, all considerations of this kind would
turn out to have been waste paper, except in so far as
they had contributed to the awakening of the popular
intelligence. But in default of either alternative, some
reconstruction of the Constitution will sooner or later be
imperatively demanded. None such can be conceived of
which would not be a considerable departure from contemporary usage. And that would be the least violent
which was conducted with the greatest regard to existing
forms and institutions.

It is perfectly possible that the peasantry and the
artizans of England, who, unlike the aristocracy and
the middle classes, have no personal interest in Parliamentary government, may solve the question of procedure
in a way of their own not at all like that which is
contemplated by Mr. Chamberlain and his party. It is
possible, of course, that the extension of Local Self-Government may solve it in another way. But this is the only
alternative. I very much doubt whether the House of Commons would long submit to any real restrictions on its freedom : I am sure that, if it did, such submission would only
be a token of decaying vigour : and I am equally sure that
in that case the people would soon grow weary of it.

Mr. Disraeli seems to have thought that the press might
come in time to do all the critical and watchful work
of Parliament better than Parliament itself; that the
municipal system would take domestic legislation off its
hands ; and that the Sovereign in Council, closely checked
by a vigilant journalism, could discharge the other func-

tions of government more promptly, uniformly, and effectively than a Minister hampered and harassed, without being really held in check, by a Parliamentary Opposition.

Let us suppose a Sovereign on the throne who had objected very strongly either to the Irish policy or the Egyptian policy of Mr. Gladstone's Government, or to the Turkish policy of Lord Beaconsfield's. Such a Prince might have insisted on a dissolution of Parliament either in 1876, 1882, or 1884. Or, suppose him to have thought, as many honest Liberals thought, that the last Reform Bill was premature, he might have required that it should stand over till another Parliament had been returned, with direct reference to the question. In all this it is idle to pretend that there would be anything unconstitutional; and, if the dormant power of the Crown in this respect were revived, we might, at all events, escape the agitation for triennial Parliaments, which is certain ere long to be renewed.

Lord Beaconsfield appears to have believed that the working classes of this country, their legitimate aspirations once satisfied, would gladly support the Constitution of their ancestors, in which the Monarchy, the Aristocracy, and the Church, while they exercised real authority, had real duties to perform, on which their tenure of power was dependent. He would have wished to see what he termed the territorial Constitution of this country rather widened and strengthened by the extension of the administrative powers now vested in the proprietors of the soil, than weakened by the withdrawal or abridgment of them. In the proposals for a County Board which his Government laid before Parliament in 1879, he followed in the main the principles adopted by the President of the Poor Law Board in 1871. In Mr. Goschen's Bill it was proposed that one half of the Board should be magistrates elected by Quarter Sessions, and the other half elected by the Chairmen of certain parochial boards which he proposed to constitute. By Mr. Sclater Booth's Bill of 1879 it was provided that one-third should be magistrates elected at Quarter Sessions, and the other two-thirds elected by the Guardians. Little more than three years ago, Mr. Heneage, a Liberal, declared himself in favour of this system of election. Matters have advanced since that time, and, by whichever party the question is settled, the principle of direct election will probably be recognized. But in any re-arrangement of our provincial administration, Lord Beaconsfield would undoubtedly have wished to preserve the influence of those classes by whom it had been conducted for centuries with acknowledged ability and success, and whom he regarded as so valuable an element in the political and social life of England. He would have made no secret of this intention, and would probably have sanctioned no measure of reform which seemed likely to defeat it. He would have known that the beneficial effects of our present rural system were counterbalanced by no such evils as made the Municipal Corporations Act of 1835 a necessity. County Government is not extravagant, not so extravagant indeed as County Boards are expected to be : it is not inefficient, for what it has had to do is allowed to have been admirably done ; it is not a prey to nepotism or venality, for had it been so it would not have been either frugal or efficient. Lord Derby has told us that county magistrates were never guilty of a job. Their administration has been " pure and economical." To " the impartiality and good sense with which they perform duties of great difficulty and delicacy," testimony has been borne even by Mr. Chamberlain.

County Government, then, stands in need of reform not on any practical grounds; not because it has been badly administered, or because its administrators, however otherwise competent, have shown themselves careless or corrupt. County Boards are demanded partly in deference to ideas,* partly because the ampler functions about to be entrusted to local authorities are supposed to require a corresponding enlargement of the machinery at our disposal. One concession to justice which the Tory Party has long persistently demanded is the assumption of certain local expenses by the Imperial exchequer. Lord Beaconsfield's Government gave some relief to the local ratepayer,† but more remains to be done; and whether this is effected by increased Government subvention or the transfer of taxes from the Imperial to the local exchequer, it is thought that some new county authority must be established before the change can be accomplished; "that no substantial relief is to be looked for by the ratepayers till some institution is provided sufficiently important and sufficiently popular to justify Government in entrusting it with these weighty functions."

The Tory Party has long been anxious to carry this scheme into effect. But it desires at the same time, if I may be allowed such an expression, to use the old materials for the new edifice; to enlarge county administration without contracting the power or the influence of the rural aristocracy who have proved themselves so competent to the task; and without impairing the foundations of our old

---

* See Mr. Chamberlain's speech at Swansea, Feb. 1, 1883.

† He took over half the cost of the County Police and Lunatic Asylums, and the whole of the cost of the County Prisons—a total of about two millions. These subventions have not led to extravagance; on the contrary, it is in those very departments which benefited by them that the greatest economy has been manifested.

county system, which, on the testimony of Liberal witnesses, is entitled on so many grounds to our respect and admiration.

If the gulf which in our large towns yawns between property and labour be one of the most threatening features of our present social state, surely that system is entitled to some esteem under which the two are brought close together, and the owner of property, known personally to all who are employed upon it, is enabled, by constant association and frequent acts of kindness, both to understand their wants and their characters, and conciliate their affection and respect. No form of society has yet been invented in which work of one kind or another must not be the lot of the majority; none in which the workman who is healthy, industrious, and well conducted, will not be a happier man than he who is idle, sickly, or dissolute. It is impossible to shut out happiness from any kind of society whatever, and no influence, no liberality, no knowledge or science can enable the landlord of an estate or the clergyman of a parish to prevent the natural consequences of moral or physical infirmity. But I do say this, and I challenge contradiction when I say it, that in an English agricultural village, with a resident squire of average good sense and good feeling, and a resident clergyman of average qualifications for the post, greater elements of happiness are gathered together than are to be found either in large towns or in villages destitute of these advantages. There is in such communities a stronger sense of fellowship than is possible in our thickly populated cities; greater consciousness of a common interest in the locality; a feeling that for all alike, from the squire downwards, it is home; and not only that it is so now, but that it has been so for generations. Amid all diversities and inequalities of life and fortune, this one bond of union makes the whole village kin. It lightens the pressure of authority by the influence of immemorial prescription, and dignifies the receipt of charity by imparting to it some flavour of the kindness which springs from a family relationship.

Now I say that, in spite of all the disintegrating agencies which have been at work during the last half century, and after full allowance has been made for the operation of social, financial, and religious causes, the old system still exists and bears fruit, and is still productive of great happiness to millions of the English people. If this is so —if the authority of the gentry, founded on their property, their jurisdiction, and their hereditary claims to respect, is still active for good, still cheerfully recognized and full of life—then I think it must be allowed that in all the changes which it may be necessary to introduce into our county administration, it should be our first object to avoid undermining or superseding this system, " this fixed and happy usage," once more to repeat the words of Mr. Gladstone, but rather to fortify and perpetuate it; and that the political party which has hitherto made this object the rule of its political conduct has deserved well of the republic.

This system is now threatened with attack from three different quarters and three converging columns ; from the reformers of land-tenure, the reformers of county government, and from those who demand the disestablishment of the national Church. It is not meant that all parties are equally hostile to the system, or that in any one of the three all are hostile to it. But in each of them there is one section to be found with whom the destruction of this influence is the real object of the legislation which they ask for ; who think that, as England has now become a great commercial country, her policy should be governed directly by the commercial and manufacturing population; who believe that the commercial aristocracy are entitled to the precedence and the influence which has been so long enjoyed by the territorial; and who are determined to take advantage of a favourable opportunity for an attack all along the line on the rivals whom they hate. To this attempt the Tory party has hitherto been the uncompromising opponent; *semper restitit semper restiturus*. Such a reform of provincial administration as commends itself alike to both Liberal Conservatives, and Conservative Liberals, that is to the great body of moderate men of both parties, so far from being injurious to the county system, by removing the management of business from the hands of the gentry, and thereby destroying the influence which naturally accompanies it, would have the directly opposite effect, and by increasing the dignity of provincial institutions, would increase the importance of all who were concerned in working them. But between the useful and practical measure of which this may be predicated, and the creation of a provincial Parliament, such as our more advanced politicians are now contemplating, the difference is immense. The Tories are for administrative reform : the Radicals for social revolution.

The practical difficulties in the way of bringing Personal Property within the meshes of Local Taxation have defied both parties in the State. But it is to the credit of the Tory Party that they have never ceased, since the repeal of the Corn Laws, to urge the injustice of the present system upon the Government of the day; and in 1872 their constant representations had made so deep an impression on the Liberal Party that, on the motion of Sir Massey Lopes, calling on the House of Commons to recognize the grievance of the ratepayers, a considerable section of them voted against the Government, which resisted it, and gave the Opposition a majority of one hundred.

I should not omit to mention that the Tory country gentlemen showed themselves the farmers' friends, at all events, on the question of Cattle Disease. The violence with which Lord Sandon's measure was resisted by the Opposition must have been witnessed to be believed. But here, again, time has been on the side of the Tories, and no one thinks of denying now that the measure was both effective and salutary.

By the Agricultural Holdings Act of 1875 the right of the tenant to compensation for unexhausted improvements was first recognized by statute. The Tory disapproval of compulsory legislation of all kinds, and of interference with freedom of contract in particular, caused Lord Beaconsfield to sanction only a permissive measure in the first instance, observing that a compulsory one would be introduced afterwards should the experiment prove to be a failure. But, according to the testimony of two leading agricultural members of the House of Commons, who, though Conservatives, are strictly independent ones, namely, Mr. Albert Pell and Mr. Clare Sewell Read, the experiment was far from being a failure. "It was a great point gained," said Mr. Read (*National Review*, June 1883), "when Parliament first gave the tenant farmer a legislative right to his improvements." It was the recognition of a great principle for which the farmers had long been solicitous, and which was now at last granted by the Tories.

To pass on to another branch of statesmanship, I think it is beyond all dispute that the Tory Party was the first to appreciate that decline in the condition of the working classes which, beginning some hundred years ago, and gradually growing deeper and deeper, had reached its climax about the beginning of the present reign. Some Tory country gentlemen, among them Mr. Wilberforce and Sir Thomas Bernard, were the first to take up the allotment system, and the first Acts of Parliament on the subject were the work of Tory administrations. A Tory member of the House of Commons, the late Sir Henry Halford, led the attack upon the truck system. And the Factory legislation of the last fifty years originated with, and has been mainly carried on by, Tories and Tory Governments. The first Factory Bill for regulating the labour of children and young persons, was introduced by the typical old Tory, Mr. Sadler, on the 15th of December 1831. The last was introduced by the Tory Home Secretary, Sir Richard Cross, in 1878. Between these two dates no less than twenty-seven Acts of Parliament have been passed for the purpose of ameliorating the position of factory operatives, the success of which may be said to be entirely due to the original exertions of Lord Ashley, Mr. Fielden, and Mr. Ferrand, all Tory Members of the House of Commons, ably seconded by the younger generation of Tories represented by Mr. Disraeli, Lord John Manners, and their associates, the result of whose inquiries, embodied in the pages of *Sybil*, first opened the eyes of the public to the great iniquities of the system.

In 1842 Lord Ashley and the Tories carried a Bill to prohibit the employment of women and girls, and to regulate the employment of boys, in mines and collieries, which was violently opposed by the Liberal Party. In 1844 he carried another Bill for " amending the Laws relating to Labour in Factories ; " but owing to the vehement resistance of Mr. John Bright, Mr. Hume, and other well-known Radicals, it was robbed of its most valuable provisions, which did not become law till three years afterwards, when Mr. Fielden and the Tory Party succeeded, after a desperate struggle, in defeating the efforts of Mr. Bright, and the Ten Hours Bill for women and children became law. This great victory, the victory of popular Toryism over class Liberalism, broke the neck of the Radical Opposition; and from that moment the course of Factory legislation began to run more smoothly. But if anyone wishes to see the tone in which, forty years ago, Mr. Bright spoke of the working classes, he has only to look to the debates of 1844 and 1847, and he will ask no more. He there predicts the ruin of the manufacturers if these measures are passed for the benefit of their workpeople, whose representations and petitions he treats with indignation and contempt. What right have Mr. Bright and the Radicals to throw stones at the Tories and the aristocracy for indulging in similar predictions when the supposed interests of their own order have been threatened? The manufacturers were opposed to Free Trade when it seemed likely to be injurious to themselves. The manufacturers were opposed to regulations for the benefit of labour when it seemed likely to be injurious to themselves. On each of these occasions the Tories took the liberal side : and who are the Radicals, therefore, to deny to them the possession of popular sympathies, and a sincere desire to promote the welfare of the people?

But the Radicals grew wiser in time. They had the sense to see which way the wind was blowing; and twenty years after the passage of the Ten Hours Bill, when a Conservative Minister, Mr. Walpole, was introducing another Factory Acts Extension Bill, the late Mr. Fawcett, denying that the Factory Acts were at variance with Political Economy, added that those who in the first instance had opposed these Acts were now the first to come forward and say that the legislation which had taken place had produced the most satisfactory results. Mr. Akroyd, the Liberal Member for Halifax, after describing his own personal experience of the beneficial effects of factory legislation, was " forced to admit the benefits which the country gentlemen had conferred upon the manufacturing interest by resolutely pressing these Acts upon them."* Sir Francis Crossley and Mr. Potter, both Radicals, said practically the same thing ; while Lord Shaftesbury, in the House of Lords, addressed the Government in the following terms : " By showing the interest in the welfare of the people, and by endeavouring in this way to advance their moral, social, and physical improvement, you will be doing more for their happiness than even by the great measure of Reform which you are now passing to enfranchise the great mass of the people, and you will make the reform more successful in its operation."

We pass over seven years, and we find another Tory Home Secretary engaged on another series of popular measures for the benefit of the working classes. In 1874 Mr. Cross introduced and carried a Factory Act, of which Mr. Baxter, the Liberal member for Montrose, declared that it would " confer incalculable benefits on the operative class of this country " ; and in 1878 he put the coping-stone to this great work of popular legislation by a consolidating Act which induced the veteran Lord Shaftesbury to declare that " two millions of the people of this country would bless the day when Mr. Cross was asked to be Secretary of State for the Home Department."

The other measures of a similar character passed by the

* Hansard, vol. 185, pp. 1071, 1078, 1281.

Tory Administration of 1874 were—the Employers and Workmen Act, abolishing imprisonment for breach of contract ; the Conspiracy and Protection to Property Act, extending workmen's rights of combination, and ensuring proper food for servants and apprentices ; the Poor Law Amendment Act, to prevent the separation of aged married couples in workhouses ; the Commons Act, for preventing illegal inclosures and securing open spaces for the people ; the Artizans' Dwellings Acts of 1875 and 1879 ; the Public Health Act ; the Rating Act ; the Contagious Diseases (Animals) Acts ; and others too numerous to mention : all intended to promote the health, comfort, and freedom of the working classes in general, and to secure to them a cheap and certain supply of the food which is an Englishman's boast.

I will conclude this summary with the compliments paid to the Tory Government by Mr. Mundella, an advanced Liberal, and Mr. Macdonald, the special representative of the working classes. On the 13th February 1879, Mr. Macdonald hoped the right honourable gentleman "would deal with the Employers and Workmen Bill as the Government had already dealt with several other important questions affecting the people." On the 29th March 1878, Mr. Macdonald said of the Factories and Workshops Bill, "he was glad the right honourable gentleman had brought in and carried that Bill—a fact which would redound to his honour and credit as a statesman." On the 16th July 1875, Mr. Mundella, speaking on the Conspiracy and Protection to Property Bill, thanked the Home Secretary, in the name of the working men, " for the very fair way in which he had met the representatives of both masters and men. He believed the course pursued by Government would prevent renewed agitation on the subject." And finally, on the same occasion, Mr. Macdonald "concurred with the honourable member for Sheffield in thanking the right honourable the Home Secretary for the patience, courtesy, and careful attention which he had given to the representations of the working men." It is not often that a statesman who has drawn so vivid a picture of social wrongs in his youth has lived to redress them in his age, and to make good, as a practical legislator, every word he had uttered thirty years before as a writer of fiction.

The welfare of the labouring classes in our large towns has now been secured. That has been one great work of the Tory Party; and men's minds have naturally been directed to the condition of the agricultural labourer. Mr. Disraeli, in 1874, pointed to the immense improvement in his condition which had taken place during the last forty years, and did not think that the extension of the franchise was necessary to secure its continuance. But at that time it may well have seemed too soon to re-open a question which had only just been settled, and which, if re-opened at all, could not be settled again without further changes even more incisive and more complicated than the Act of 1867. And this, in fact, was the ground which Mr. Disraeli took. Another Bill for the extension of the suffrage must be accompanied by another redistribution of seats, involving a larger measure of disfranchisement than the country had ever seriously contemplated; and on this ground, and this ground alone, Mr. Disraeli opposed the Bill introduced by Mr. Trevelyan in 1874 for the Enfranchisement of the Agricultural Labourers. All that he said in his speech on this occasion has been amply borne out by what has occurred since. The Tory Party saw at a glance that if the Liberals insisted on an extension of the suffrage, they in turn must insist on the simultaneous production of a Redistribution Bill, as they had done in 1866 ; and the course of events turned out exactly as Mr. Disraeli had predicted. He also thought—and to this argument, I think, too much weight can hardly be attached—that it was " an unwise thing for a State always to be speculating on organic change, especially in a country like this, an old country, a country influenced greatly by tradition, a country which respects authority from habit, a country which expects in the redistribution of political power that it should be invested as much as possible with a venerable character."

So far from objecting to the principle of Mr. Trevelyan's Bill, he said that his Government " were pledged to it."* So far from being afraid of the agricultural labourer, he had no doubt " that the rated householder in the county was just as competent to exercise the franchise with advantage to the country as the rated householder in the towns." " I have not the slightest doubt," he said, " that he possesses all those virtues which generally characterize the British people ; and I have as little doubt that if he possessed the franchise he would exercise it with the same prudence and the same benefit to the community as the rated householder in the town.' But " the distribution of political power in the community is an affair of convention, not of moral or abstract right." And we must always consider, when invited to any fresh arrangement of it, whether it is worth the price we may be called upon to pay. He was not of opinion at that time that the enfranchisement of the peasantry was so urgent a need as to compensate for the total derangement and reconstruction of our electoral system which would be its necessary

* May 13th, 1874

consequence. The Tory Party, by its action in 1867, had recognized the principle. The time for carrying it into effect was a matter of expediency. He, for one, did not think that only five years after the last great settlement that time had arrived. Such was the attitude of Lord Beaconsfield and the Tory Party on the subject of the county franchise down to the day of his death.

If the Tories, down to 1881, made no attempt to effect the restoration of yeomen, peasant proprietors, and small occupiers by means of legislation, it is because they doubted whether it were possible to restore by Parliamentary enactment a class which has disappeared in obedience to a natural law; and, secondly, because all practical experience seems to show that petty farming at the present day is not an economical success. The idea of the compulsory purchase of land by local authorities to be resold to peasant proprietors had not obtained currency during the life-time of Lord Beaconsfield, whose sympathies were all with the peasantry, but who was too good a man of business not to see at a glance the financial fallacies involved in it. On the general question I can add nothing to what I wrote some years ago.* I believe the moral and political effects of the multiplication of peasant proprietors would, if they could be secured against indigence and pauperism, be admirable. If it is condemned by Conservatives it is not because it would be hostile to the landed interest. On the contrary the influence of the country gentlemen would be largely increased by the restoration of a system which was originally called into existence for the service of their ancestors. The way to possess influence, said Dr. Johnson, is to have a multitude of small tenants at a low rent. Country gen-

---

* *The Agricultural Labourer*, chaps. iii., viii., ix. (1870)

tlemen, who have excellent means of judging, think, rightly or wrongly, that a system of large farms pays better ; that the rent is safer, and, some would say, higher ; what is more, that the soil is much better cultivated ; and that all the trouble and distress of getting rid of poverty-stricken tenants, who are ruining the soil without bene-fiting themselves, is avoided by it. But if it came to the question of political and social influence, there cannot be a doubt to which side they would incline.

Peasant proprietors are as great an economic failure as peasant occupiers. There is abundance of evidence to prove this. But one question surely is enough. Why have they disappeared ? Why, for the last hundred years, have they been steadily selling their possessions and lapsing into the rank of labourers ? If the system answered, why has it been abandoned ? The reply is that it did not answer ; and we see, by examination of such fragments of it as still remain among us, that it answers worse and worse every year. With the example before them of the " statesmen of Cumberland and Westmoreland," and the peasant proprietors of the fens, where every condition favourable to peasant farming is to be found, no wonder that the Tory Party has declined to hold it up as a panacea for the agricultural labourer.

On the connection of the Tory Party with the Church of England it is unnecessary to write at any length. Their old hereditary alliance is one of the leading facts of modern history, and one of the chief titles of the Tory Party to the confidence of the English people. On this subject Lord Beaconsfield's opinions followed the course of his political opinions. He, too, found, like Mr. Gladstone,*

---

* *Autobiography*, p. 25.

that it was one thing to propound a theory and another to reduce it to practice. His theory of the Monarchy could not be carried out when he succeeded to political power, and his theory of the Church had to be modified in conformity with existing circumstances. In 1844, looking at the Church of England as part of that ideal system which it might be possible to realise in the future, he was favourable to the separation of the Church from State control, but only on condition that she still retained possession of her estates; and he suggested that, even if the State cast her off, the people would protect her property, which was mainly held in trust for their benefit. It is needless to say that if the people do not ask for disestablishment there can be no fear of disendowment. But forty years of agitation and misrepresentation, practically unchecked by any counter efforts, have done their work, and though I believe it will gradually be undone, we would not answer for the effect of a plebiscite at the present moment. No more, were he living, would Lord Beaconsfield have done; and he saw clearly enough, in his later years, that the enemies of the Church had been allowed their own way too long among the lower orders to justify her in relying on that allegiance which was really her due, and which he still believed to be only in abeyance.

Latterly, therefore, there was no warmer supporter of the connection between Church and State than the author of *Coningsby*; and he laid great stress on the connection of the clergy with the land, as bringing within the class of small freeholders a highly-educated and intellectual body of men, who added greatly to the strength of that fabric of local jurisdictions and local independence to which he was, on principle, attached. He deplored the inroad on the old parochial system which was effected by the new

Poor Law, and nobody would have joined more heartily in the work of decentralization than the statesman who saw in " a vast pile of municipalities," both urban and rural, the administrative method of the future. There can be no manner of doubt that the party which specially represents the landed interest, and, therefore, the territorial aristocracy, is, and ever has been, the natural guardian of that system of local self-government of which they have been the recognized administrators, and of all kindred forms which repose upon the same principle. To the Church, accordingly, as one branch of the great territorial interest, he gave his support on political and constitutional grounds, independently of his strong conviction that she was the best, if not the only agency, for evangelizing the masses, and that her connection with the State was in the highest degree advantageous, if not absolutely indispensable, to the fulfilment of this great duty. " The principles of divine truth, I admit, do not depend upon property ; but the inculcation of the principles of divine truth by human machinery depends upon property for its organization."* But he also said, in a speech delivered at Aylesbury the year before : " Broadly and deeply planted in the land, mixed up with all our manners and customs, one of the main guarantees of our local government, and therefore one of the prime securities of our common liberties, the Church of England is part of our history, part of our life, part of England itself." The speeches from which these extracts are taken, combined with one on the Act of Uniformity in 1863, and another delivered at Oxford just after the publication of *Essays and Reviews* in 1864, form a complete representation of his opinion on the subject of the

* Speech at High Wycombe, October 30th, 1862.

Church of England at that period of his life. On the duty
of the clergy when the Church is threatened with any great
danger from without his remarks apply to all times. He
was not in favour of the political activity of the clergy, as
a general rule. " But there was a limit to this reserve."*
From purely party struggles he thought they would do well
to abstain. " But where the interests of the Church of
which they are the sacred ministers are concerned, the
clergy would be guilty of indefensible apathy if they remained silent and idle." " Can anyone," he said, " now
pretend that the union between Church and State in this
country is not assailed and endangered? It is assailed in
the chief place of the realm, its Parliament; and it is endangered in an assembly where, if Churchmen were united,
the Church would be irresistible. Nothing can exceed the
preparation, the perseverance, the ability, and, I am willing
to admit, the conscience with which the assault upon the
Church is now conducted in the House of Commons.
Churchmen would do wrong to treat lightly these efforts
because they believe that they are only the action of a
minority in the country. The history of success is the
history of minorities." And then " what would happen? "
" Why, it is very obvious what would happen. The State
of England would take care, after the Church was spoiled,
to enlist in its services what are called the ministers of all
religions. The ministers of all religions would be salaried
by the State, and the consequences of the dissolution of
the alliance between Church and State would be only
equally disastrous to the Churchman and to the Non-
conformist. It would place the ministers of all spiritual
influences under the control of the civil power, and it

* Speech at Aylesbury, November 12th, 1861.

would, in reality, effect a revolution in the national character." " The clergy of the Church of England have, at this moment, one of the greatest and most glorious opportunities for accomplishing a great public service that was probably ever offered to any body of men. It is in their power to determine and ensure that Church questions in this country shall no longer be party questions. They, and they alone, can effect this immense result, and that by a simple process—I mean by being united."*

When Lord Beaconsfield became Prime Minister he was induced, by the representations of the bishops, to give his consent and support to the Public Worship Regulation Bill, to which he was personally opposed. But, though he may have been justified in giving up his own judgment to the superior authority of the Episcopal Bench, he need not have thrown himself into the cause with such unnecessary zeal as to proclaim his sympathy with a Bill for "putting down Ritualism." With these three words he sowed the seeds of hostility and distrust among the English clergy which cost him dear, and of which even his successors are, to some extent, feeling the effects.

The accusations of extravagance which one Party brings against another I have never thought worthy of much attention. Both Parties are anxious to keep down the estimates ; and there is no more common error that all Governments commit than that of being penny wise and pound foolish. No Minister is wilfully extravagant ; but the expenses of government and administration increase every year, partly because more is expected of the Government, and partly because the cost of national insurance, the defence of our Empire, and the protection of our own

* Speech at Aylesbury, November 12th, 1861.

country is likewise much higher than it used to be. No Government is able to prevent this. But, as the Tories are constantly accused of being the more expensive party of the two, it may be well to repeat that the Tory Administrations which preceded the Reform Bill are allowed, even by their enemies, to have excelled in the virtue of economy.*

The Estimates of 1835, under Sir Robert Peel and the Duke of Wellington were exceptionally low. Peel's financial measures from 1841 to 1846 needed no repentance, though as much cannot be said for the Whig finance which followed, when Sir Charles Wood withdrew three budgets in the same year. Mr. Gladstone's finance from 1853 to 1862 has been reviewed by a master hand, who shows, at least, that in his case, as in that of so many others, all was not gold that glittered. And, finally, if we come down to the three last Administrations, from 1868 to 1874, from 1874 to 1880, and from 1880 to the present year, we shall see that the Tories have no reason whatever to shun comparison with their rivals, but rather every reason to court it. The Liberal Party, which was never tired of attacking the financial measures of Sir Stafford Northcote, have now enough to do to defend their own. The evidence supplied by their five years of office is the best vindication of their predecessors, and they ought at least to have learned the lesson by this time that those who live in glass houses had better not throw stones.

One fertile source of error in the judgment of the people on finance questions lies in their failure to recognize the difference between realised and estimated surpluses. For instance, it is commonly believed that Mr. Gladstone, in

* Cf. *Gladstone Gleanings*, vol. i. pp. 130, 131.

1874, left a surplus of six millions to Lord Beaconsfield. He did nothing of the kind. He left £870,000. This was a realised surplus. The state of the Revenue when he quitted office justified Sir Stafford Northcote in assuming that the excess of income over expenditure for the ensuing year would be about five millions and a half. This was an estimated surplus: and the people had the benefit of it beforehand, in the shape of a remission of taxation to the amount of nearly five millions. Then began the period of agricultural and commercial depression, and no more such estimates were possible.

The apparent excess of the Conservative expenditure 1874–1880 over the Liberal expenditure of 1869–74 was between seven and eight millions. Of this a large part, about two millions, was due to subvention in aid of local rates, which leave the expenditure of the country at large exactly where it was before. Two millions more are to be accounted for by the Sinking Fund, and converting the permanent debt into terminable annuities. Six hundred and forty-three thousand consisted of money borrowed at 3 per cent. to be advanced to municipalities, School Boards, sanitary authorities, and town councils at $3\frac{1}{2}$ per cent. So that this was merely a profitable investment of money, not the waste of it. Some three millions more went to the improvement of the army and navy, the condition of which, in the year 1873, had become a public scandal. The war expenditure stands on a separate ground, and must be judged by considerations of policy. But, whether we judge of it by policy, or by magnitude, it is much to be preferred to the war expenditure of Lord Beaconsfield's successors, which exceeded it by nearly one-half. The average expenditure of the Tory Government from 1874 to 1880 was £78,709,937, that of the

Liberal Government from 1880 to 1885 £87,777,911.* But I altogether object to comparisons of this nature; the only question is whether the money which is raised by Govern ments is wisely or unwisely spent. For their own sakes they are not likely to raise more than they want. They are much more likely to raise less.

There are in this country at the present time three schools of Foreign Policy, sufficiently distinct from each other, though the differences between them are of very unequal magnitude. The enthusiastic school, who would have gone to war for an idea, and of whom Burke on the one side and Mackintosh† on the other may be considered representatives, has, I think, nearly died out : at all events, it exercises no appreciable influence on English politics. The two main theories which contend for the mastery at the present moment are the Imperial theory and the Insular theory. But the upholders of the former are again divided into those who believe in the doctrine of insurance, and those who think it better on the whole to run the risk; so that we have, in effect, three diffe- rent systems to choose between. There are those who think our Empire only an encumbrance to us ; who hold that England has no real interests beyond her own shores, and no business with any military expenditure beyond what is necessary to protect ourselves from foreign invasion. This is one party. I believe it to be perfectly honest ; and, what is more, I believe that on one theory of the ends of national existence, and the nature of human happiness, there is much to be said for it. It is not, however, my own, nor has it ever been entertained

---

* These figures are supplied by the Conservative Association, and, though I do not vouch for their literal accuracy, there can be no doubt of their sub- stantial correctness

† Cf. p. 236

by any party or set of statesmen to whom the English people have confided the destinies of their country. There is, secondly, the party which, while friendly to the maintenance of the Empire, recoils from the trouble and expense which others think necessary to that end, and would rather trust to the benevolence of our neighbours than to our own readiness for action. And there is, thirdly, the party which, in the face of great military Powers, anxious to extend their dominions in all quarters of the globe, sees our only security in a policy of vigilance and preparation, and the maintenance of our fleets and armies on a thoroughly efficient footing. Of the first of these parties it is unnecessary to say more ; nor shall we find that the second has ever permanently commanded the confidence of the nation. Whenever the attention of the country has been directed to the results of its policy, whenever the public have been fairly called upon to choose between the two, they have invariably proclaimed their preference for the third theory which I have described, which is virtually founded on the old Roman maxim, *Si vis pacem para bellum*. However dazzled for the moment by visions of retrenchment and immunity from taxation, they have always reverted in the end to the principle of insurance, and have recognized with characteristic common sense that a cheap Foreign Policy, like so many other cheap articles, is sure to be the dearest in the long run.

This, then, may be called the traditional policy of Great Britain : the defence of our Empire and its interests by nipping encroachment in the bud, and the preservation of peace by showing our readiness for war. Whigs and Tories alike, with one exception, have pursued this policy on the Eastern Question since the question first came into being. Canning, Wellington, Peel, Melbourne, and Palmerston, have all alike seen in the policy of Russia a distinct threat to British interests, and in the maintenance of the Turkish Empire the best answer to it. Had Lord Aberdeen recognized the truth in time, we should have escaped the Crimean War; and that disastrous event, however glorious to our arms, is the best vindication of the maxim which he foolishly disregarded till it had become too late to act upon it.

The first thing to be remembered, then, in connection with Lord Beaconsfield's Foreign Policy, is that it was the traditional policy of this country; the national policy, always supported by the nation, and recommended by the example of a long line of illustrious statesmen. It was no novelty, no new-fangled scheme or ambition. It was simply the adoption of recognized principles on the revival of the international difficulty to which they had always been applied. The end which Lord Beaconsfield had in view was the same as had been pursued by all the great statesmen whose policy I have previously described; and if it was a mistake, he and they must come under one common condemnation.

The question divides itself into two parts. Could England have prevented the war between Turkey and Russia in the first instance, without sacrificing Turkey; and could she have counteracted the results of the Russian victory more effectually than was done by the Treaty of Berlin. The first of these questions we must answer by another. Would England have been justified in going to war by herself when France and Austria refused to co-operate with her in carrying out the Tripartite Treaty? This was a question of calculation. But in the then temper of the public mind in England it was clearly impossible for the Government to decide in the affirmative. The British people have grown ashamed by this time of the fit of madness into which they allowed themselves to be lashed by the tale of the Bulgarian atrocities, reminding one as it does of the story of " Jenkin's ears," in the last century, which produced a somewhat similar effect. But in 1876 the report of the outrages committed by the Bashi-Bazouks in suppressing the Bulgarian insurrection, being turned to good account by the Opposition, created an anti-Turkish feeling in the country, which paralysed the Government, and is thought to have unnerved for a time even some members of the Cabinet. At the Conference of Constantinople, in 1875, the Turks, while refusing to accept the scheme of reforms then proposed to it, undertook to carry out others which, it is not denied, would have had a very salutary effect. The English Government would have allowed time for the value of this promise to be tested. But Russia would not : and proposed the adoption of a Protocol leaving it to the Powers to watch events, and reserve their action in the matter. As this was merely giving to Russia the right to choose her own moment for going to war, England declined to be a party to it unless Russia would disarm. Unfortunately, this condition was abandoned, Russia merely offering to Turkey the choice of sending an ambassador to St. Petersburg to treat of disarmament. Turkey refused to sign the Protocol, and Russia resolved to treat her refusal as a *casus belli*. England protested. against this high-handed proceeding, which Lord Derby declared to be a gross breach of Treaty obligations.* But the Government resolved to remain neutral unless the British interests particularly specified by Lord Derby should appear to be endangered.

---

* May 1st, 1877,

Whether to a firmer attitude on the part of England at more than one stage of these negotiations Russia might not have yielded, as she did a year afterwards, when her grasp was on her victim's throat, it is impossible to say with any certainty. But it is a prevalent belief that she would have done; and that what alone prevented that firmer attitude from being adopted was the outcry against Turkey which had been raised in the preceding year. But in 1878 the tide had turned. The British public was beginning to suspect that, in the matter of the Bulgarian atrocities, it had been made a cat's-paw. The Sultan had been utterly defeated. But the gallantry of the Turkish soldiers had revived public sympathy with our old ally, and the imminent danger of a general European war, and the jeopardy in which the highest interests of this country were involved when Russia was at the gates of Constantinople, had aroused the old English spirit, and Lord Beaconsfield was himself again.

When the contents of the Treaty of San Stefano, by which the Empire of Turkey in Europe was virtually annihilated, first became known to the British Government,* Lord Beaconsfield demanded that it should be submitted to a European Congress. Russia refused: our fleet passed the Dardanelles; and Lord Beaconsfield called out the Reserves. Russia hesitated; and a division of our native Indian army was summoned to the Mediterranean. Convinced at last that we were in earnest, and conscious that she would have other enemies to face as well, Russia reluctantly yielded; and by so doing showed perhaps what she would have done before had she been confronted by similar demonstrations.

* In the spring of 1878.

The magnitude of the perils with which the Treaty of San Stefano threatened Europe is described in detail by Lord Beaconsfield in his speech on calling out the Reserve Forces, April 8th, 1878. It would have made Turkey in Europe a Russian province, and the Black Sea a Russian lake :—

A vast Slav state was to stretch from the Danube to the Ægean shores, extending inwards from Salonica to the mountains of Albania—a state which, when formed, would have crushed the Greek population, exterminated the Mussulmans, and exercised over the celebrated Straits that have so long been the scene of political interest the baneful and irresistible influence of the Slavs.

Elsewhere Lord Beaconsfield summed up the dangers which he apprehended from Russian conquest in the following words :—

There was danger that the balance of power in the Mediterranean might be subverted; that Russia might establish ports in the Ægean; that the restrictions on the navigation of the Straits might be removed; that Asia Minor might be conquered; and the establishments and influence of Great Britain on the Persian Gulf might be seriously endangered.

The Treaty of Berlin foiled the Russian projects in Europe.

By the Treaty of Berlin, Bulgaria was confined to the north of the Balkans instead of the arrangement that was made under the Treaty of San Stefano; Thrace, Macedonia, and the littoral of the Ægean were restored to the Sultan; the Slav principalities of Servia and Montenegro were restricted within reasonable limits; the disturbed districts of Bosnia and Herzegovina were placed under the administration of Austria, which was thus offered to Slav aggression; and Eastern Roumelia was created with an organic statute which, if wisely accepted by the people of that province, would make them one of the most prosperous communities in the world.

The Anglo-Turkish Convention, by taking guarantees for the good government of Asia Minor, and enabling England, through the occupation of Cyprus, to command the valley of the Euphrates, barred the advance of Russia through Asia Minor either towards Constantinople or India. The means by which these ends were gained cost Lord Beaconsfield the services of Lord Derby and Lord Carnarvon, who did not see the necessity for either. It is enough to say here that they were followed by the desired consequences, if they did not produce them; and we have seen since that time what misfortunes may ensue from the neglect of England to act with vigour at the proper moment.

Early in June Lord Beaconsfield and Lord Salisbury went out as the English Plenipotentiaries to the Congress of Berlin. They returned to London on the 15th July, and at that moment there were hardly any limits to their popularity. "Peace with Honour" became a household word; and Mr. Gladstone himself, in the admirable speech which he delivered over his great rival's tomb, referred to this as the culminating moment of his career.

Of the general policy of the Treaty of Berlin thus much may be said. Its primary object was to bar the advance of Russia to the Mediterranean. The best means to that end lay in the creation of a powerful independent State between the Adriatic and the Black Sea. But such a State could not be established in a day. It must be really, as well as nominally, independent: a free Power, and not a Russian Province. Lord Beaconsfield fully recognized the superiority of such a barrier over any other that could be created against Muscovite aggression. But in 1878 no materials existed for such an edifice. If we turn back to what Mr. Canning told the Greeks in 1826, and the conditions on which he was prepared to acknowledge their independence,* we shall see that he at all events would have recognized the futility of attempting at that moment to erect an independent kingdom out of the ruins of the Turkish Empire in Europe. It was impossible. But Lord Beaconsfield's policy was distinctly shaped with a view to the realisation of this idea at some

*Cf. p. 166.

future time. For this purpose the grasp of Russia must at once be loosened from these provinces, and leisure must be secured for them to develop their internal resources, and gradually fit themselves for the independence which it was hoped would one day be their portion. To this end precise instructions were given to our Ambassador at Constantinople, and to Mr. Michel, our representative at Sofia, to nurse the spirit of nationality wherever they found it among the inhabitants of these countries, and to encourage them by every means in their power to acquire the faculty of self-government. In carrying out these instructions they naturally gave umbrage to the many Russian officers who still lingered on the spot; and as soon as Lord Beaconsfield was driven from office, and the complaints of Russia reached the ears of Mr. Gladstone, Sir Henry Layard and Mr. Michel were recalled.

As an independent State could not at that time be formed, it was necessary in the mean time to take other steps for providing against Russian conquest; and the only alternative was to persevere in the support of Turkey, and to strengthen the hands of Austria. Should it eventually turn out that no new State could be constructed, and that the territory in question must be absorbed into one or other of the adjoining empires, it was better that it should fall into the hands of Austria than into the hands of Russia. An Austrian Empire stretching from Ragusa to Varna, and from the Carpathians to the Balkans, or possibly further still, would keep the Cossack from the Mediterranean for as many generations as statesmen are called on to forecast.

On December 5th, 1878, Parliament was called together to receive a message from the Queen requesting that provision might be made for an expeditionary force to be despatched against the Ameer of Afghanistan. He had received a Russian envoy, and had declined to admit an English one. Explanations were demanded and refused, and war was the result. The Tory policy in the Afghan War was to secure a barrier against Russia while it was in our power to do so. We had offered the Ameer our friendship, and had asked only what other native princes had usually conceded, that we might have a minister at his court, and Residents at some of his chief towns. We want "eyes to see and ears to hear," said Lord Beaconsfield, "what is going on in Afghanistan," and with these concessions we might perhaps have secured ourselves without further operations. These being refused, while the same privilege was conceded to Russia, England was compelled to protect herself by other means; and when, in consequence of the war which followed we were able to occupy Candahar, the opportunity was taken of constructing that "scientific frontier" which military officers and engineers well acquainted with the country, no less than the most experienced Indian statesmen, had long recommended. The value of the frontier which was abandoned by Lord Beaconsfield's successors has since his death been abundantly demonstrated. It comprised not only the city of Candahar, but also the completion of a line of railway from that fortress to the Indus. The position was abandoned on an undertaking given by Russia early in 1881 that she intended to advance no further. In the three following years she advanced five hundred miles; and the loss of Candahar has consequently entailed upon us far more onerous responsibilities than the retention of it could possibly have involved.

The questions raised by the Zulu War of 1879 are scarcely questions of policy. As Lord Beaconsfield said when the continuation of Mr. Bartle Frere as High Commissioner was called in question in the House of Lords, " It is not the policy of England with regard to South Africa now for some years that is called in question. Different Cabinets and different schools of political opinion are equally interested in maintaining that policy."* The chief charge brought against Lord Beaconsfield's Government was the retention of Sir Bartle Frere at his post after he had declared war against Cetewayo without consulting the Home Government. It was easy for Lord Beaconsfield to answer this charge, not only by appealing to precedent, but by showing that Sir Bartle Frere's fitness for the discharge of the duties now devolving on him was not affected by this single error of judgment. His own "policy," he said, was a policy of confederation, which he conceived to be directly opposed to a policy of annexation. Annexation was forced upon states very often by a weak frontier. Confederation was sure to provide a strong one.

I now come to Ireland ; and if I may be allowed to say so without incurring the charge of great presumption, I cannot think that the Irish policy of either the Whigs or the Tories, the Conservatives or the Liberals, has been a wise one since the death of Mr. Pitt. Perhaps, for the sake of justice, I should say since the beginning of the Regency ; for it was not till then that either party had its hands free. But the Tories, by that time, had fallen into the hands of the ultra-Protestant section of the Party, while the Whigs, in turning the Roman Catholic question into a party weapon, were careless what spirit they

* March 2nd 1879.

encouraged among the Irish, and fostered the trade of
agitation which since that time has attained such formidable dimensions. Sixty years ago it was still possible,
perhaps, to have stamped it out, and to have succeeded
in placing the Protestant interest in a position of permanent
ascendancy ; to have governed Ireland, in fact, as Cromwell meant it should be governed. But to do so required
another Cromwell ; and as that scheme became impossible,
the opposite one should have been tried in its integrity.
Roman Catholic Emancipation only, after all, left the two
systems in a position of irritating rivalry; and the means
by which the emancipation of the one church and the disestablishment of the other were alike carried were far
more mischievous than the evils they were intended to
remove. The Irish agitators had now learned their full
strength, and soon began to apply it to something much
nearer to their hearts than the sympathies or antipathies
of religion.

Lord Beaconsfield's speeches on the subject in 1843,
1869, 1870, and 1871 are extremely suggestive and instructive. In 1843 he gives the fullest expression to those
convictions which are perceptible in *Coningsby* and *Sybil*,
and which suggest a recurrence to the ancient Tory policy
in favour of the Roman Catholics.

> The Whig Party for seventy years had the command of the Government,
> and the course of their policy was hostile to the Roman Catholics of Ireland.
> That was an historical fact which no one could controvert. But even at the
> time when the Tory Party was overthrown, and prescribed, and when it was
> led by an attainted and exiled leader, principles were always advocated in
> harmony with those to which he had referred, and on all occasions of
> political contest the Roman Catholic population of this country supported
> the claims of the Tory Party. *

* *Speeches*, vol. ii. p. 289. It was on this speech and the rebuke which it
drew down on Mr. Disraeli from the Treasury Bench, that the following
leading article was published by the *Times*, which sufficiently shows the

In 1844 he places the following reply in the mouth of *Coningsby*, when taxed by Sir Joseph Wallinger with being "a regular Orangeman." "I look on an Orange-

---

estimation in which "Young England" was held by a thoroughly competent and independent witness.

"It appears that some honourable members who have come lately into notice, and, we will add, into favourable notice—so far, at least, as honourable character and talent is concerned—choose to combine with a general declared support of the administration opposition to it upon certain particular subjects. Lord John Manners, Mr. Smyth, Mr. Disraeli, Mr. Cochrane, and others animadverted during the late debate upon the policy of Ministers, and on Tuesday night Mr. Disraeli reflected upon some of the measures of Government in the Servian affair. Upon this Lord Sandon rose up and made a furious attack upon Mr. Disraeli for daring to show such disagreement with Government, and went on to make most invidious and uncalled-for observations upon other honourable members who had been recently using the same liberty.

"Is it really come to this, that in a House of Commons, in which every man has for years thought himself at full liberty to talk as much nonsense as he likes, for as long as he likes, gentlemen of some sense and talent are not to be allowed to express their opinions upon points, whether of foreign or Irish legislation, without being taunted and silenced? Is the Magna Charta of the House to be invaded, and that at the expense of speakers who really have not as yet needed its indulgence? Have these gentlemen, we ask, spoken more diffusely, tediously, lengthily than they should? If they had, the example of members would have borne them out; but we do not hear that they have. When they have spoken they have spoken to the point, and because they had something to say. Everybody allows this.

"It is not to defend 'Young England,' who are amply able to defend themselves, that we make these remarks, but to maintain the principle of free and fair debate against such attempts to cow and bully as have lately been exhibited. It is not for the benefit of the public, or really for the Minister himself (however much for his temporary convenience), that he should be completely independent of, and above all questions from, his own party. Above all, it is not for the public good that *any* talent should be kept down, and excluded from a fair field of exercise and training which the debates afford. The country is not in a state to dispense with any rising intellect and vigour—any heads that give promise. The latter may not be ready for service yet—most public men require years of labour and drudgery to bring them into action. There may be ideas that require maturing, and principles that require moulding and accommodating, before they can be brought to bear upon the present state of things. Parties have been stiffened into a certain attitude for the last two centuries, and certain men man," said Coningsby, "as a pure Whig; the only professor and practiser of unadulterated Whiggism." My own opinion, founded exclusively on his writings and his speeches, is that in his famous summing up of "the Irish Question," as "a starving population, an absentee aristocracy, and an alien Church," we see the nearest approach to his real convictions that is anywhere to be found. But as leader of the Conservative Party, he had to deal with Protestantism of various hues, embarrassed by the fact that parties in Ireland had changed sides, and that the interest created by the Whigs for the maintenance of English ascendancy had now passed over to the Tories, while the interest which had most in common with pure Toryism had passed over to the Whigs. Lord Beaconsfield found it useless to struggle against accomplished facts, and, therefore, like a sensible man, tried to make the best of them. But even in 1869 he preferred concurrent endowment to Disestablishment, and his language on the subject was almost exactly the same as Sir Robert Peel's in 1835.*

If the right honourable gentleman had proposed to confiscate the property of the Irish Protestant Church and transfer it to the Roman Catholic Church, though I should consider that an unjust and unwise measure, it would be an intelligible proposition. It would be a proposition for which arguments could be offered, and which at least would be consistent with the principle of property.†

He clearly foresaw, both in 1869 and in 1870, that neither the Church Bill nor the Land Bill would bring peace to Ireland. He foretold the rise of fresh agitation

seem wanted politically, and others not, and that is all that your superficial statesman says. But who knows when a thaw and loosening may come, and when older heads may have gone, new events may have happened, and new modes of thinking may be demanded and come into play?"

   * *Cf.* p. 287.

   † *Speeches*, vol. ii. p. 308

ending in the severance of the Union. " It is very possible,"
he said, " that after a period of great disquietude, doubt,
and passion, events may occur which may complete that
severance of the Union which to-night we are com-
mencing."* The Land Bill followed, and Lord Beaconsfield condemned it upon grounds which possess peculiar
interest for us at the present moment, when it is the desire
of a political party to extend its provisions to this
country.

"I now proceed," he says (March 11, 1870) " to another point of the Bill,
of which I entirely disapprove and that is the compensation that is to be
given for occupation. We have heard many objections to the principle of
the clause. I may touch upon them, but I wish at once to state the
reason why I particularly object to that clause. It is not upon the interest
peculiarly of the landlord that I found my objection. My objection to this
clause, which, at the first blush, recognizes property in occupation, and
which, therefore, I am not surprised has alarmed many gentlemen, is that
this is a proposition which terminates at one fell swoop all moral relations
between the owner and occupier."†

Finally, in 1881, in the last speech which he ever made
upon the subject, he sums up the various failures of this
country to allay Irish discontent, the inference being that
we had always overlooked its real cause. At first we were
told that the dissatisfaction of Ireland was political, and
that it would be allayed at once by admitting the Roman
Catholic part of the population to the same civil rights as
were enjoyed by the Protestants. This remedy was tried
and failed. Then we were told that the cause was
ecclesiastical : reformers began by abolishing tithes, and
ended by abolishing the Church. That remedy was a
failure. Then we were told that the mischief was
agrarian : and could only be cured by a sweeping reform
of the Land Laws. This experiment, likewise, had been

* House of Commons, May 31, 1869.
† *Speeches*, vol. ii. p. 349

tried and failed. And we can only gather from the remainder of his speech that " the conclusion of the whole matter " was in his opinion this, that all that Ireland needed was rest—rest from the intrigues of foreign conspirators, who, without representing the feelings of the great body of the people, kept them continually unsettled; rest from the agitation of professional grievance-mongers who taught Ireland that the ordinary calamities of life, bad harvests, bad trade, poverty, and sickness, were all the faults of the Government, and could be averted by legislation in accordance with Irish ideas. He seems to have believed that if Ireland could have been left in peace after 1848, and time allowed for the more favourable circumstances in which she was then placed to produce their natural effect, Ireland by this time might have been as tranquil as Scotland. He seems to have thought that after the suppression of the Fenian conspiracy in 1867 there was a second opportunity for the development of Irish prosperity, if only Ireland could have been left alone instead of the passions of the people being again stirred up by recourse to revolutionary legislation. The Parliament of 1869 created a second Irish question worse than the first, and taught the disloyal party where to find the weapons which they have since used with such effect. Such seem to have been the final conclusions at which the old statesman had arrived. The curse of Ireland amounted to no more than this, that she had been made the battle-ground of English parties. The Irish Question of 1843 was not the Irish Question of 1881. A great deal had happened in the interval. The Estates Act, the Land Acts, the Disestablishment and Disendowment of the Church, had altered the conditions of the problem, though not after the fashion which Lord Beaconsfield himself would have desired. These were accomplished facts; and he wished their efficacy to be fairly tested. This, he thought, could not be done unless the legislation of 1870 was allowed time to bear fruit, and if the minds of the people were constantly being unsettled by fresh concessions to intimidation.

Lord Beaconsfield survived his Ministry only one year. But one year was quite long enough to bring back to him all his former popularity, augmented by the rare dignity and self-control which he displayed under the momentary loss of it. Nor did his services to his party terminate with his retirement from office. His advice on more than one critical emergency saved them from false steps which would have weakened their powers of resistance, now more than ever needed for the defence of the Constitution; while he pointed out to them at the same time the duty which they owed as Conservatives to the liberties of Parliament, now for the first time threatened by a Liberal administration. The two speeches on Ireland and on India which he delivered in the House of Lords some three weeks before the commencement of his last illness, are remarkable for the precision and conciseness with which he sums up the general character of our Foreign Policy during the last hundred years, and the causes of Irish discontent which prevailed at that particular moment. His last epigram, one of the finest which ever fell from his lips, spoke the gallant spirit and truly English heart which distinguished him through life : "But, my Lords, the key of India is not Herat or Candahar; the key of India is London."

Lord Beaconsfield died on the 19th of April 1881, and his death left a blank in the public life of England which is too recent to need any illustration, or to become the

subject of a comparison. It was felt that a deep and
original thinker, a great orator, and a wise and fearless
statesman had been removed from among us at a time
when we could least spare him; one who, by the force of
his character and the breadth of his sympathies, had
regained for the principle of authority much of that
popular affection which had been gradually estranged from
it; had taught the people of England that the classes
which they had been educated to distrust were still worthy
of their allegiance; and had re-awakened them at the
same time to a sense of the greatness, the beneficence, and
the priceless national value of the Empire they had inherited from their fathers. Men knew that he was not
faultless. He had borne the burden and heat of the day;
had fought a battle such as few have ever fought, against
foes such as few have ever known. If the passion of the
moment had sometimes blinded him to higher interests,
and in the eagerness of retaliation he had cared more for
victory than justice, they felt that great allowance must
be made for one whose provocations had been almost un-
paralleled, who for years, it may be said, had carried his
life in his hand, and whose wit supplied him with a
weapon which was always springing from its sheath. But
they felt more than this: they felt that with all his
faults he stood before the world as a true lover of his
country, a firm believer in the greatness and the glory
of her Imperial mission, and interested to the bottom of
his heart in the past history and future welfare of her
venerable and still vigorous institutions.

It has been said that Lord Beaconsfield was rather a
debater than an orator. But this seems an idle question
to discuss till we find some definition of an orator in
which everyone can agree, and some definition of invective

which shall exclude the quality of eloquence. In his earlier days, notably in 1867, his power of debate was the admiration of all who heard him.* But when this power is combined with wit and sarcasm of the keenest and most brilliant order, surely we have the orator before us. No doubt, however, it is the humorous rather than the serious qualities of his eloquence that posterity will remember best; for while in the latter he has many equals, and doubtless some superiors, in the former he shines without a rival. Nature had furnished him with the weapons most suitable to the kind of warfare in which he was destined to engage. Epigrams served him better than syllogisms. He did more for his party by turning the laugh against their opponents than he could ever have hoped to accomplish by the most elaborate and cogent logic; and men winced at his irony on whom the highest flights of imagination would have been expended in vain.

As a political writer he ranks with Bolingbroke and Burke. We may think him inferior or superior to either or to both of these distinguished men. But that is the class in which he will always be enrolled; the class of great statesmen who brought the highest literary ability to bear on practical politics, and whose writings, whether on history, constitutional principles, or the questions of

* "One of the most remarkable examples of his eminence in this branch of oratory is his speech of April 12th, 1867, in answer to a hostile motion of Mr. Gladstone, which was the first real trial of strength between the two parties. The Government majority was twenty-one, and it was of this occasion that Lady Beaconsfield loved to tell how her husband, refusing an invitation to supper pressed upon him by the members of the Carlton, hurried home to the 'best of wives,' and ate half the raised pie and finished the bottle of champagne which she had prepared for his reception."—*Speeches*, vol. i. p. 592.

One of the finest specimens of his higher style of eloquence is to be found also, in a speech upon Reform, May 8th, 1865. "England cannot begin again," is the text of the peroration.

the day, had direct and immediate reference to the state
of parties and the conduct of Parliamentary campaigns.
Whatever the relative effect of *Coningsby* and *Sybil*, as
compared with that of the *Patriot King* or the *Reflections
on the French Revolution*, absolutely it was enormous. It
infused, by degrees, an entirely new spirit into the Conservative creed, which veteran politicians, "the grey-
haired Privy Councillors" who sighed for the days of
Lord Liverpool, might stigmatize as fanciful, romantic, or
puerile, but which was the one thing wanted, nevertheless,
in order to harmonize Toryism with the progress of national
opinions, and bring it within the range of modern sympathies and aspirations.

In Vol. LXXX. of the *Edinburgh Review*, in a critique on
Coningsby, we find the contributor quite in agreement with
Mr. Disraeli as to the decay of political faith. Writing
of the old *régime*, he says : " This was a system on which
one's moral nature could repose, a solid temple in which
one could sincerely worship." Faith in such a system
may be an erroneous faith ; but it is better than none at
all ; and to none at all, in the opinion of the Reviewer,
had the Conservative Party now been brought. At vol. i.
p. 137 of Mr. Gladstone's *Gleanings*, we find that " the
convictions of men like Mr. Burke, Lord Grenville, Mr.
Canning, Mr. Hallam, in favour of the old system represent something much higher, much more historical than
has since been, or could be, arrayed against schemes
essentially intermediate and provisional, against further
modification." Between the years 1828 and 1832 a
revolution had been accomplished by which the two
great principles—the religious and the political principles—of the old Constitution were virtually abro-
gated. The Tory revival was but the twin sister of the

Anglican revival. Both sprang from one common source, the necessity of providing some antidote against the religious and political scepticism which this, like all other revolutions, had confessedly engendered. The want was as perceptible to Mr. Gladstone as it was to Mr. Disraeli; and " the State in its relations to the Church," was but another mode of giving utterance to the same convictions which found their political exponent in the author of *Coningsby* and *Sybil*. We have only to read Cardinal Newman's account of his own feeling towards Liberalism in his *History of My Religious Opinions* to understand how it was regarded by Tories of the same stamp. The remedy* which all alike seemed to acknowledge as the only one possible was a return to primitive principles— to primitive Toryism on the one hand, and primitive Anglicanism on the other. Mr. Disraeli and Mr. Gladstone, Keble and Newman, were all working in different parts of the same field for the same great object.

---

* *Cf.* the following very interesting letter written by Mr. Disraeli to the *Times*, August 11th, 1843, immediately after the publication of the leading article which I have already quoted:—

" I voted for ' the Industrial measures ' of Sir Robert Peel last year, and defended them during the present, because I believed, and still believe, that they were founded on sound principles of commercial policy: principles which were advocated by that great Tory statesman, Lord Bolingbroke, in 1713, principles which, in abeyance during the Whig Government of seventy years, were revived by that great Tory statesman, Mr. Pitt, and, though their progress was disturbed by war and revolution, were faithful to the traditional policy of the Tory Party, sanctioned and developed, on the return of peace and order, by Lord Liverpool.

" It is not merely with reference to commercial policy that I believe that a recurrence to old Tory principles would be of great advantage to this country. It is a specific, in my opinion, and the only one, for many of those disquietudes which now perplex our society. I see no other remedy for that war of classes and creeds which now agitates and menaces us; but in an earnest return to a system which may be described generally as one of loyalty and reverence, of popular rights and social sympathies."

As the Churchman, therefore, fell back upon the ecclesiastical writers of the seventeenth century, so did the statesman fall back upon the political writers of the eighteenth. The latter were to the Revolution what the former were to the Reformation. The task of each was reconstruction without retrogression. The task of the Caroline Divines was to reassert the Catholic element in the Church which had not been expelled by the Genevans. The task of the Georgian Tories was to reassert the monarchical element in the State which had not been expelled by the Republicans. To restore the symmetry of the Church after the first great convulsion without retrograding towards Popery, was the object of Laud and Andrews. To restore the symmetry of the Constitution after the second, without retrograding towards despotism, was the object of Bolingbroke and Wyndham. Newman, writing in 1837, says:

> Protestantism and Popery are real religions . . . but the *via media*, viewed as an integral system, has scarcely had existence except on paper. . . . It still remains to be tried whether what is called Anglo-Catholicism, the religion of Andrews, Laud, Hammond, Butler, and Wilson, is capable of being professed, acted on, and maintained on a large sphere of action, or whether it be a mere modification or transition state of either Romanism or popular Protestantism.

Similarly, the political *via media* represented by the Patriot King was something intermediate between a practically absolute and a practically impotent sovereignty, between an autocrat and a puppet. And at Bolingbroke's death in 1752 it still " remained to be seen " whether the ideal could be anything more than a mere "paper constitution "; whether " it was capable of being professed, acted on, and maintained on a large sphere of action, or whether it was a mere modification " of other forms of government which had already stood the test of experience.

The English clergy certainly would not allow that the religious movement had been a failure; nor can it truly be said that George the Third's attempt to act on the theory of Bolingbroke was a failure either. It ended in a compromise. But he certainly laid the foundation of a new system which, had his successors been men like himself, would probably have been established for some generations on a permanent and popular basis. But we must picture to ourselves Lord Beaconsfield looking back to the writings of Bolingbroke and seeing in them "a paper Constitution" which had never had a really fair trial, and which it still might be possible to adapt to the changed conditions of the age in which he lived himself. Of the practical bearings of this interesting question I have said what I had to say on a previous page. With much in it that was fanciful and would not stand the shock of experience, it was founded, nevertheless, on a truth which perhaps only its author understood; the tendency, namely, of the Reform Bill to place more and more power in the hands of individuals, and so to accomplish by degrees some approximation to that personal rule to which democracies have never been unfavourable. Lord Beaconsfield thought to give this tendency a monarchical bias. I am not sure that his writings have not borne fruit, or that they may not in the future bear more. But whether they do or do not, they represent one of those reactions which are sure to occur periodically in an age of progress, and from which the returning wave, though it may not take a new direction, not unfrequently takes a new colour.

CHAPTER IX.

CONCLUSION.

An exhaustive history of the Tory Party must be looked for in a history of England. It has been my object in the present volume to endeavour to meet some of the more popular prejudices against Tories and Toryism, which have been allowed to grow up during the last fifty years with so little protest or remonstrance that they have glided by degrees into political truisms, to be accepted as a matter of course by all who think or talk about such matters. Lord Beaconsfield, who has put to rout so many popular errors on this subject, is not always himself a perfectly trustworthy guide. We must at least remember that in reading *Coningsby* and *Sybil* we are reading novels, and that even in the purely political dissertations attached to them the lights and shades may be marked more strongly than they would have been in a regular history. After a tolerably careful study, extending over some years, of the period in question, I cannot accept as literally true his picture of what he terms "The Mediocrities," calculated, as it seems to me, to deepen rather than to dissipate prevailing errors with respect to Lord Liverpool's administration. I do not think it can be proved that either the Foreign Policy or the domestic legislation of the statesmen who governed England from the Peace to the Reform Bill was deficient in that practical common-sense which is nine times out of ten the best guide a statesman can possess. No Ministry could have lived through the domestic ordeal which awaited this country on the conclusion of the great war without becoming more or less unpopular. And while we recognize the firmness and courage which steered us through so many difficulties, both social and commercial, we should make allowances for errors which, considering the circumstances of the time, were neither numerous nor grave.

I have endeavoured to show that the Tory Party has throughout been true to certain leading principles, and that the successive statesmen by whom it has at times been represented have always acted on what they conceived to be its traditional Foreign Policy; that policy being one which a small island with a great empire is necessarily compelled to follow if it would preserve itself from being plundered or dismembered. I have shown that till very recent times this was not even a party question,* and that, although the Tory view may have differed from the Whig view in some important particulars, the necessity of foreign alliances, and of maintaining the integrity of our influence on the continent of Europe, was recognized by both. I have shown, or endeavoured to show, that Lord Castlereagh and the Duke of Wellington were equally guided by this principle, and that there is no ground for charging either of them with participating in the schemes of the continental monarchies for the suppression of popular liberty. I have likewise pointed out—what is too often overlooked—that at the Congress of

* *Vide* p. 108.

Vienna England could not have materially altered the terms agreed upon by the Powers without imminent danger of another European war, and that, short of running this risk, she protested as strongly as she could against the treatment of both Saxony and Poland.

It has seldom been sufficiently considered that in the adoption of those repressive measures which have been singled out for special abuse by the hostile critics of Lord Liverpool, Government was face to face with seditions and insurrectionary plots which culminated in a scheme for the assassination of the whole Cabinet. I see little or no justification for the various Arms Bills and Crimes Bills, and other precautionary measures which have been demanded for Ireland, which did not equally exist for the Six Acts. Governments are answerable for the preservation of peace and the security of life and property; and I doubt whether impartial men, after the experience of the last ten years, would be disposed to judge as harshly of these measures as was the fashion forty years ago, when public danger of this kind had come to seem almost like a dream.

Of the three great questions of Parliamentary Reform, Free Trade, and Roman Catholic Emancipation, on the two last the Tory Party was divided; what I should have called the orthodox Tories, who adhered to the principles of Mr. Pitt, being favourable to Free Trade, and the newer school of Tories, who traced their lineage to Mr. Addington, being opposed to it. Mr. Pitt was a thorough Free-trader; and in attempting to carry out his principles met with the most violent opposition from the Whigs. The orthodox Tories, Castlereagh and Canning among the number, were also favourable to Roman Catholic Emancipation. Against Lord Grey's Reform Bill the whole Tory

Party was united; but they were not opposed to all reform; and, had it not been for the unlucky declaration of the Duke of Wellington, would most likely have settled the Reform Question, as they had recently settled the Roman Catholic Question.

In legislation affecting the special interests of the working classes it is a simple fact that the Tories took the lead of the Liberals. Not only with regard to the physical condition of the manufacturing operatives were the Tories the first to introduce a series of remedial measures, but it was reserved for them also to complete their own work some forty years afterwards by the measures which Lord Beaconsfield adopted for the protection of the rights of labour, and the final adjustment of the relations between employers and employed.

The Tories have always been opposed to the three principles of compulsion, centralization, and confiscation. Lord Beaconsfield acknowledged in more than one of his speeches upon Ireland that it might be necessary at times, and in the presence of peculiar national diseases, to have recourse to these violent remedies; but he strongly condemned the introduction of them into the ordinary legislation of the country, as injurious alike to the national character, to local independence, and to those rights of property which are the best incentives to industry. State interference with personal morality, with private enterprise, with freedom of contract, has, according to Toryism, an enervating effect both on the community and the individuals who compose it. Centralization is incompatible with that system of local jurisdiction which has been the political education of Englishmen; which softens the harshness of authority by the influence of neighbourly associations; widens the basis of aristocracy by investing it with the discharge of visible and important duties ;* and knits class to class, from the highest to the lowest, by the constant intercourse and acquaintanceship which it establishes between them. Confiscation is a word that is liable to be much misunderstood. The transference of a man's private property to the public treasury is, properly speaking, the punishment of a crime. We require some other word at the present day to signify the forcible appropriation by the State of the property of the innocent. It may be quite true that in great national emergencies arguments may be found even for that. What the Tories have always contended for is that it should not be reduced to a system, and invoked without scruple as often as the State is perplexed by the pressure of some new social difficulty. Security for capital means security for labour, for wages, for general prosperity. It is not merely the interest of the rich. Those who begin by attacking large properties will end by attacking small ones. And the time would come, by an inevitable process, when the yeoman or peasant farmer with his ten, twenty, or a hundred acres would be as much an object of cupidity as the owner of Woburn or Chatsworth, and would be called on in his turn to give up his possessions for the benefit of those who had none. We may be told that to appropriate private property for public purposes is justified by a thousand precedents, and that it is childish to call it confiscation. But for property so taken compensation has hitherto been paid according to those recognized rules which govern the sale and purchase of land between private individuals. The forced sale of land at a price to be fixed by the purchasers, when markets may be glutted, and in total disregard of either its potential or its moral value is now proposed for the first

* See again Mr. Gladstone's Speech of Feb. 17th, 1870

time ; and as the vendor would certainly be robbed by it of some part of the value of his property, it is to that extent, if words have a meaning, confiscation.

The Tory Party has almost always been in England the popular party. That it was so throughout the eighteenth century, and, in spite of the disturbances which occurred under the Regency, down even to the repeal of the Roman Catholic disabilities, requires no demonstration. But even since the first Reform Bill, in by far the greater number of General Elections the Tory Party has had the majority of English votes. Ever since the second Reform Bill it has commanded a majority in Lancashire, of which it has been said that what that county says to-day England will say to-morrow. The saying is not literally true ; but the mere fact that in this great centre of industry the Tories are the popular party, is a singular comment on the wisdom and veracity of those persons who are for ever assuring us that between the people and the Tory Party there is a natural antagonism, which neither policy nor kindness can ever hope to overcome.

The Tories have involved us in fewer wars, and have kept the expenditure of the country at a lower level, than the Liberals. But to pursue these points at any length would involve a history of Liberalism as well as of Toryism, which is quite beyond my present purpose. In conclusion, I will merely add that parties must be judged by the policy of their leaders and most prominent members, and not by the prejudices or projects of the rank and file. Fox, Grey, Melbourne, Russell, and Palmerston did a great many things of which their followers disapproved. But the policy of the Whig Party was the policy of Fox, Grey, Melbourne, Russell, and Palmerston. Similarly, in the case of the Tories, Pitt, Canning, and Peel, Lord Derby and Lord

Beaconsfield did many things of which their followers disapproved. But it is to Pitt, Canning, and Peel, Lord Derby, and Lord Beaconsfield, that we must look for the policy of the Tory Party. The acts of the leader are the acts of the Party. We do not deny that the victories of the Peninsular War were the victories of the British army, because a few colonels and brigadiers may have disputed the tactics of the Duke of Wellington; and I utterly deny the right of a historian to draw any similar line of distinction between political parties and their leaders. No party can long be led by its extreme men. The Conservative leaders must be the most liberal men of their connection, and the Liberal leaders the most conservative. But the work which they respectively accomplish is the work of the party which they lead; and when it ceases to be considered so, the Party system will expire.

In its defence of the Monarchy, the Church, and the territorial Constitution of this country, the Tory Party has never faltered. Personal liberty, the rights of property, and the rights of labour have, in more recent days, found their warmest supporters in the Tories. And with these words inscribed upon its banner, Toryism need not be ashamed to speak with its enemies in the gate.